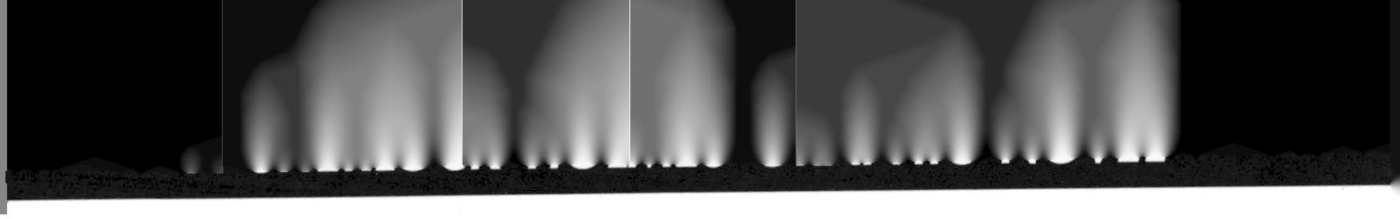

THE SIGN OF FOUR

THE SIGN OF THE FOUR

ADAPTED FROM THE ORIGINAL NOVEL BY
SIR ARTHUR CONAN DOYLE
ILLUSTRATED BY
I.N.J. CULBARD
TEXT ADAPTED BY
IAN EDGINTON

STERLING

New York / London
www.sterlingpublishing.com

STERLING and the distinctive Sterling logo are registered trademarks of
Sterling Publishing Co., Inc.

Library of Congress Cataloging-in-Publication Data Available

10 9 8 7 6 5 4 3 2 1

Published by Sterling Publishing Co., Inc.
387 Park Avenue South, New York, NY 10016

© 2010 SelfMadeHero

First published 2010
by SelfMadeHero
A division of Metro Media Ltd
5 Upper Wimpole Street
London W1G 6BP
www.selfmadehero.com

Distributed in Canada by Sterling Publishing
c/o Canadian Manda Group, 165 Dufferin Street,
Toronto, Ontario, Canada M6K 3H6

Illustrator: I. N. J. Culbard
Adaptor: Ian Edginton
Cover Designer: I. N. J. Culbard
Designer: Andy Huckle
Textual Consultant: Nick de Somogyi
Publishing Director: Emma Hayley
With thanks to: Catherine Cooke, John Corbett, Jane Laporte,
and Doug Wallace

Dedications
For Katy, Joseph, and Benjamin
– I. N. J. Culbard

To the trio of lovely ladies in my life: my wife, Jane, and daughters,
Constance and Corinthia – Ian Edginton

ISBN 978-1-4027-8003-5

For information about custom editions, special sales, premium
and corporate purchases, please contact Sterling Special Sales
Department at 800-805-5489 or specialsales@sterlingpublishing.com.

FOREWORD

"THERE IS SOMETHING DEVILISH IN THIS, WATSON . . ."

The Sign of the Four was only the second Sherlock Holmes adventure penned by Arthur Conan Doyle—and, judged as an adventure story alone, it's probably the best. Lengthy flashbacks in Doyle's other long-form Holmes tales necessitate a slowing in pace; the short story form, meanwhile, requires ruthless economy of incident. That's not the case here. The story is every bit as intriguing, perplexing, and exciting as its three main literary sources: Wilkie Collins' *The Moonstone*, Poe's *The Murders in the Rue Morgue*, and Stevenson's *Treasure Island*. Investigating "The Problem of the Sholtos" (as Doyle's original subtitle had it), Holmes and Watson dash about at a frenetic pace, culminating in a thrilling shoot-out on the River Thames. Unsurprising, therefore, that *The Sign of the Four* ranks just behind the gothic horrors of *The Hound of the Baskervilles* as the second most-filmed Holmes story—as zippily realized in the silent Stoll Picture Productions version of 1923 as in the Granada TV film of 1987, with Jeremy Brett's Holmes in breathless pursuit of John Thaw's especially fine Jonathan Small.

Doyle's supporting characters are translated with no less style in Messrs. Edginton and Culbard's graphical retelling. Readers of Mr. Edginton's "steampunk" comic strip *Stickleback*, as serialized in *2000 AD*, will recall the devilish imp "Little Tonga," whose no-less-vile antecedent may be found herein. We are as struck as any Watson by the charms of Mr. Culbard's luminous Mary Morstan, without a doubt Doyle's loving pen portrait of his first wife, Louisa. My favorite remains the bizarre, aesthetic Thaddeus Sholto. Fascinatingly, Doyle only came to write this second Holmes adventure after a dinner at the Langham Hotel—his host, the managing editor of *Lippincott's Magazine*, who wished to recruit London's most promising literary lights to author new books for serialization in a forthcoming English edition. Doyle's fellow guest on that occasion was none other than Oscar Wilde, and it seems certain that the divine Thaddeus was created in the reflection of Doyle's notorious dining companion.

Out of that one dinner, therefore, came not only *The Sign of the Four*, but also Wilde's *The Picture of Dorian Gray*. Unlike that infamous portrait, however, this latest retelling proves that *The Sign of the Four* grows fresher with age.

—Alan Barnes
author, *Sherlock Holmes on Screen*

THE SCIENCE OF DEDUCTION

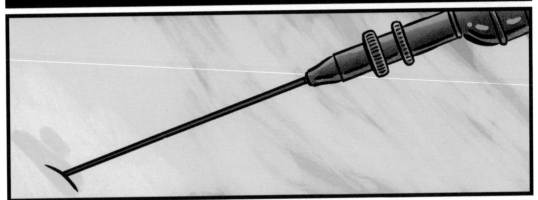

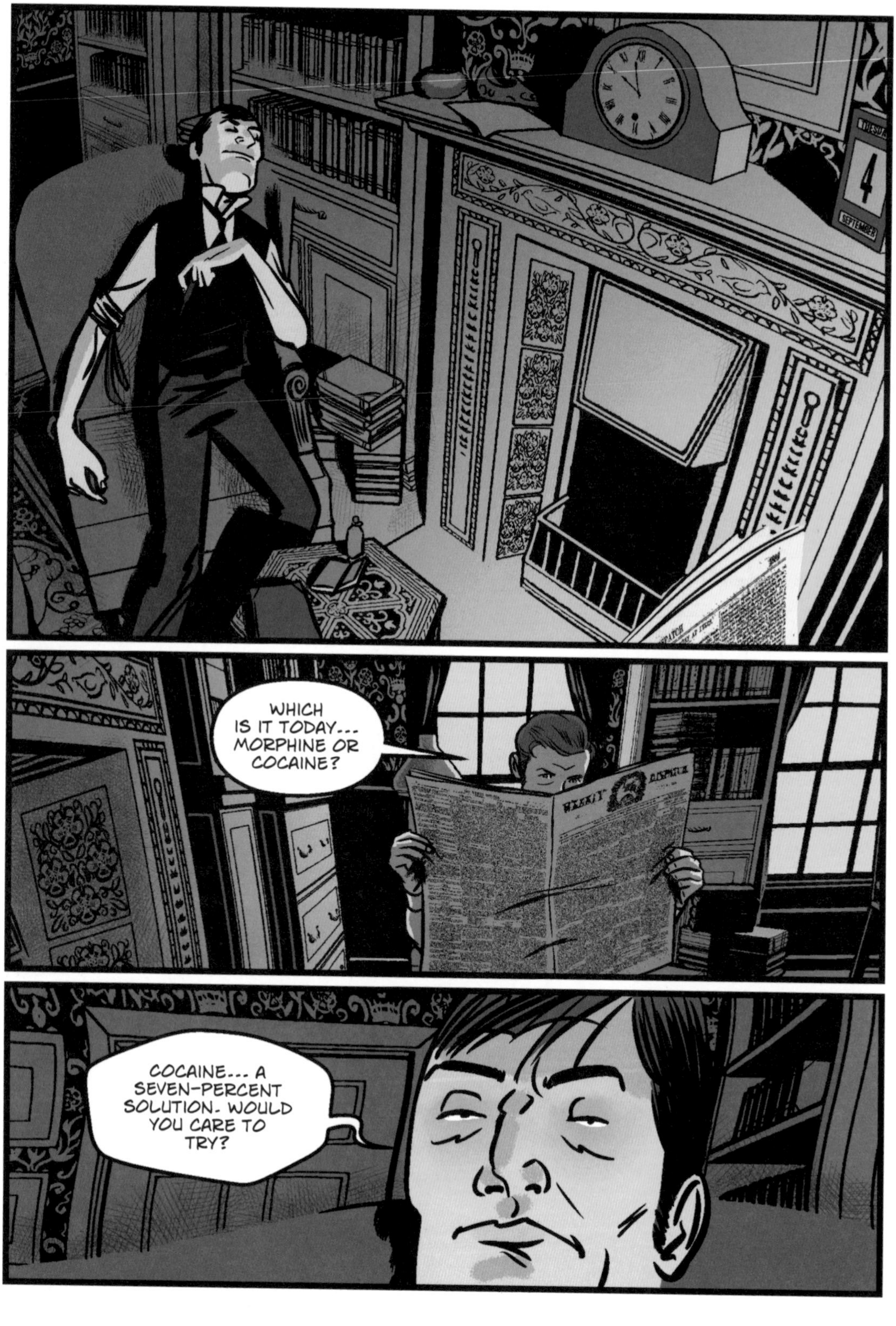
WHICH IS IT TODAY... MORPHINE OR COCAINE?
COCAINE... A SEVEN-PERCENT SOLUTION. WOULD YOU CARE TO TRY?

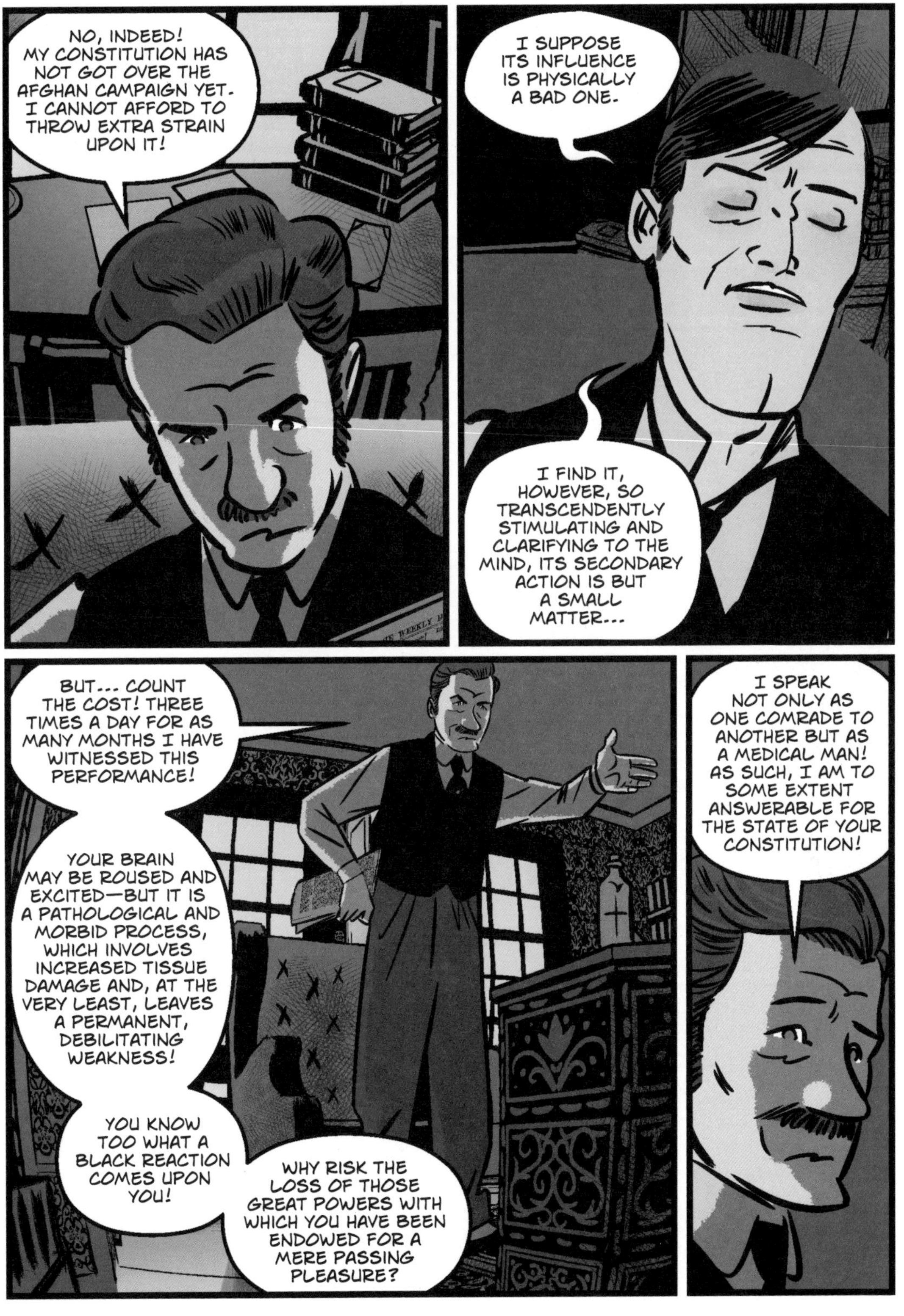
NO, INDEED! MY CONSTITUTION HAS NOT GOT OVER THE AFGHAN CAMPAIGN YET. I CANNOT AFFORD TO THROW EXTRA STRAIN UPON IT!
I SUPPOSE ITS INFLUENCE IS PHYSICALLY A BAD ONE.
I FIND IT, HOWEVER, SO TRANSCENDENTLY STIMULATING AND CLARIFYING TO THE MIND, ITS SECONDARY ACTION IS BUT A SMALL MATTER...
BUT... COUNT THE COST! THREE TIMES A DAY FOR AS MANY MONTHS I HAVE WITNESSED THIS PERFORMANCE!
YOUR BRAIN MAY BE ROUSED AND EXCITED—BUT IT IS A PATHOLOGICAL AND MORBID PROCESS, WHICH INVOLVES INCREASED TISSUE DAMAGE AND, AT THE VERY LEAST, LEAVES A PERMANENT, DEBILITATING WEAKNESS!
YOU KNOW TOO WHAT A BLACK REACTION COMES UPON YOU!
WHY RISK THE LOSS OF THOSE GREAT POWERS WITH WHICH YOU HAVE BEEN ENDOWED FOR A MERE PASSING PLEASURE?
I SPEAK NOT ONLY AS ONE COMRADE TO ANOTHER BUT AS A MEDICAL MAN! AS SUCH, I AM TO SOME EXTENT ANSWERABLE FOR THE STATE OF YOUR CONSTITUTION!

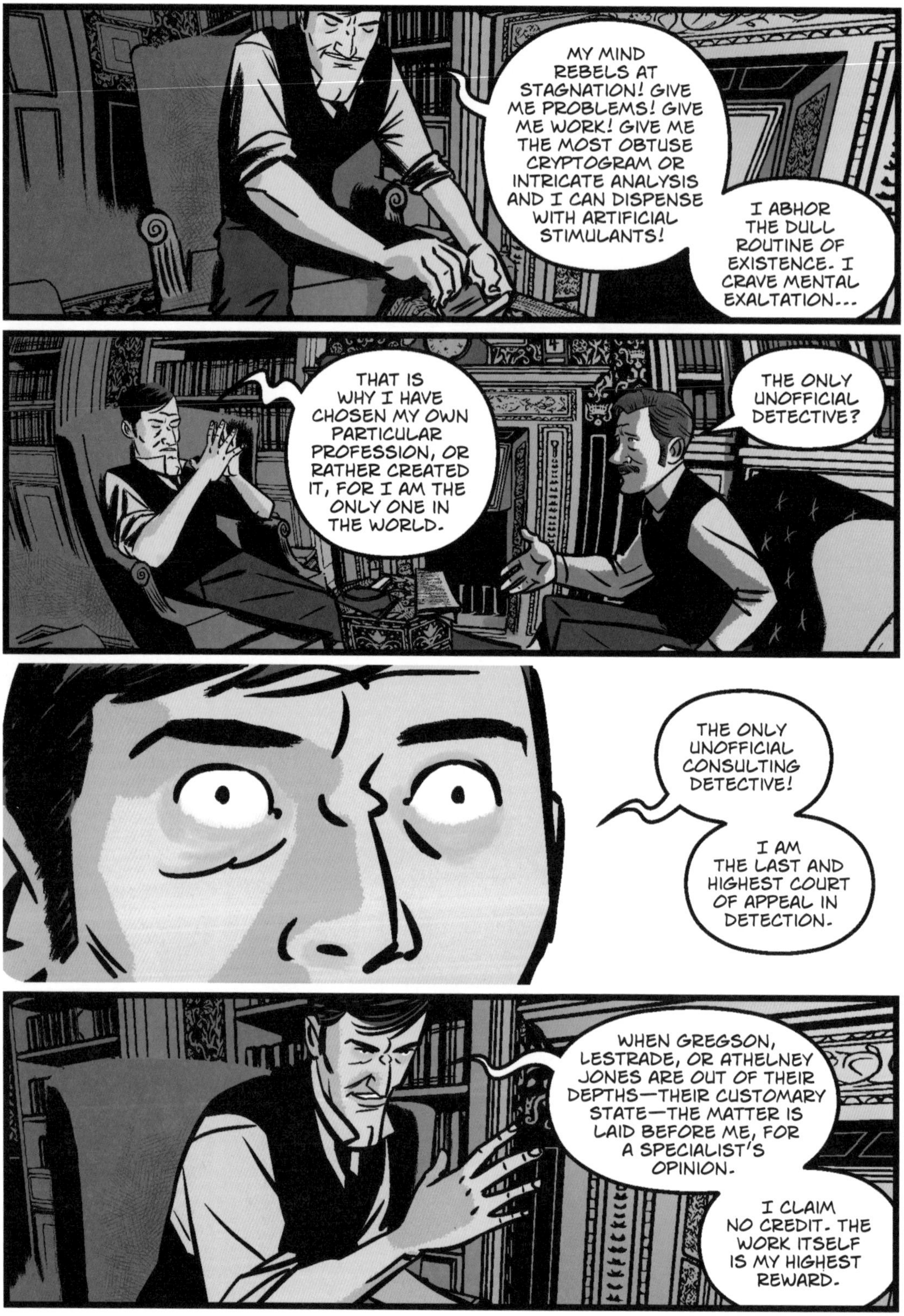
MY MIND REBELS AT STAGNATION! GIVE ME PROBLEMS! GIVE ME WORK! GIVE ME THE MOST OBTUSE CRYPTOGRAM OR INTRICATE ANALYSIS AND I CAN DISPENSE WITH ARTIFICIAL STIMULANTS!
I ABHOR THE DULL ROUTINE OF EXISTENCE. I CRAVE MENTAL EXALTATION...
THAT IS WHY I HAVE CHOSEN MY OWN PARTICULAR PROFESSION, OR RATHER CREATED IT, FOR I AM THE ONLY ONE IN THE WORLD.
THE ONLY UNOFFICIAL DETECTIVE?
THE ONLY UNOFFICIAL CONSULTING DETECTIVE!
I AM THE LAST AND HIGHEST COURT OF APPEAL IN DETECTION.
WHEN GREGSON, LESTRADE, OR ATHELNEY JONES ARE OUT OF THEIR DEPTHS—THEIR CUSTOMARY STATE—THE MATTER IS LAID BEFORE ME, FOR A SPECIALIST'S OPINION.
I CLAIM NO CREDIT. THE WORK ITSELF IS MY HIGHEST REWARD.

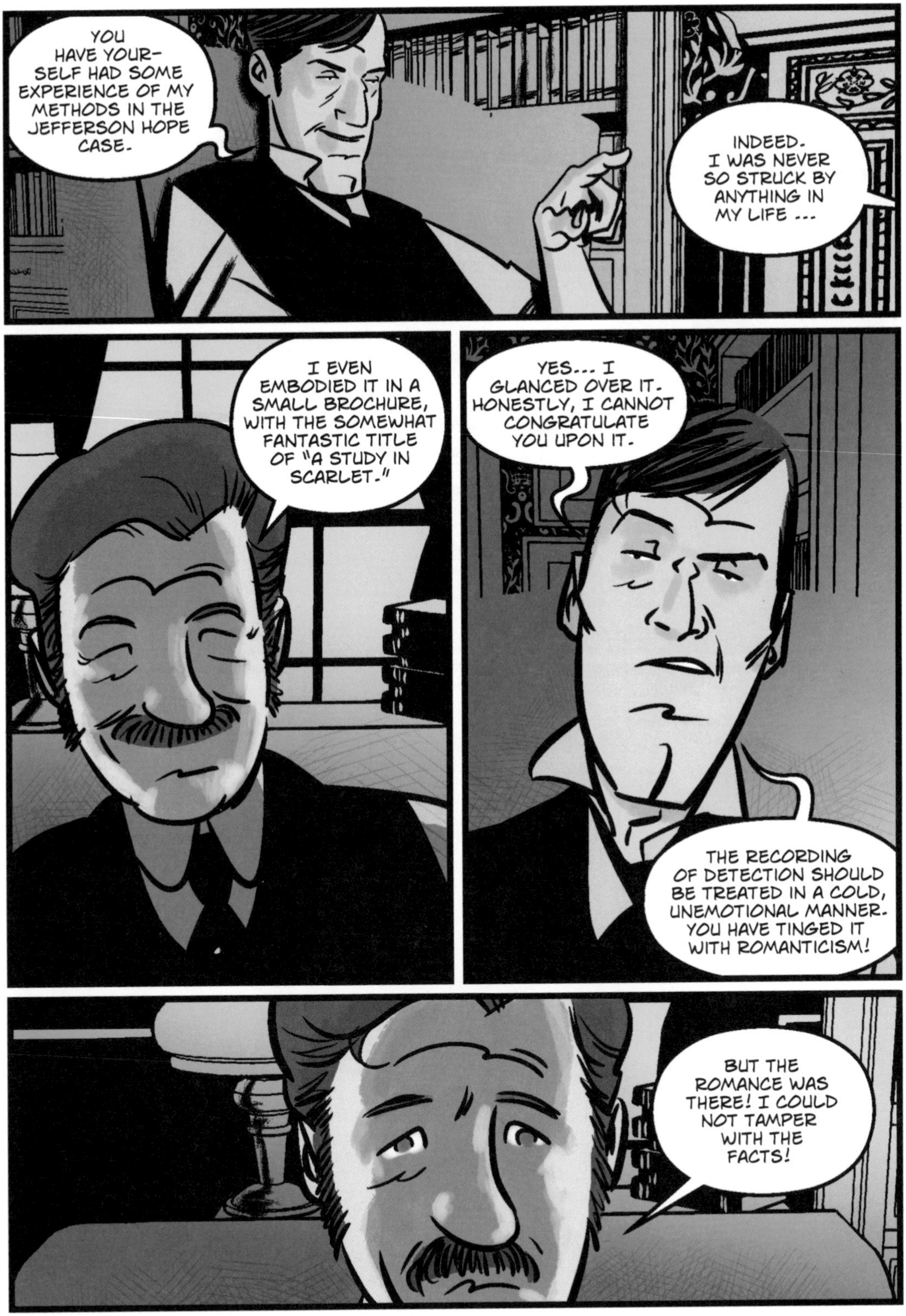
YOU HAVE YOUR-SELF HAD SOME EXPERIENCE OF MY METHODS IN THE JEFFERSON HOPE CASE.
INDEED. I WAS NEVER SO STRUCK BY ANYTHING IN MY LIFE ...
I EVEN EMBODIED IT IN A SMALL BROCHURE, WITH THE SOMEWHAT FANTASTIC TITLE OF "A STUDY IN SCARLET."
YES... I GLANCED OVER IT. HONESTLY, I CANNOT CONGRATULATE YOU UPON IT.
THE RECORDING OF DETECTION SHOULD BE TREATED IN A COLD, UNEMOTIONAL MANNER. YOU HAVE TINGED IT WITH ROMANTICISM!
BUT THE ROMANCE WAS THERE! I COULD NOT TAMPER WITH THE FACTS!

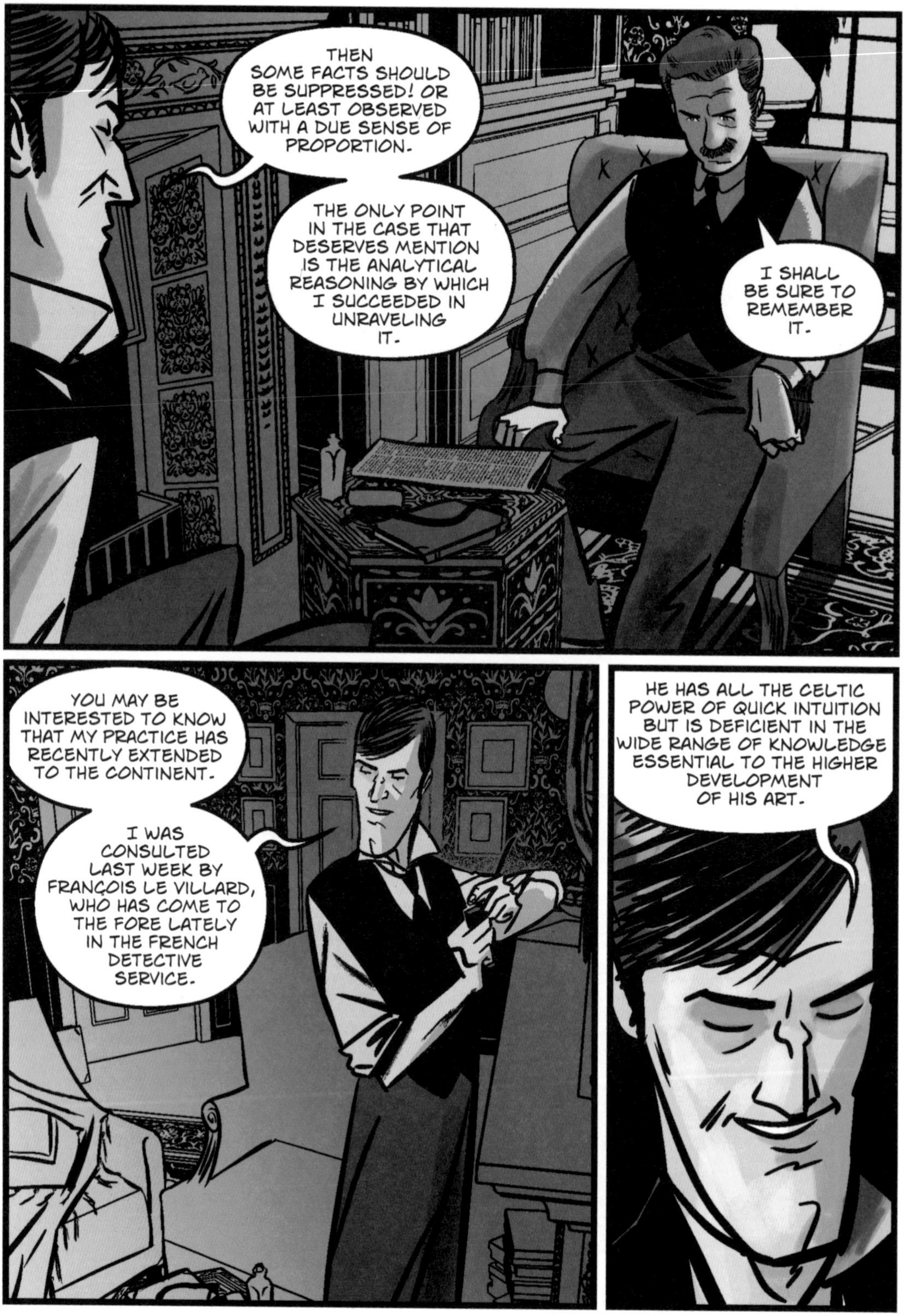
THEN SOME FACTS SHOULD BE SUPPRESSED! OR AT LEAST OBSERVED WITH A DUE SENSE OF PROPORTION.
THE ONLY POINT IN THE CASE THAT DESERVES MENTION IS THE ANALYTICAL REASONING BY WHICH I SUCCEEDED IN UNRAVELING IT.
I SHALL BE SURE TO REMEMBER IT.
YOU MAY BE INTERESTED TO KNOW THAT MY PRACTICE HAS RECENTLY EXTENDED TO THE CONTINENT.
I WAS CONSULTED LAST WEEK BY FRANÇOIS LE VILLARD, WHO HAS COME TO THE FORE LATELY IN THE FRENCH DETECTIVE SERVICE.
HE HAS ALL THE CELTIC POWER OF QUICK INTUITION BUT IS DEFICIENT IN THE WIDE RANGE OF KNOWLEDGE ESSENTIAL TO THE HIGHER DEVELOPMENT OF HIS ART.

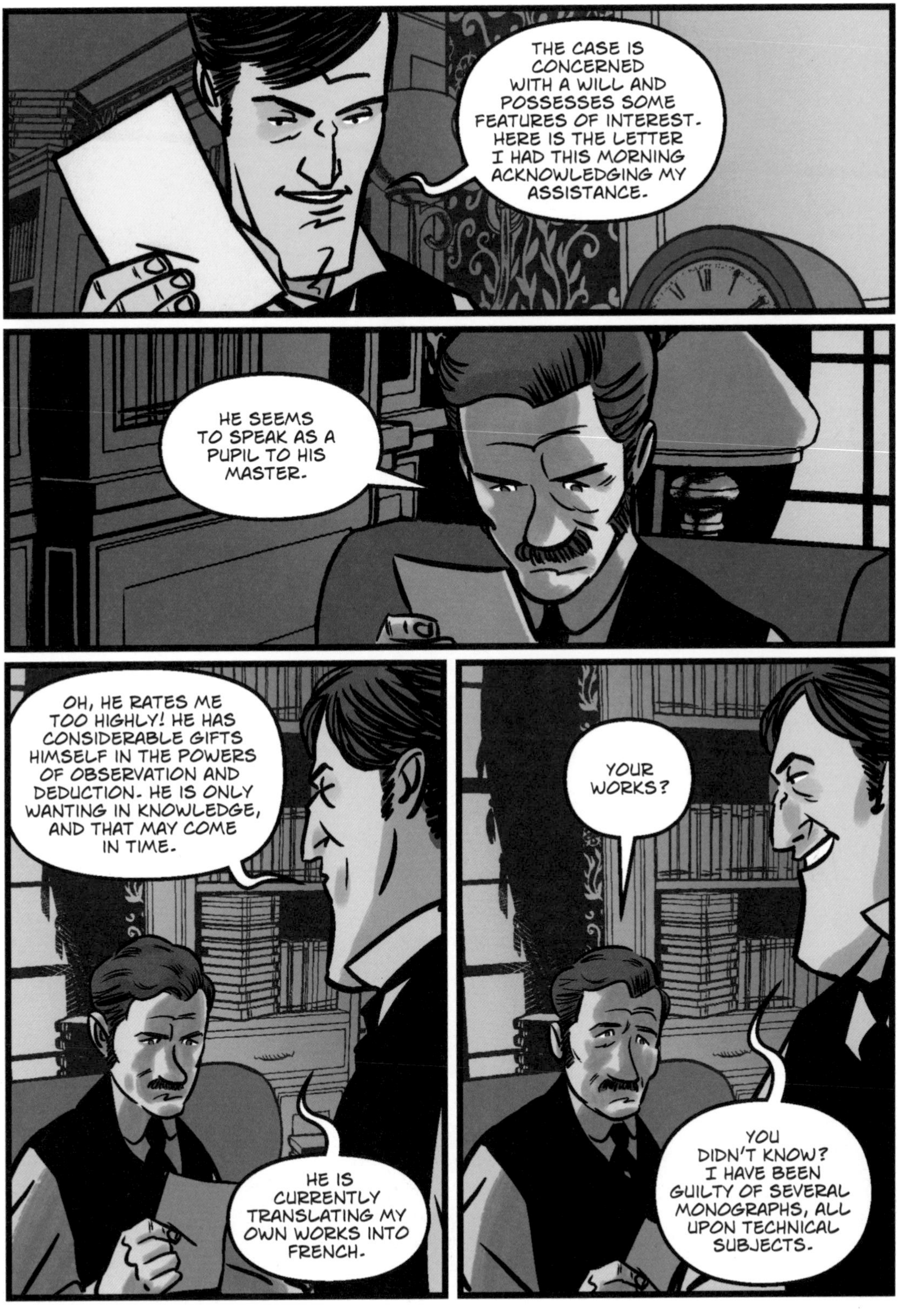
THE CASE IS CONCERNED WITH A WILL AND POSSESSES SOME FEATURES OF INTEREST. HERE IS THE LETTER I HAD THIS MORNING ACKNOWLEDGING MY ASSISTANCE.
HE SEEMS TO SPEAK AS A PUPIL TO HIS MASTER.
OH, HE RATES ME TOO HIGHLY! HE HAS CONSIDERABLE GIFTS HIMSELF IN THE POWERS OF OBSERVATION AND DEDUCTION. HE IS ONLY WANTING IN KNOWLEDGE, AND THAT MAY COME IN TIME.
HE IS CURRENTLY TRANSLATING MY OWN WORKS INTO FRENCH.
YOUR WORKS?
YOU DIDN'T KNOW? I HAVE BEEN GUILTY OF SEVERAL MONOGRAPHS, ALL UPON TECHNICAL SUBJECTS.

HERE IS ONE, "UPON THE DISTINCTION BETWEEN THE ASHES OF THE VARIOUS TOBACCOS."

IN IT I ENUMERATE A HUNDRED AND FORTY FORMS OF CIGAR, CIGARETTE, AND PIPE TOBACCO, WITH COLORED PLATES ILLUSTRATING THE DIFFERENCE IN THE ASH.

IT IS A POINT CONTINUALLY TURNING UP IN CRIMINAL TRIALS AND CAN BE OF SUPREME IMPORTANCE AS A CLUE.

TO THE TRAINED EYE, THERE IS AS MUCH DIFFERENCE BETWEEN THE BLACK ASH OF A TRICHINOPOLY AND THE WHITE FLUFF OF A BIRD'S-EYE AS THERE IS BETWEEN A CABBAGE AND A POTATO.

YOU CERTAINLY HAVE AN EXTRAORDINARY GENIUS FOR MINUTIAE!

I SIMPLY APPRECIATE THEIR IMPORTANCE.

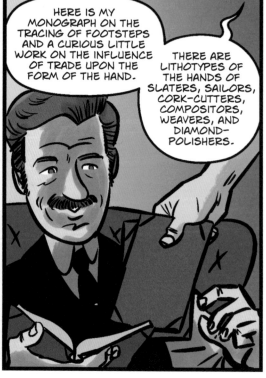

HERE IS MY MONOGRAPH ON THE TRACING OF FOOTSTEPS AND A CURIOUS LITTLE WORK ON THE INFLUENCE OF TRADE UPON THE FORM OF THE HAND.

THERE ARE LITHOTYPES OF THE HANDS OF SLATERS, SAILORS, CORK-CUTTERS, COMPOSITORS, WEAVERS, AND DIAMOND-POLISHERS.

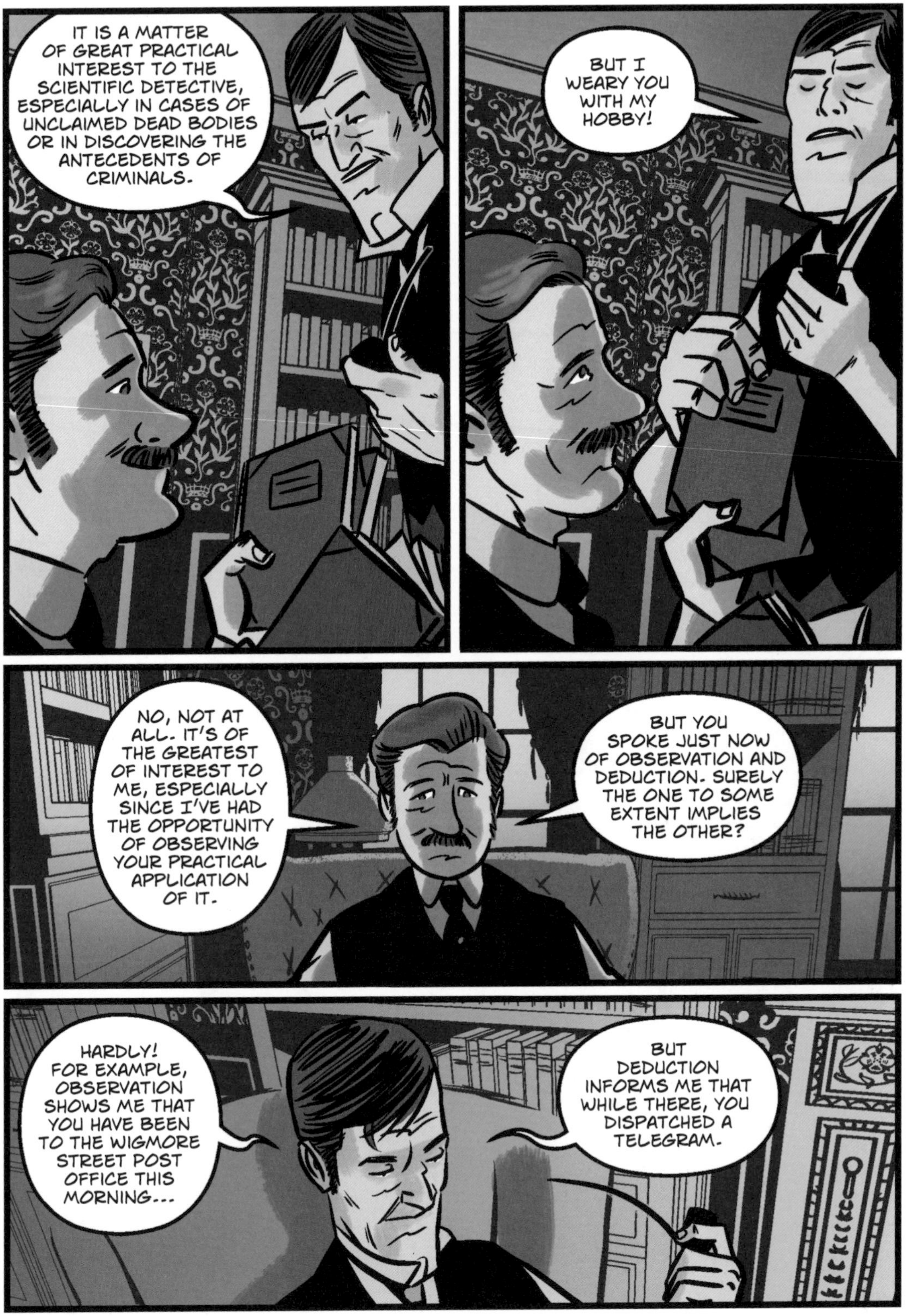
IT IS A MATTER OF GREAT PRACTICAL INTEREST TO THE SCIENTIFIC DETECTIVE, ESPECIALLY IN CASES OF UNCLAIMED DEAD BODIES OR IN DISCOVERING THE ANTECEDENTS OF CRIMINALS.
BUT I WEARY YOU WITH MY HOBBY!
NO, NOT AT ALL. IT'S OF THE GREATEST OF INTEREST TO ME, ESPECIALLY SINCE I'VE HAD THE OPPORTUNITY OF OBSERVING YOUR PRACTICAL APPLICATION OF IT.
BUT YOU SPOKE JUST NOW OF OBSERVATION AND DEDUCTION. SURELY THE ONE TO SOME EXTENT IMPLIES THE OTHER?
HARDLY! FOR EXAMPLE, OBSERVATION SHOWS ME THAT YOU HAVE BEEN TO THE WIGMORE STREET POST OFFICE THIS MORNING...
BUT DEDUCTION INFORMS ME THAT WHILE THERE, YOU DISPATCHED A TELEGRAM.

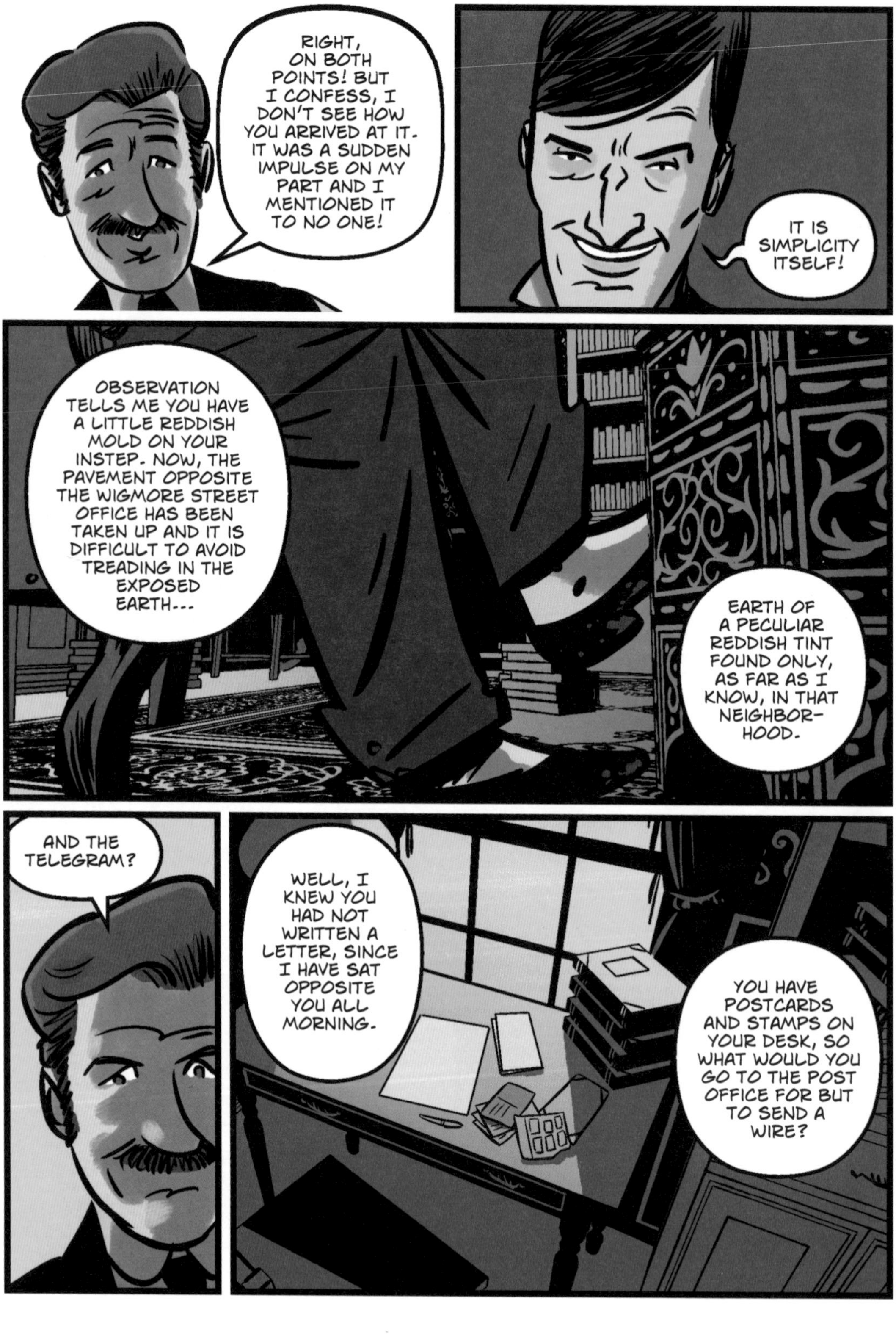
RIGHT, ON BOTH POINTS! BUT I CONFESS, I DON'T SEE HOW YOU ARRIVED AT IT. IT WAS A SUDDEN IMPULSE ON MY PART AND I MENTIONED IT TO NO ONE!
IT IS SIMPLICITY ITSELF!
OBSERVATION TELLS ME YOU HAVE A LITTLE REDDISH MOLD ON YOUR INSTEP. NOW, THE PAVEMENT OPPOSITE THE WIGMORE STREET OFFICE HAS BEEN TAKEN UP AND IT IS DIFFICULT TO AVOID TREADING IN THE EXPOSED EARTH...
EARTH OF A PECULIAR REDDISH TINT FOUND ONLY, AS FAR AS I KNOW, IN THAT NEIGHBOR-HOOD.
AND THE TELEGRAM?
WELL, I KNEW YOU HAD NOT WRITTEN A LETTER, SINCE I HAVE SAT OPPOSITE YOU ALL MORNING.
YOU HAVE POSTCARDS AND STAMPS ON YOUR DESK, SO WHAT WOULD YOU GO TO THE POST OFFICE FOR BUT TO SEND A WIRE?

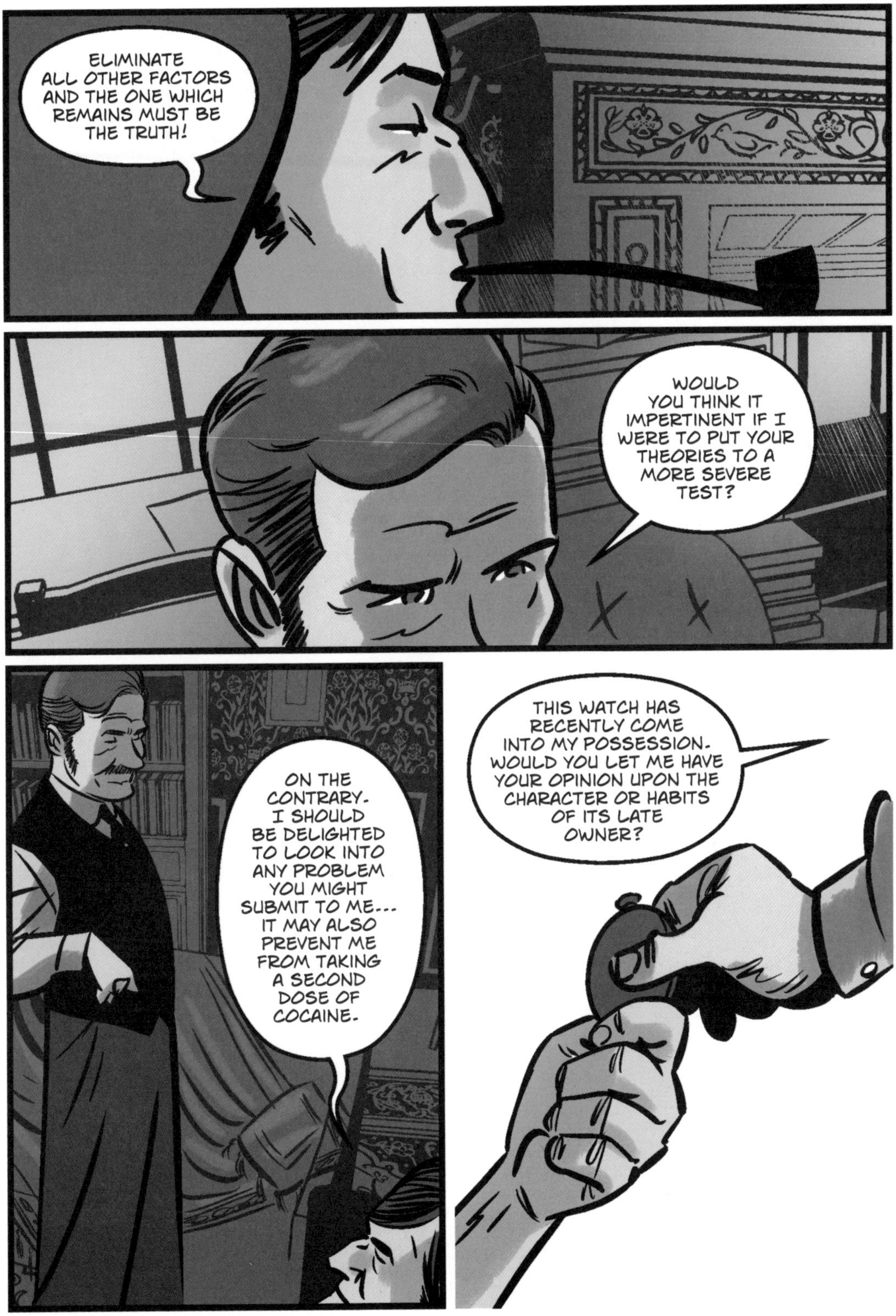
ELIMINATE ALL OTHER FACTORS AND THE ONE WHICH REMAINS MUST BE THE TRUTH!
WOULD YOU THINK IT IMPERTINENT IF I WERE TO PUT YOUR THEORIES TO A MORE SEVERE TEST?
ON THE CONTRARY. I SHOULD BE DELIGHTED TO LOOK INTO ANY PROBLEM YOU MIGHT SUBMIT TO ME... IT MAY ALSO PREVENT ME FROM TAKING A SECOND DOSE OF COCAINE.
THIS WATCH HAS RECENTLY COME INTO MY POSSESSION. WOULD YOU LET ME HAVE YOUR OPINION UPON THE CHARACTER OR HABITS OF ITS LATE OWNER?

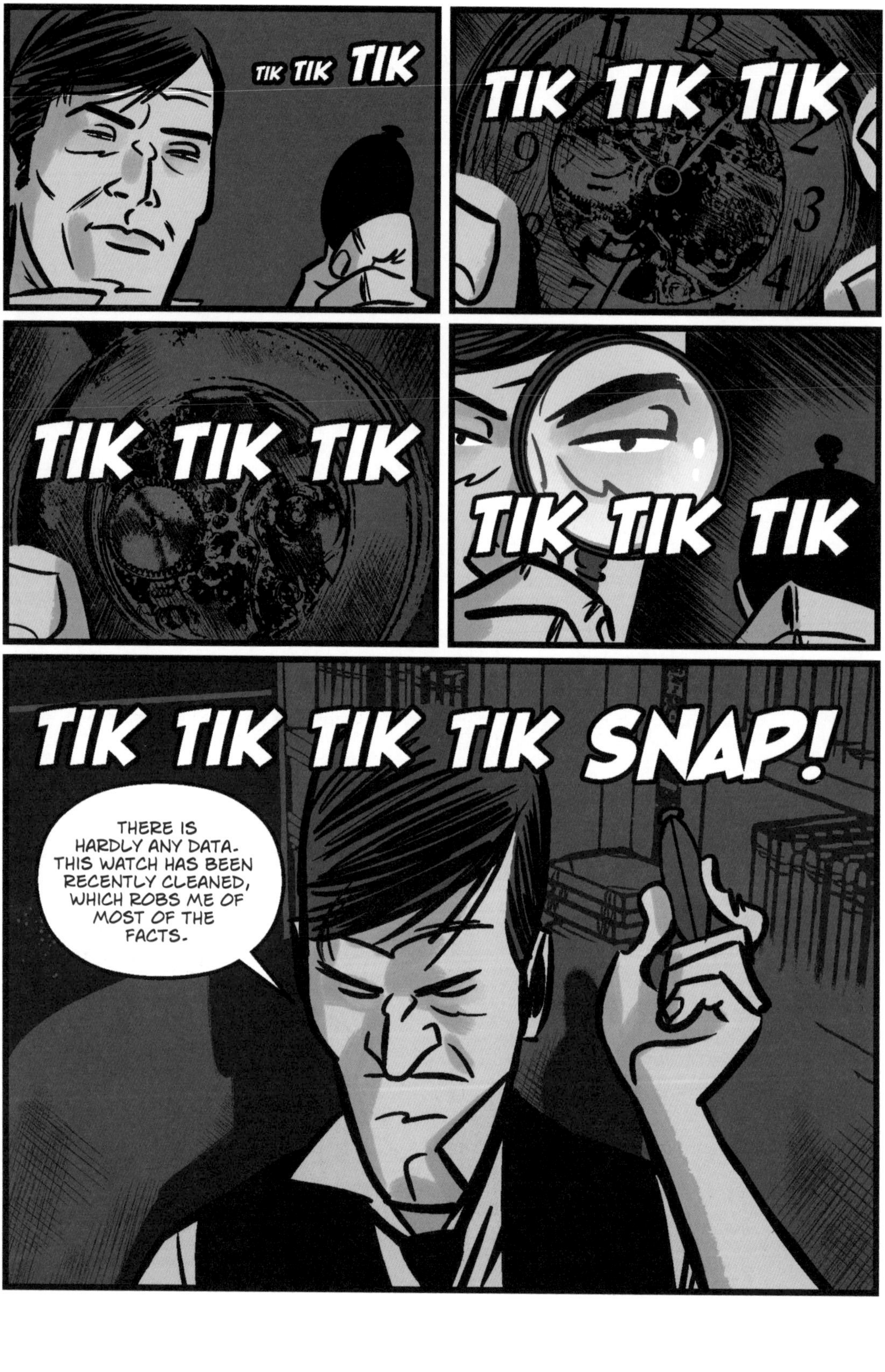
TIK TIK TIK
TIK TIK TIK
TIK TIK TIK
TIK TIK TIK
TIK TIK TIK TIK SNAP!
THERE IS HARDLY ANY DATA. THIS WATCH HAS BEEN RECENTLY CLEANED, WHICH ROBS ME OF MOST OF THE FACTS.

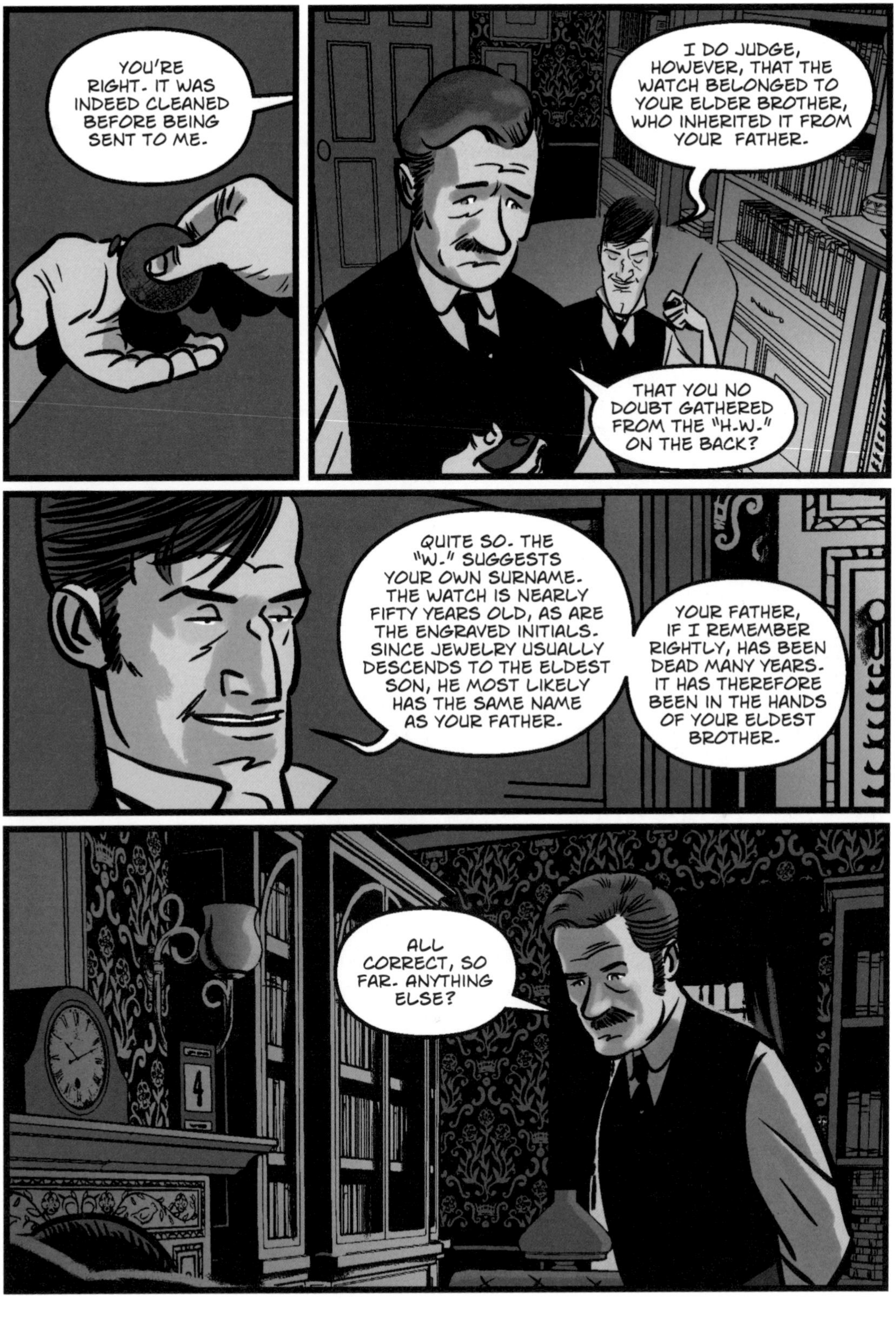
YOU'RE RIGHT. IT WAS INDEED CLEANED BEFORE BEING SENT TO ME.
I DO JUDGE, HOWEVER, THAT THE WATCH BELONGED TO YOUR ELDER BROTHER, WHO INHERITED IT FROM YOUR FATHER.
THAT YOU NO DOUBT GATHERED FROM THE "H.W." ON THE BACK?
QUITE SO. THE "W." SUGGESTS YOUR OWN SURNAME. THE WATCH IS NEARLY FIFTY YEARS OLD, AS ARE THE ENGRAVED INITIALS. SINCE JEWELRY USUALLY DESCENDS TO THE ELDEST SON, HE MOST LIKELY HAS THE SAME NAME AS YOUR FATHER.
YOUR FATHER, IF I REMEMBER RIGHTLY, HAS BEEN DEAD MANY YEARS. IT HAS THEREFORE BEEN IN THE HANDS OF YOUR ELDEST BROTHER.
ALL CORRECT, SO FAR. ANYTHING ELSE?

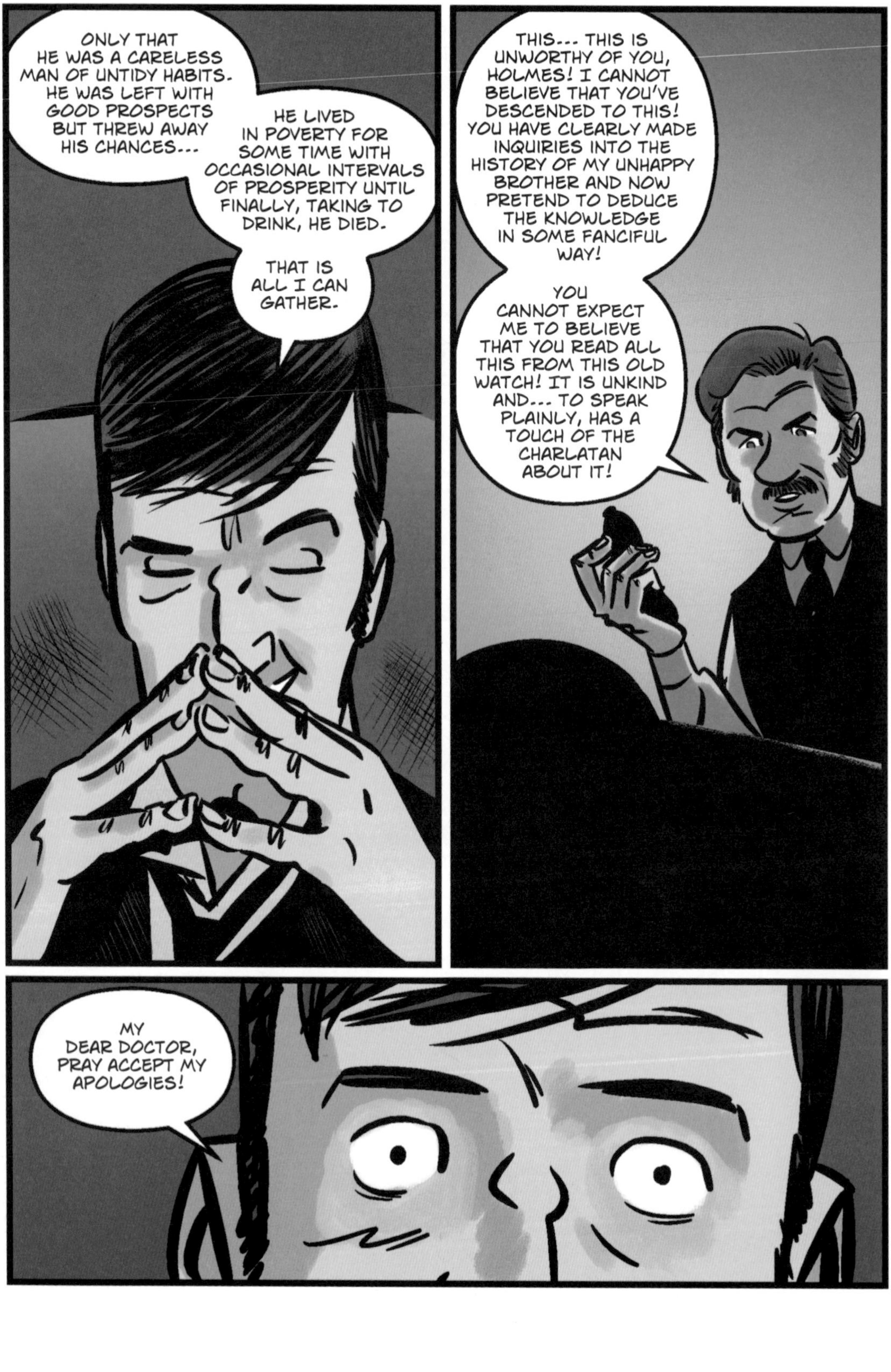
ONLY THAT HE WAS A CARELESS MAN OF UNTIDY HABITS. HE WAS LEFT WITH GOOD PROSPECTS BUT THREW AWAY HIS CHANCES...
HE LIVED IN POVERTY FOR SOME TIME WITH OCCASIONAL INTERVALS OF PROSPERITY UNTIL FINALLY, TAKING TO DRINK, HE DIED.
THAT IS ALL I CAN GATHER.
THIS... THIS IS UNWORTHY OF YOU, HOLMES! I CANNOT BELIEVE THAT YOU'VE DESCENDED TO THIS! YOU HAVE CLEARLY MADE INQUIRIES INTO THE HISTORY OF MY UNHAPPY BROTHER AND NOW PRETEND TO DEDUCE THE KNOWLEDGE IN SOME FANCIFUL WAY!
YOU CANNOT EXPECT ME TO BELIEVE THAT YOU READ ALL THIS FROM THIS OLD WATCH! IT IS UNKIND AND... TO SPEAK PLAINLY, HAS A TOUCH OF THE CHARLATAN ABOUT IT!
MY DEAR DOCTOR, PRAY ACCEPT MY APOLOGIES!

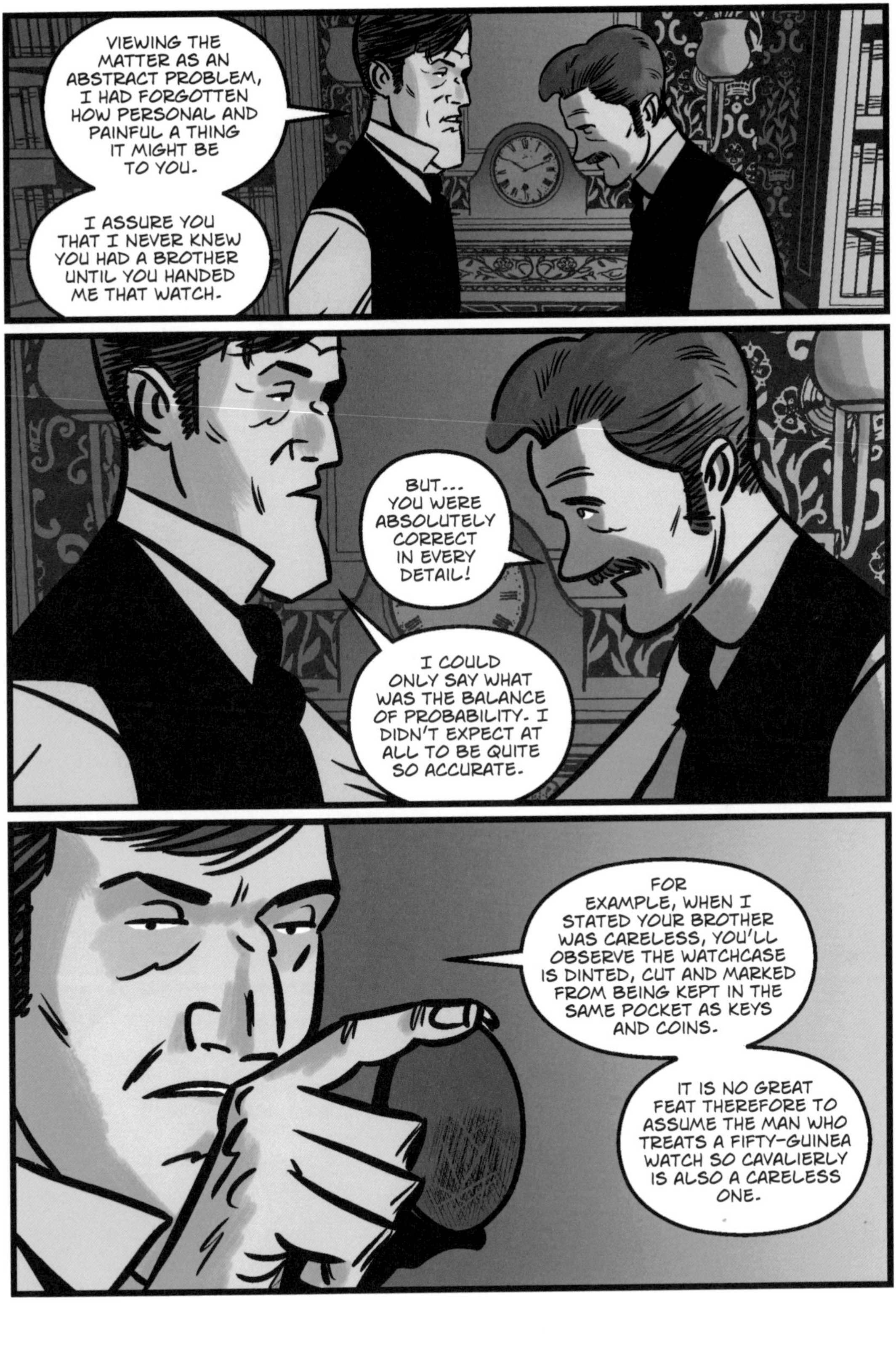
VIEWING THE MATTER AS AN ABSTRACT PROBLEM, I HAD FORGOTTEN HOW PERSONAL AND PAINFUL A THING IT MIGHT BE TO YOU.
I ASSURE YOU THAT I NEVER KNEW YOU HAD A BROTHER UNTIL YOU HANDED ME THAT WATCH.
BUT... YOU WERE ABSOLUTELY CORRECT IN EVERY DETAIL!
I COULD ONLY SAY WHAT WAS THE BALANCE OF PROBABILITY. I DIDN'T EXPECT AT ALL TO BE QUITE SO ACCURATE.
FOR EXAMPLE, WHEN I STATED YOUR BROTHER WAS CARELESS, YOU'LL OBSERVE THE WATCHCASE IS DINTED, CUT AND MARKED FROM BEING KEPT IN THE SAME POCKET AS KEYS AND COINS.
IT IS NO GREAT FEAT THEREFORE TO ASSUME THE MAN WHO TREATS A FIFTY-GUINEA WATCH SO CAVALIERLY IS ALSO A CARELESS ONE.

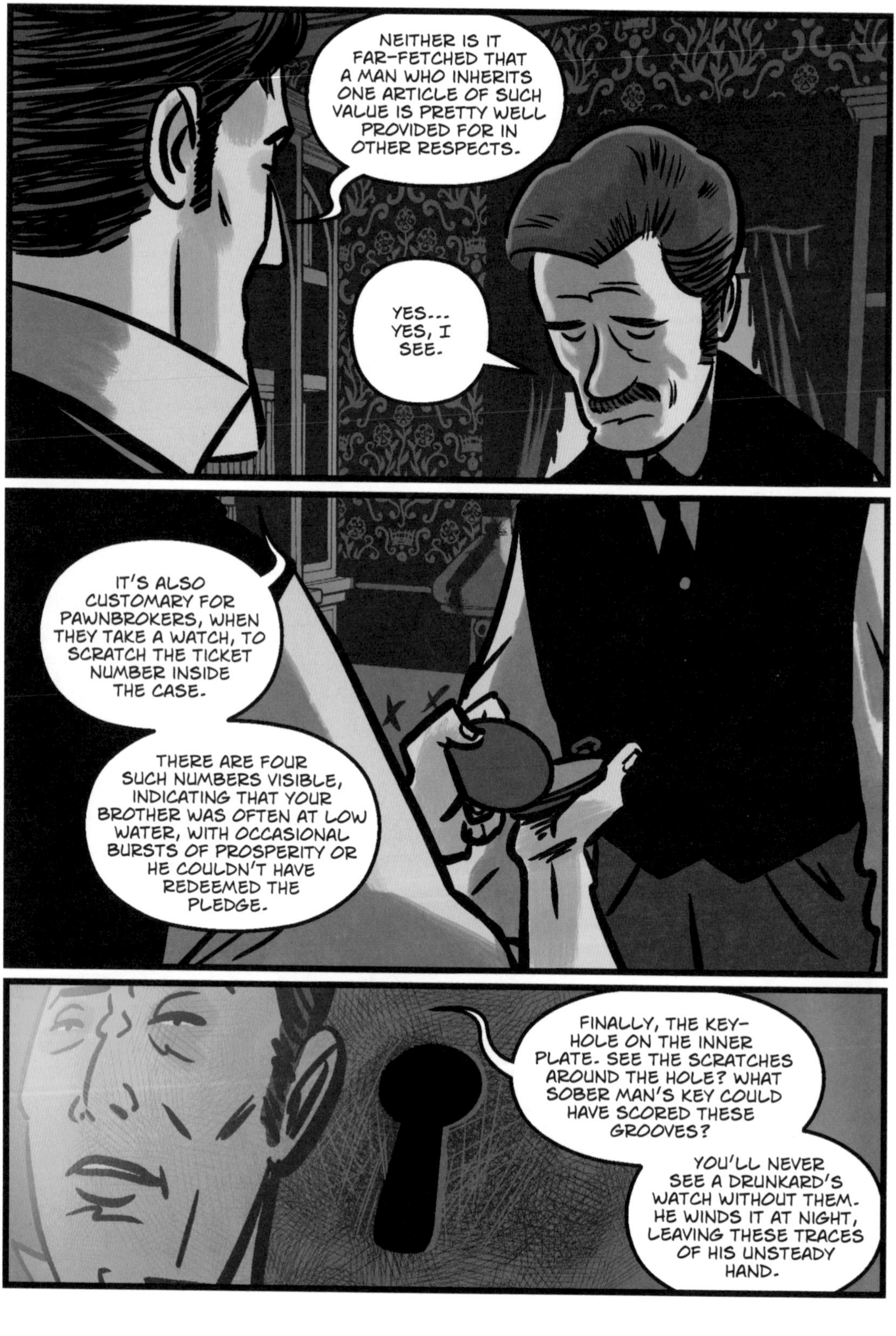
NEITHER IS IT FAR-FETCHED THAT A MAN WHO INHERITS ONE ARTICLE OF SUCH VALUE IS PRETTY WELL PROVIDED FOR IN OTHER RESPECTS.
YES... YES, I SEE.
IT'S ALSO CUSTOMARY FOR PAWNBROKERS, WHEN THEY TAKE A WATCH, TO SCRATCH THE TICKET NUMBER INSIDE THE CASE.
THERE ARE FOUR SUCH NUMBERS VISIBLE, INDICATING THAT YOUR BROTHER WAS OFTEN AT LOW WATER, WITH OCCASIONAL BURSTS OF PROSPERITY OR HE COULDN'T HAVE REDEEMED THE PLEDGE.
FINALLY, THE KEY-HOLE ON THE INNER PLATE. SEE THE SCRATCHES AROUND THE HOLE? WHAT SOBER MAN'S KEY COULD HAVE SCORED THESE GROOVES?
YOU'LL NEVER SEE A DRUNKARD'S WATCH WITHOUT THEM. HE WINDS IT AT NIGHT, LEAVING THESE TRACES OF HIS UNSTEADY HAND.

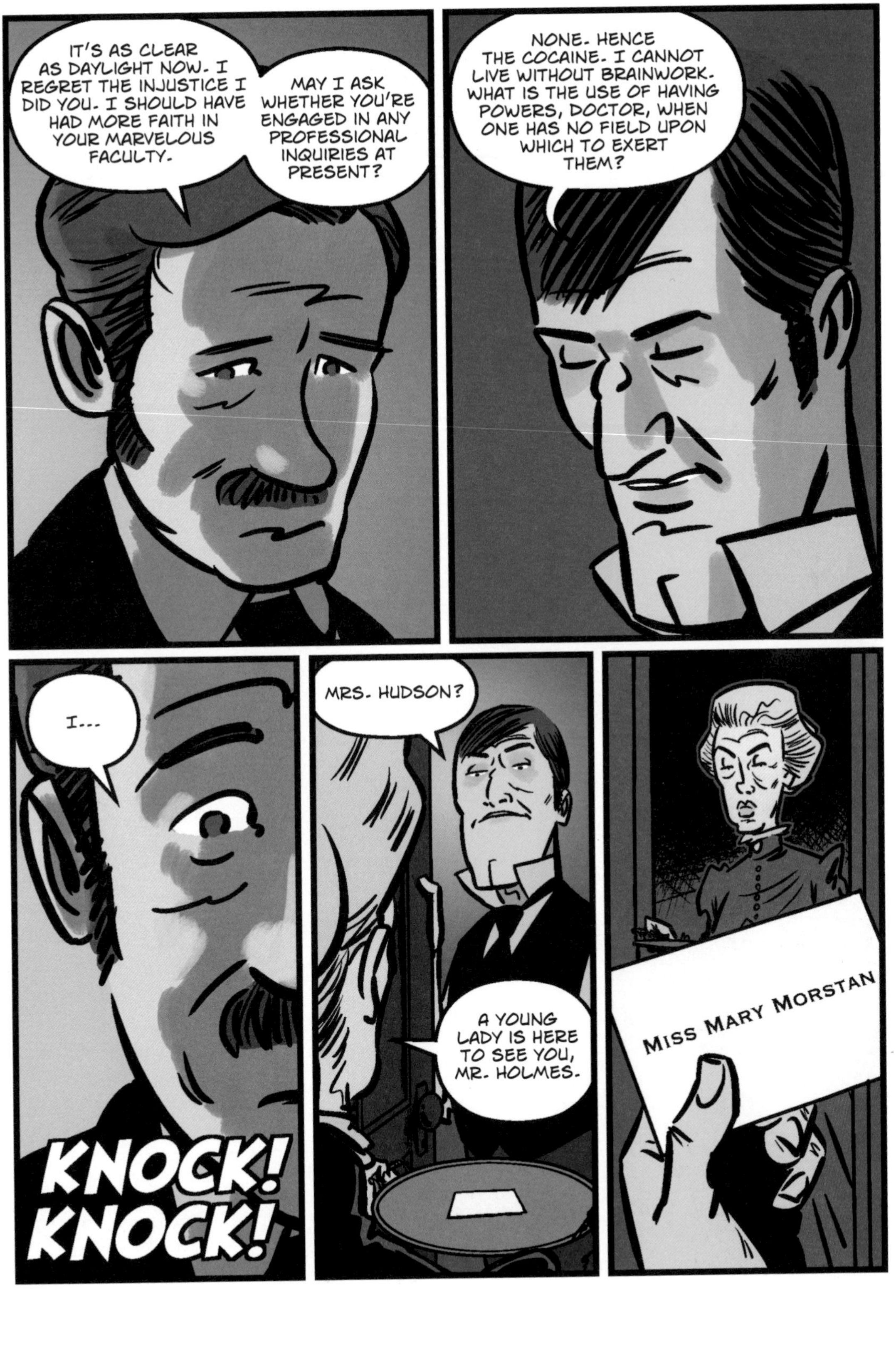
IT'S AS CLEAR AS DAYLIGHT NOW. I REGRET THE INJUSTICE I DID YOU. I SHOULD HAVE HAD MORE FAITH IN YOUR MARVELOUS FACULTY.
MAY I ASK WHETHER YOU'RE ENGAGED IN ANY PROFESSIONAL INQUIRIES AT PRESENT?
NONE. HENCE THE COCAINE. I CANNOT LIVE WITHOUT BRAINWORK. WHAT IS THE USE OF HAVING POWERS, DOCTOR, WHEN ONE HAS NO FIELD UPON WHICH TO EXERT THEM?
I...
KNOCK! KNOCK!
MRS. HUDSON?
A YOUNG LADY IS HERE TO SEE YOU, MR. HOLMES.
MISS MARY MORSTAN

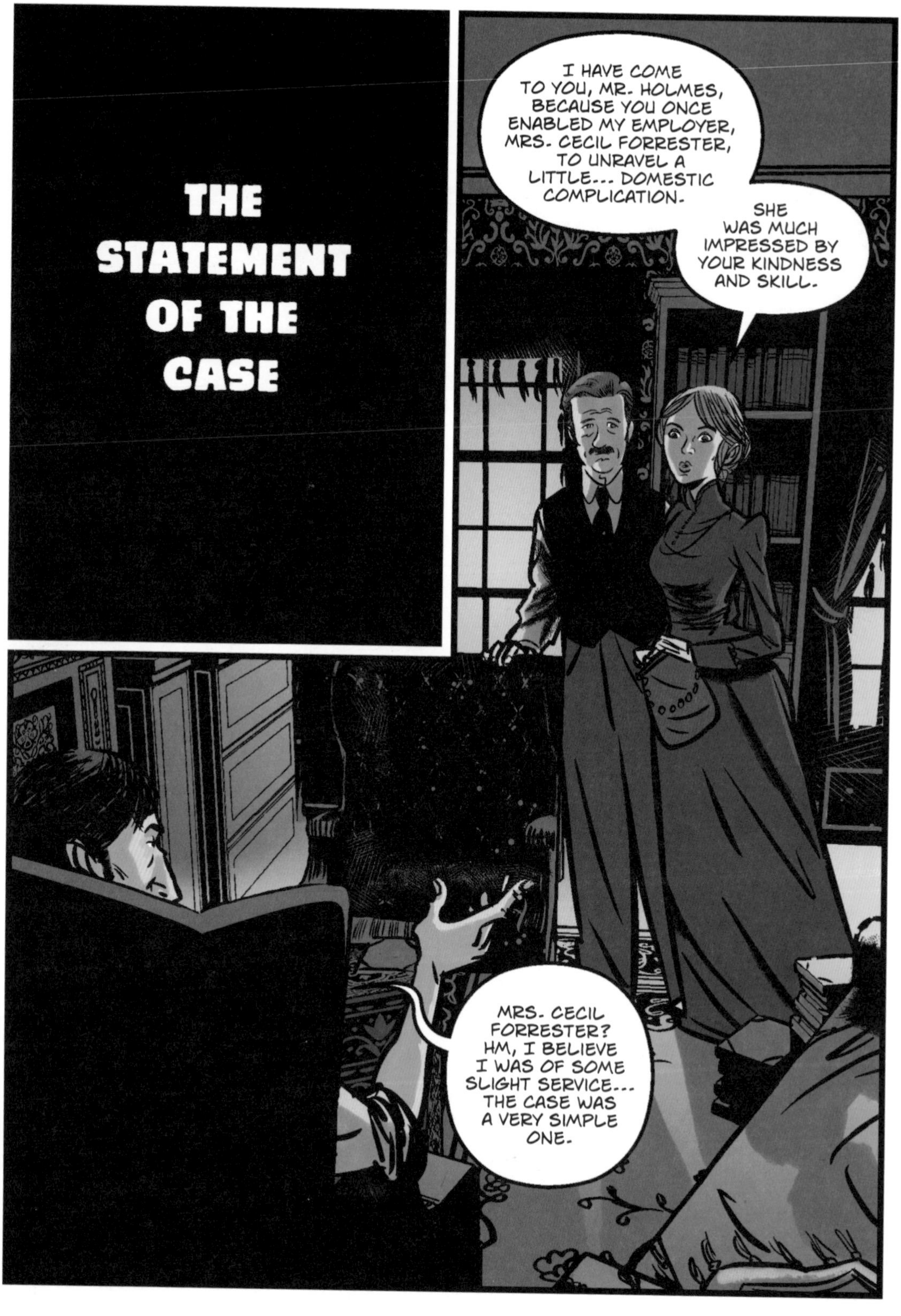
THE STATEMENT OF THE CASE
I HAVE COME TO YOU, MR. HOLMES, BECAUSE YOU ONCE ENABLED MY EMPLOYER, MRS. CECIL FORRESTER, TO UNRAVEL A LITTLE... DOMESTIC COMPLICATION.
SHE WAS MUCH IMPRESSED BY YOUR KINDNESS AND SKILL.
MRS. CECIL FORRESTER? HM, I BELIEVE I WAS OF SOME SLIGHT SERVICE... THE CASE WAS A VERY SIMPLE ONE.

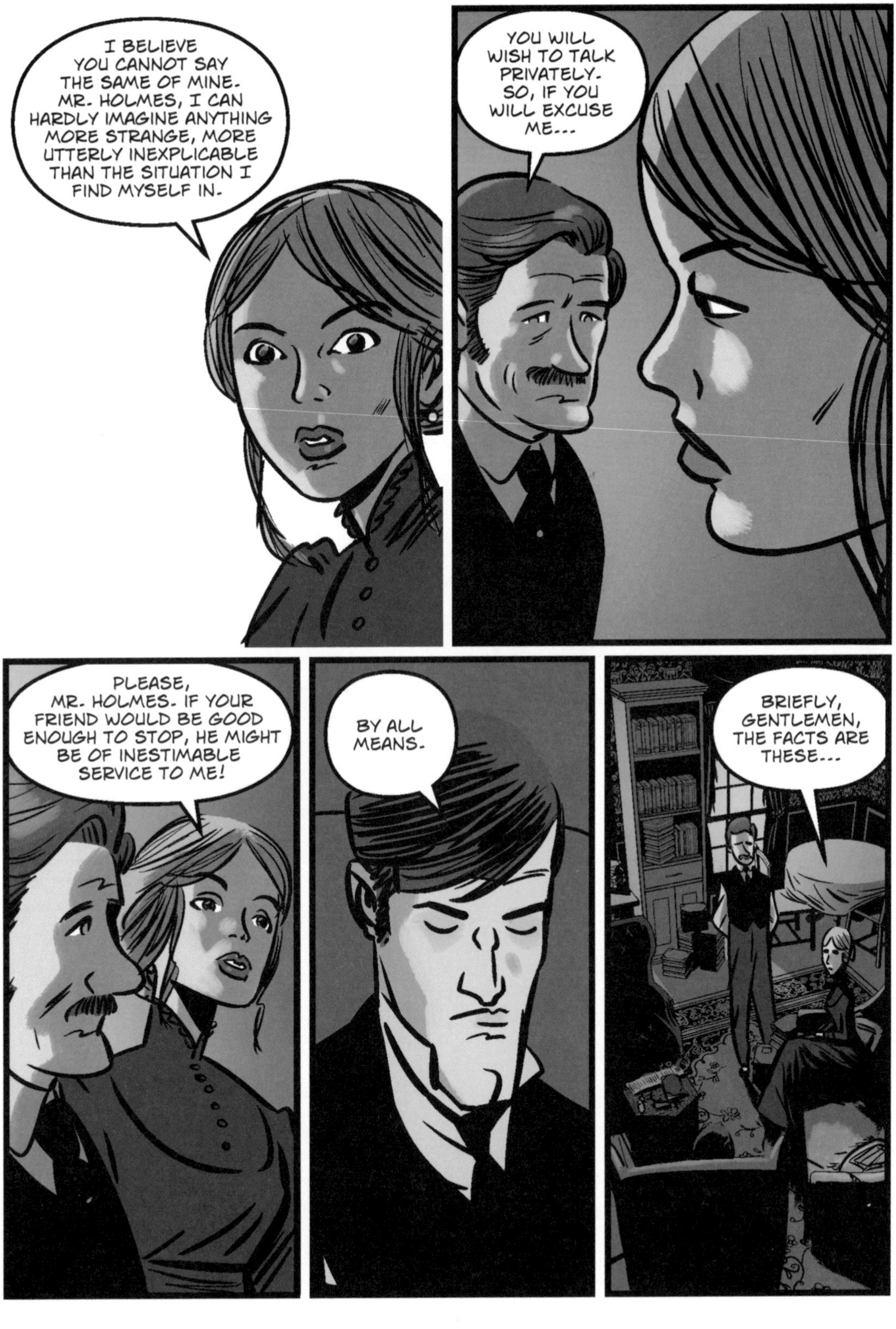
I BELIEVE YOU CANNOT SAY THE SAME OF MINE. MR. HOLMES, I CAN HARDLY IMAGINE ANYTHING MORE STRANGE, MORE UTTERLY INEXPLICABLE THAN THE SITUATION I FIND MYSELF IN.
YOU WILL WISH TO TALK PRIVATELY. SO, IF YOU WILL EXCUSE ME...
PLEASE, MR. HOLMES. IF YOUR FRIEND WOULD BE GOOD ENOUGH TO STOP, HE MIGHT BE OF INESTIMABLE SERVICE TO ME!
BY ALL MEANS.
BRIEFLY, GENTLEMEN, THE FACTS ARE THESE...

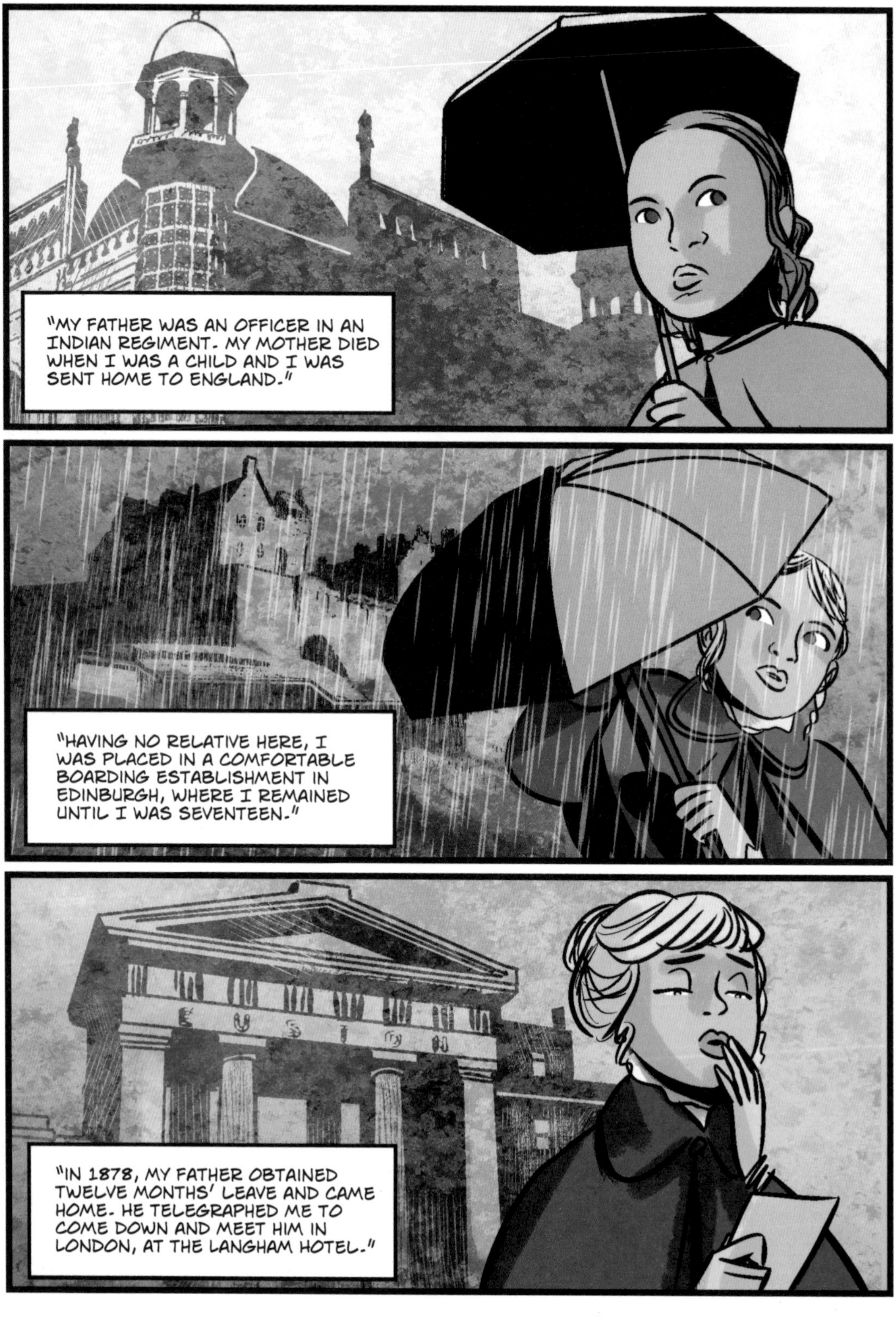
"MY FATHER WAS AN OFFICER IN AN INDIAN REGIMENT. MY MOTHER DIED WHEN I WAS A CHILD AND I WAS SENT HOME TO ENGLAND."
"HAVING NO RELATIVE HERE, I WAS PLACED IN A COMFORTABLE BOARDING ESTABLISHMENT IN EDINBURGH, WHERE I REMAINED UNTIL I WAS SEVENTEEN."
"IN 1878, MY FATHER OBTAINED TWELVE MONTHS' LEAVE AND CAME HOME. HE TELEGRAPHED ME TO COME DOWN AND MEET HIM IN LONDON, AT THE LANGHAM HOTEL."

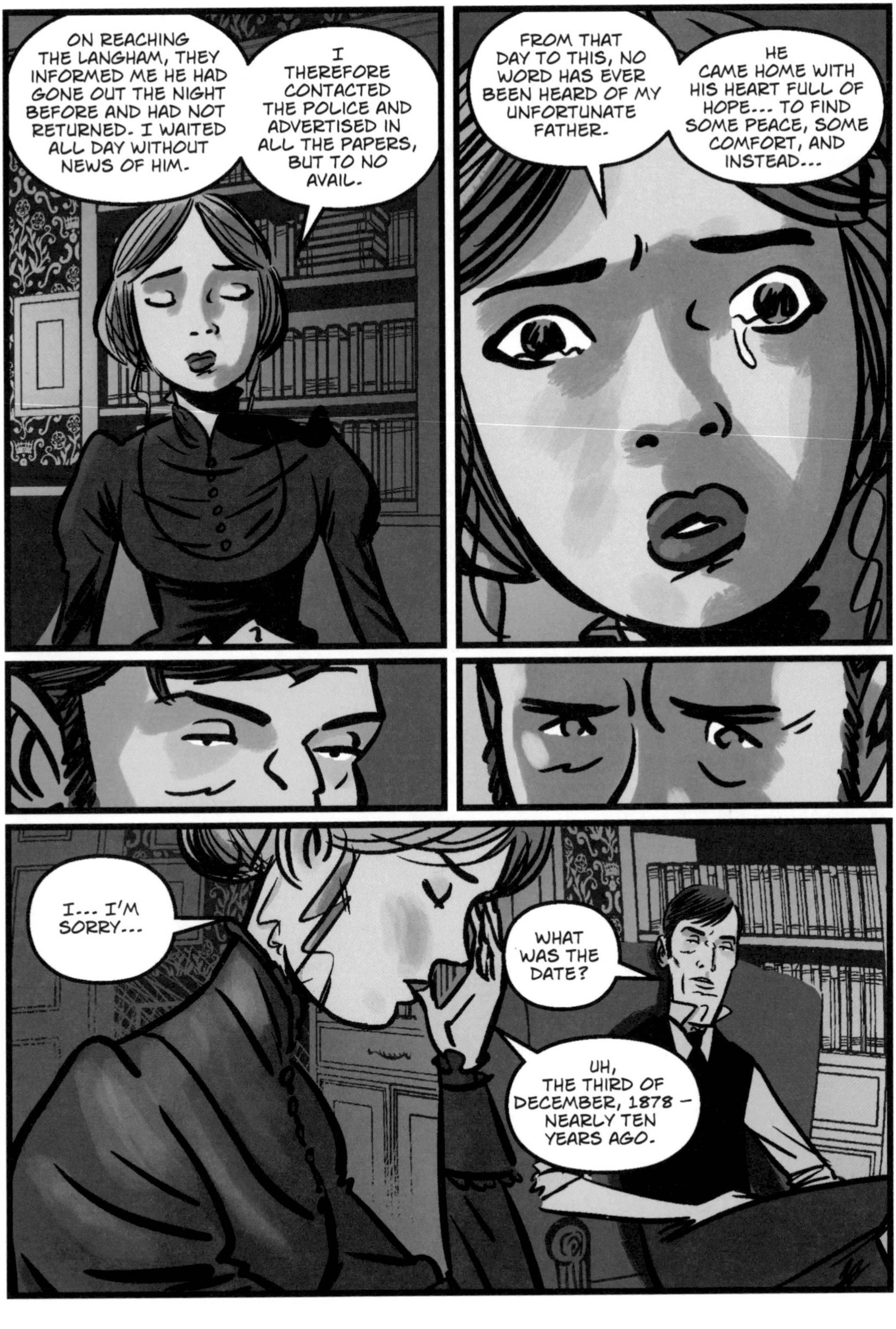
ON REACHING THE LANGHAM, THEY INFORMED ME HE HAD GONE OUT THE NIGHT BEFORE AND HAD NOT RETURNED. I WAITED ALL DAY WITHOUT NEWS OF HIM.
I THEREFORE CONTACTED THE POLICE AND ADVERTISED IN ALL THE PAPERS, BUT TO NO AVAIL.
FROM THAT DAY TO THIS, NO WORD HAS EVER BEEN HEARD OF MY UNFORTUNATE FATHER.
HE CAME HOME WITH HIS HEART FULL OF HOPE... TO FIND SOME PEACE, SOME COMFORT, AND INSTEAD...
I... I'M SORRY...
WHAT WAS THE DATE?
UH, THE THIRD OF DECEMBER, 1878 — NEARLY TEN YEARS AGO.

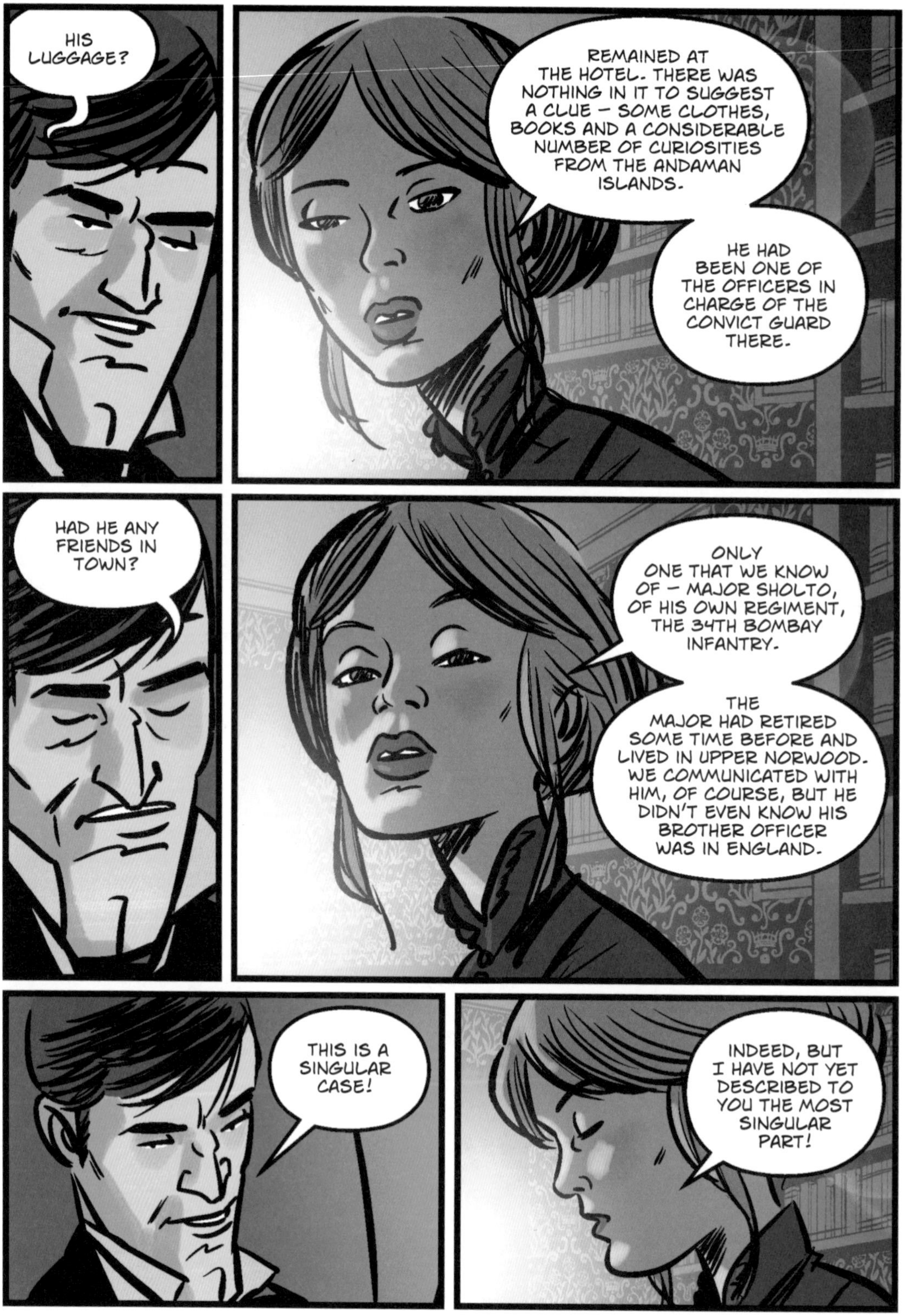
HIS LUGGAGE?
REMAINED AT THE HOTEL. THERE WAS NOTHING IN IT TO SUGGEST A CLUE — SOME CLOTHES, BOOKS AND A CONSIDERABLE NUMBER OF CURIOSITIES FROM THE ANDAMAN ISLANDS.
HE HAD BEEN ONE OF THE OFFICERS IN CHARGE OF THE CONVICT GUARD THERE.
HAD HE ANY FRIENDS IN TOWN?
ONLY ONE THAT WE KNOW OF — MAJOR SHOLTO, OF HIS OWN REGIMENT, THE 34TH BOMBAY INFANTRY.
THE MAJOR HAD RETIRED SOME TIME BEFORE AND LIVED IN UPPER NORWOOD. WE COMMUNICATED WITH HIM, OF COURSE, BUT HE DIDN'T EVEN KNOW HIS BROTHER OFFICER WAS IN ENGLAND.
THIS IS A SINGULAR CASE!
INDEED, BUT I HAVE NOT YET DESCRIBED TO YOU THE MOST SINGULAR PART!

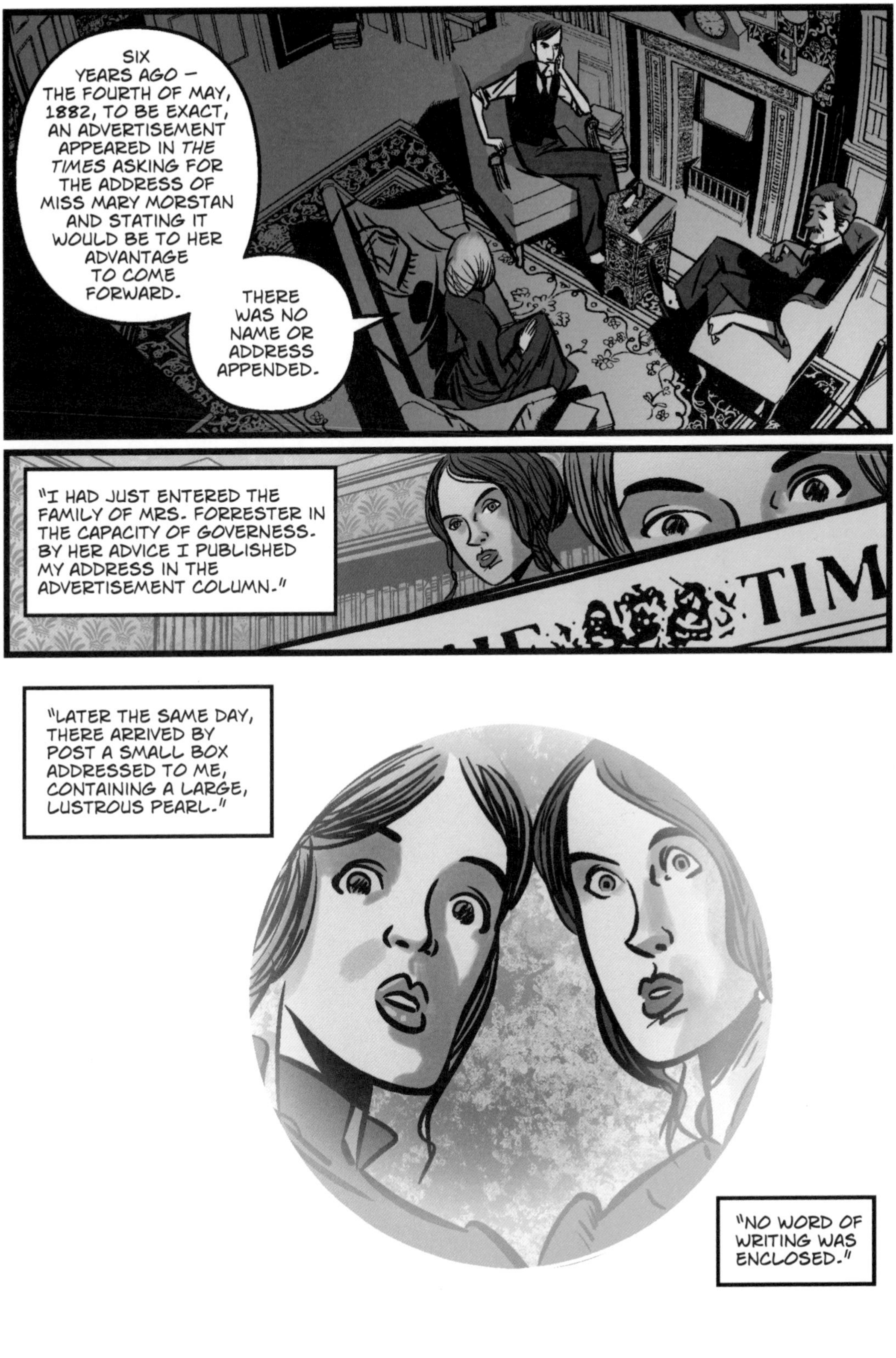
SIX YEARS AGO — THE FOURTH OF MAY, 1882, TO BE EXACT, AN ADVERTISEMENT APPEARED IN *THE TIMES* ASKING FOR THE ADDRESS OF MISS MARY MORSTAN AND STATING IT WOULD BE TO HER ADVANTAGE TO COME FORWARD.
THERE WAS NO NAME OR ADDRESS APPENDED.
"I HAD JUST ENTERED THE FAMILY OF MRS. FORRESTER IN THE CAPACITY OF GOVERNESS. BY HER ADVICE I PUBLISHED MY ADDRESS IN THE ADVERTISEMENT COLUMN."
"LATER THE SAME DAY, THERE ARRIVED BY POST A SMALL BOX ADDRESSED TO ME, CONTAINING A LARGE, LUSTROUS PEARL."
"NO WORD OF WRITING WAS ENCLOSED."

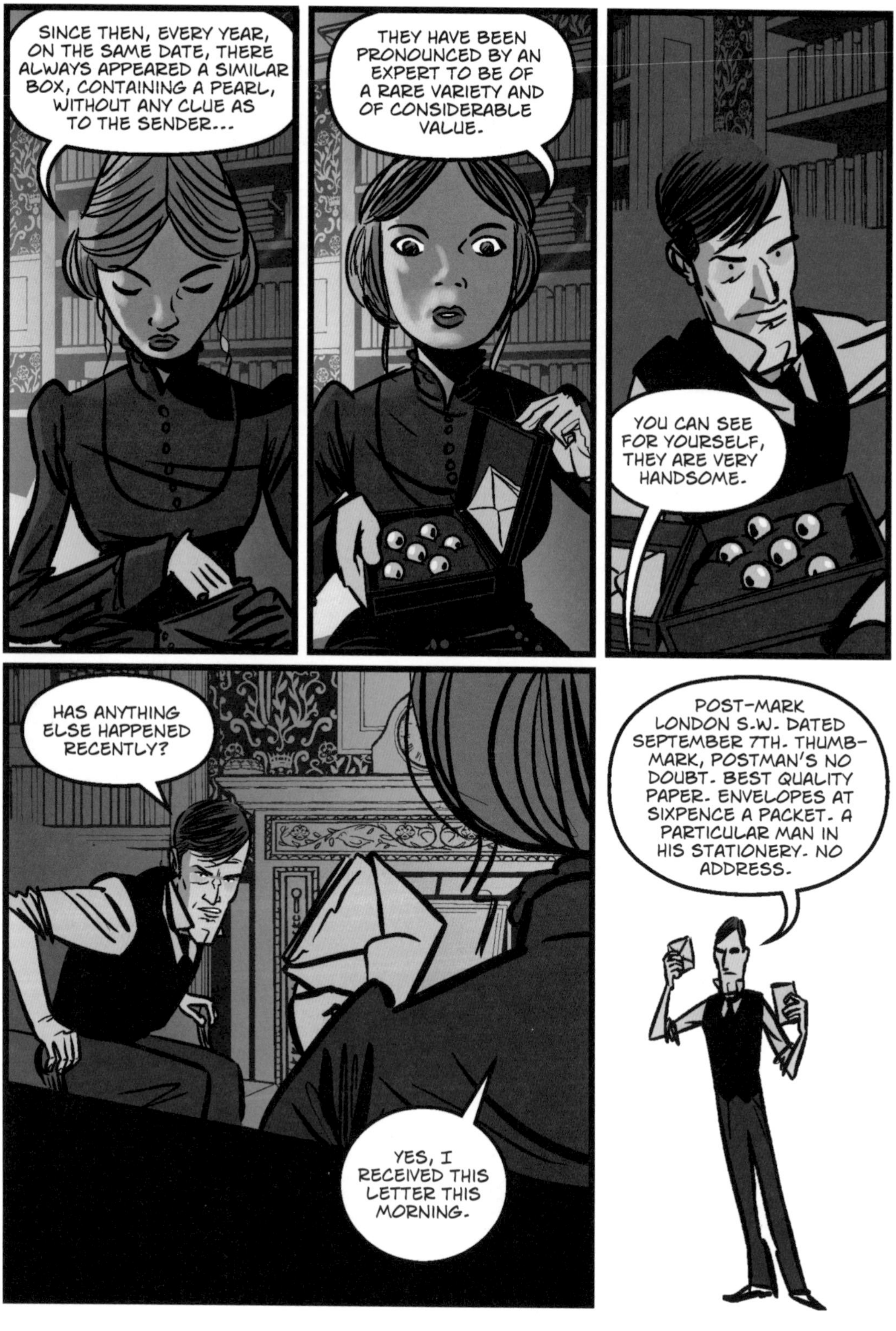
SINCE THEN, EVERY YEAR, ON THE SAME DATE, THERE ALWAYS APPEARED A SIMILAR BOX, CONTAINING A PEARL, WITHOUT ANY CLUE AS TO THE SENDER...
THEY HAVE BEEN PRONOUNCED BY AN EXPERT TO BE OF A RARE VARIETY AND OF CONSIDERABLE VALUE.
YOU CAN SEE FOR YOURSELF, THEY ARE VERY HANDSOME.
HAS ANYTHING ELSE HAPPENED RECENTLY?
YES, I RECEIVED THIS LETTER THIS MORNING.
POST-MARK LONDON S.W. DATED SEPTEMBER 7TH. THUMB-MARK, POSTMAN'S NO DOUBT. BEST QUALITY PAPER. ENVELOPES AT SIXPENCE A PACKET. A PARTICULAR MAN IN HIS STATIONERY. NO ADDRESS.

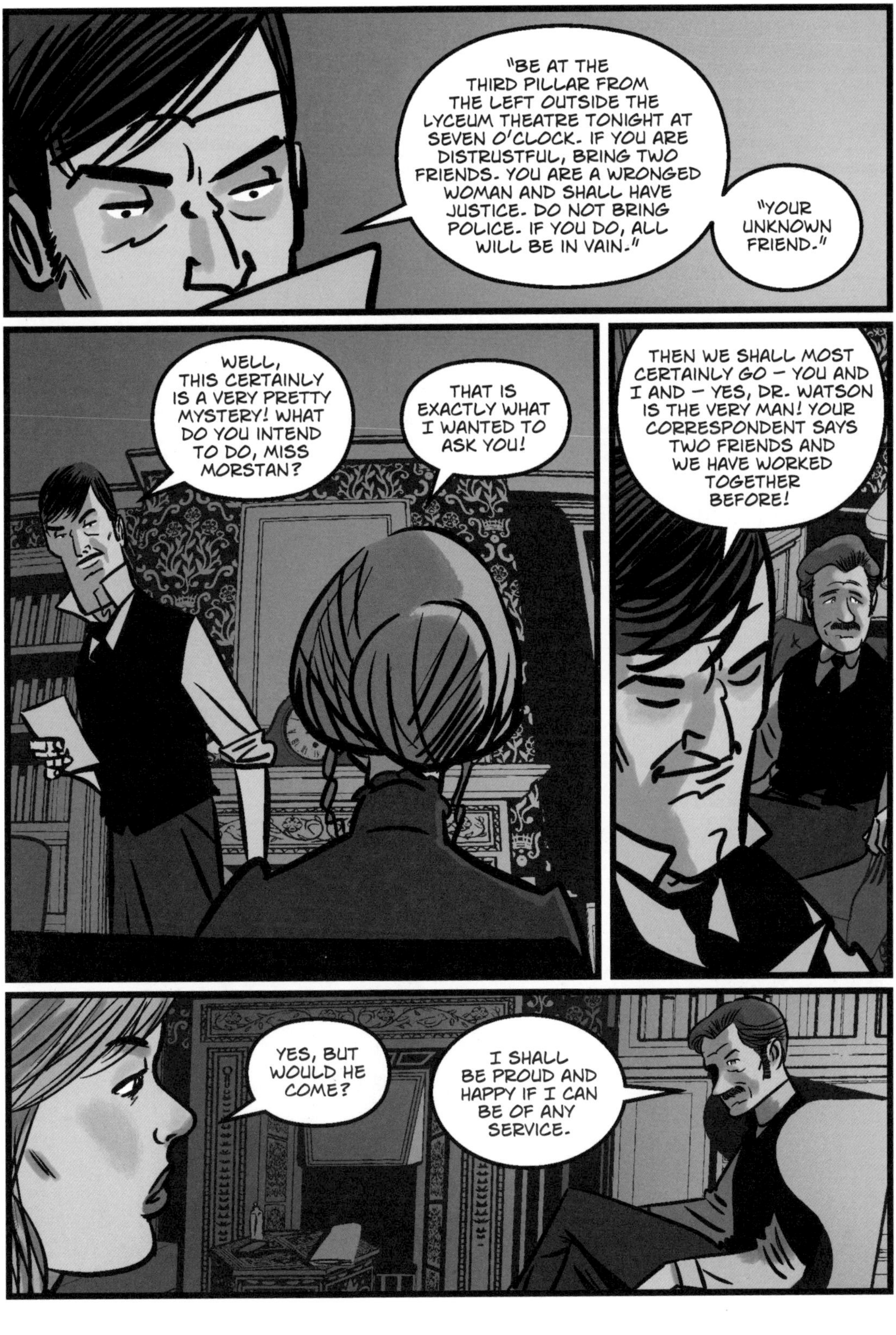
"BE AT THE THIRD PILLAR FROM THE LEFT OUTSIDE THE LYCEUM THEATRE TONIGHT AT SEVEN O'CLOCK. IF YOU ARE DISTRUSTFUL, BRING TWO FRIENDS. YOU ARE A WRONGED WOMAN AND SHALL HAVE JUSTICE. DO NOT BRING POLICE. IF YOU DO, ALL WILL BE IN VAIN."
"YOUR UNKNOWN FRIEND."
WELL, THIS CERTAINLY IS A VERY PRETTY MYSTERY! WHAT DO YOU INTEND TO DO, MISS MORSTAN?
THAT IS EXACTLY WHAT I WANTED TO ASK YOU!
THEN WE SHALL MOST CERTAINLY GO – YOU AND I AND – YES, DR. WATSON IS THE VERY MAN! YOUR CORRESPONDENT SAYS TWO FRIENDS AND WE HAVE WORKED TOGETHER BEFORE!
YES, BUT WOULD HE COME?
I SHALL BE PROUD AND HAPPY IF I CAN BE OF ANY SERVICE.

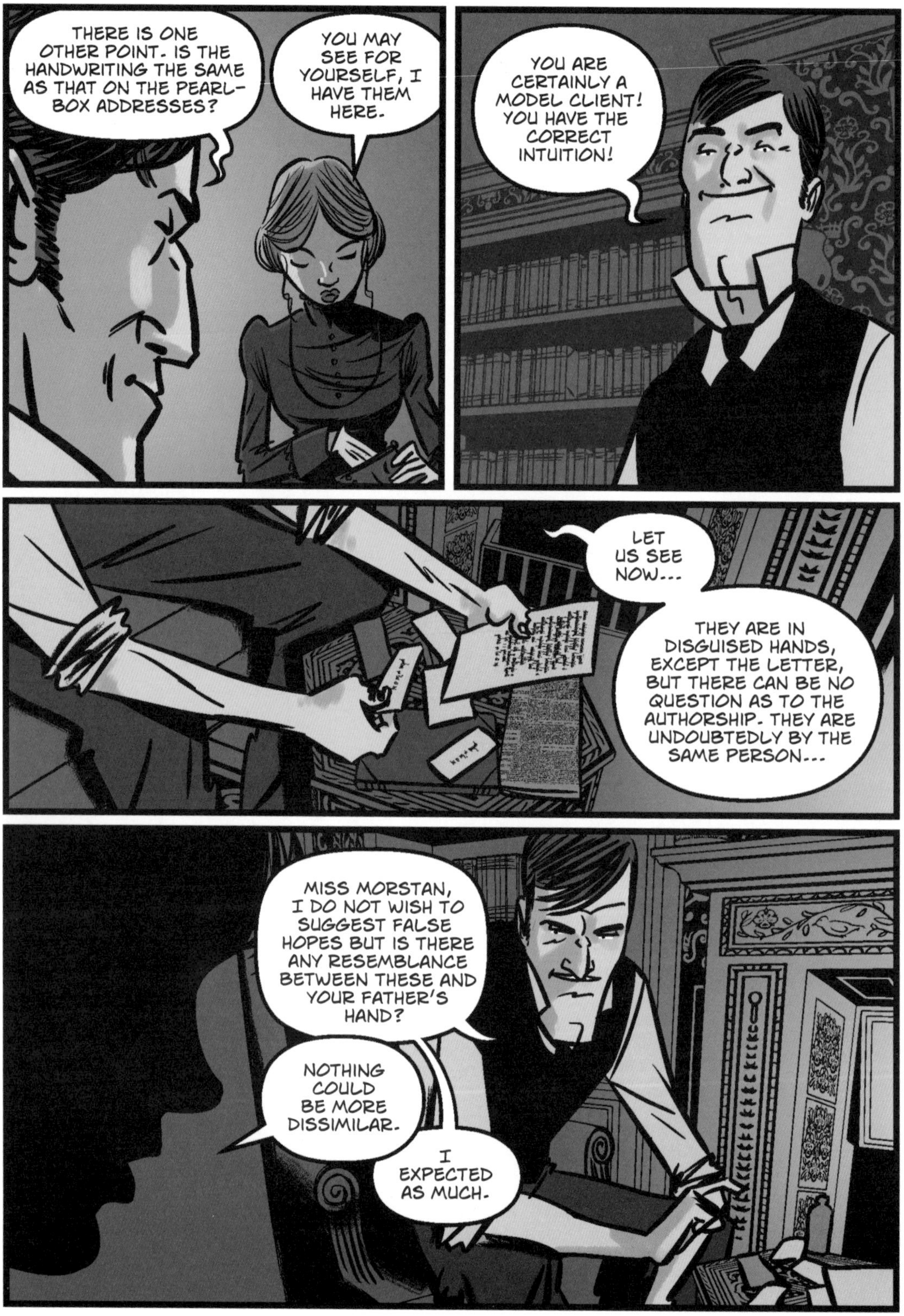
THERE IS ONE OTHER POINT. IS THE HANDWRITING THE SAME AS THAT ON THE PEARL-BOX ADDRESSES?
YOU MAY SEE FOR YOURSELF, I HAVE THEM HERE.
YOU ARE CERTAINLY A MODEL CLIENT! YOU HAVE THE CORRECT INTUITION!
LET US SEE NOW...
THEY ARE IN DISGUISED HANDS, EXCEPT THE LETTER, BUT THERE CAN BE NO QUESTION AS TO THE AUTHORSHIP. THEY ARE UNDOUBTEDLY BY THE SAME PERSON...
MISS MORSTAN, I DO NOT WISH TO SUGGEST FALSE HOPES BUT IS THERE ANY RESEMBLANCE BETWEEN THESE AND YOUR FATHER'S HAND?
NOTHING COULD BE MORE DISSIMILAR.
I EXPECTED AS MUCH.

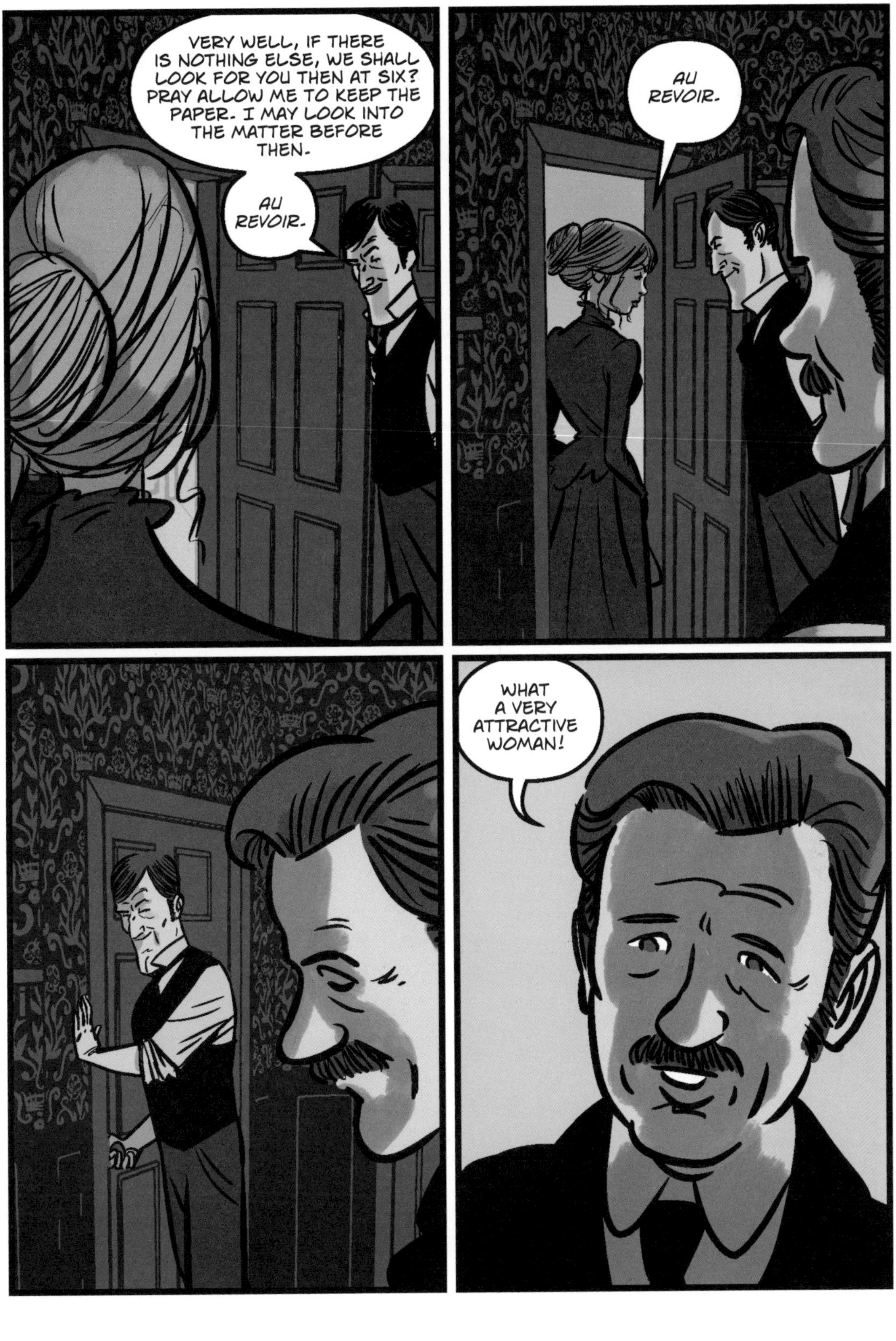
VERY WELL, IF THERE IS NOTHING ELSE, WE SHALL LOOK FOR YOU THEN AT SIX? PRAY ALLOW ME TO KEEP THE PAPER. I MAY LOOK INTO THE MATTER BEFORE THEN.
AU REVOIR.
AU REVOIR.
WHAT A VERY ATTRACTIVE WOMAN!

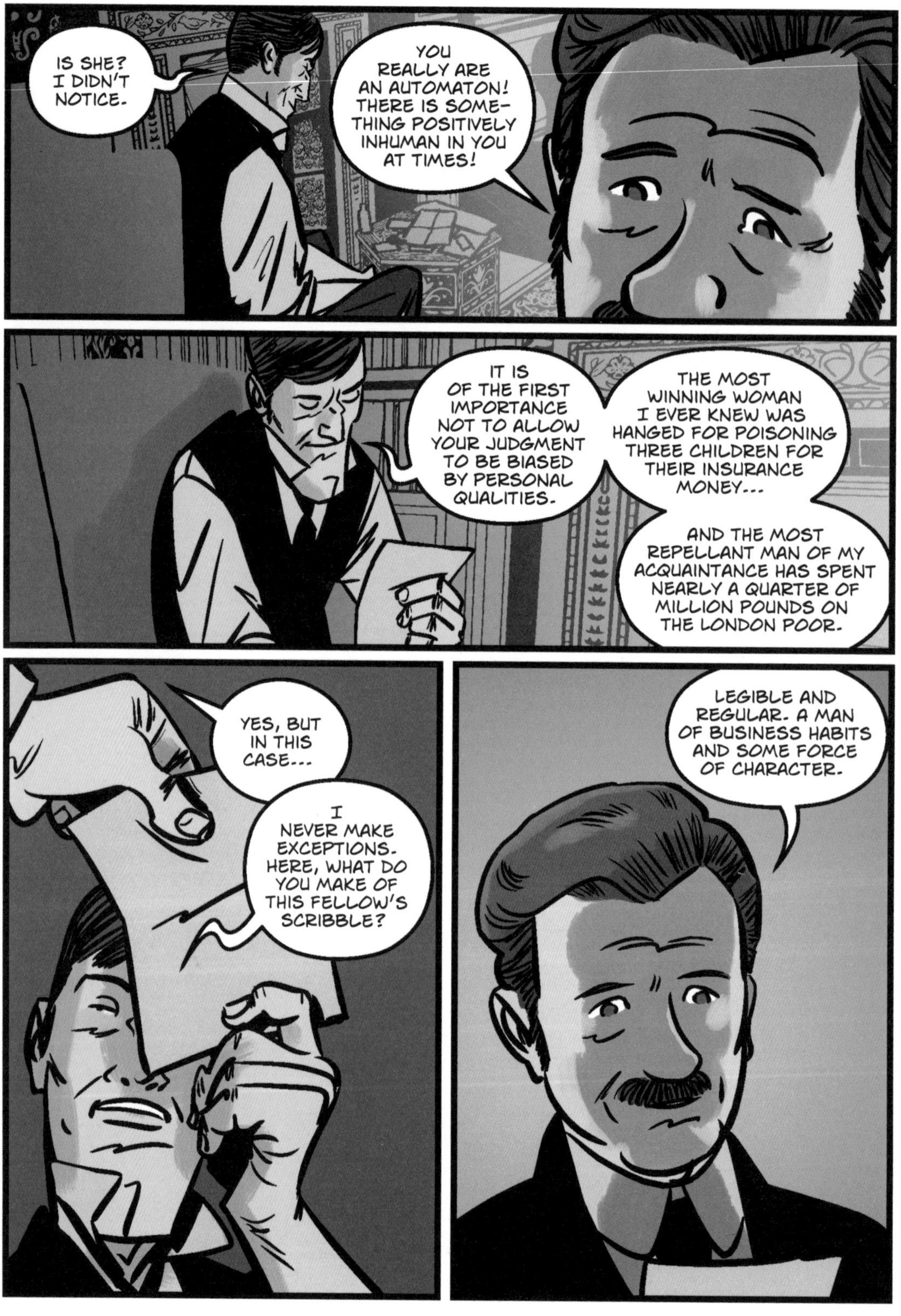
IS SHE? I DIDN'T NOTICE.
YOU REALLY ARE AN AUTOMATON! THERE IS SOME-THING POSITIVELY INHUMAN IN YOU AT TIMES!
IT IS OF THE FIRST IMPORTANCE NOT TO ALLOW YOUR JUDGMENT TO BE BIASED BY PERSONAL QUALITIES.
THE MOST WINNING WOMAN I EVER KNEW WAS HANGED FOR POISONING THREE CHILDREN FOR THEIR INSURANCE MONEY...
AND THE MOST REPELLANT MAN OF MY ACQUAINTANCE HAS SPENT NEARLY A QUARTER OF MILLION POUNDS ON THE LONDON POOR.
YES, BUT IN THIS CASE...
I NEVER MAKE EXCEPTIONS. HERE, WHAT DO YOU MAKE OF THIS FELLOW'S SCRIBBLE?
LEGIBLE AND REGULAR. A MAN OF BUSINESS HABITS AND SOME FORCE OF CHARACTER.

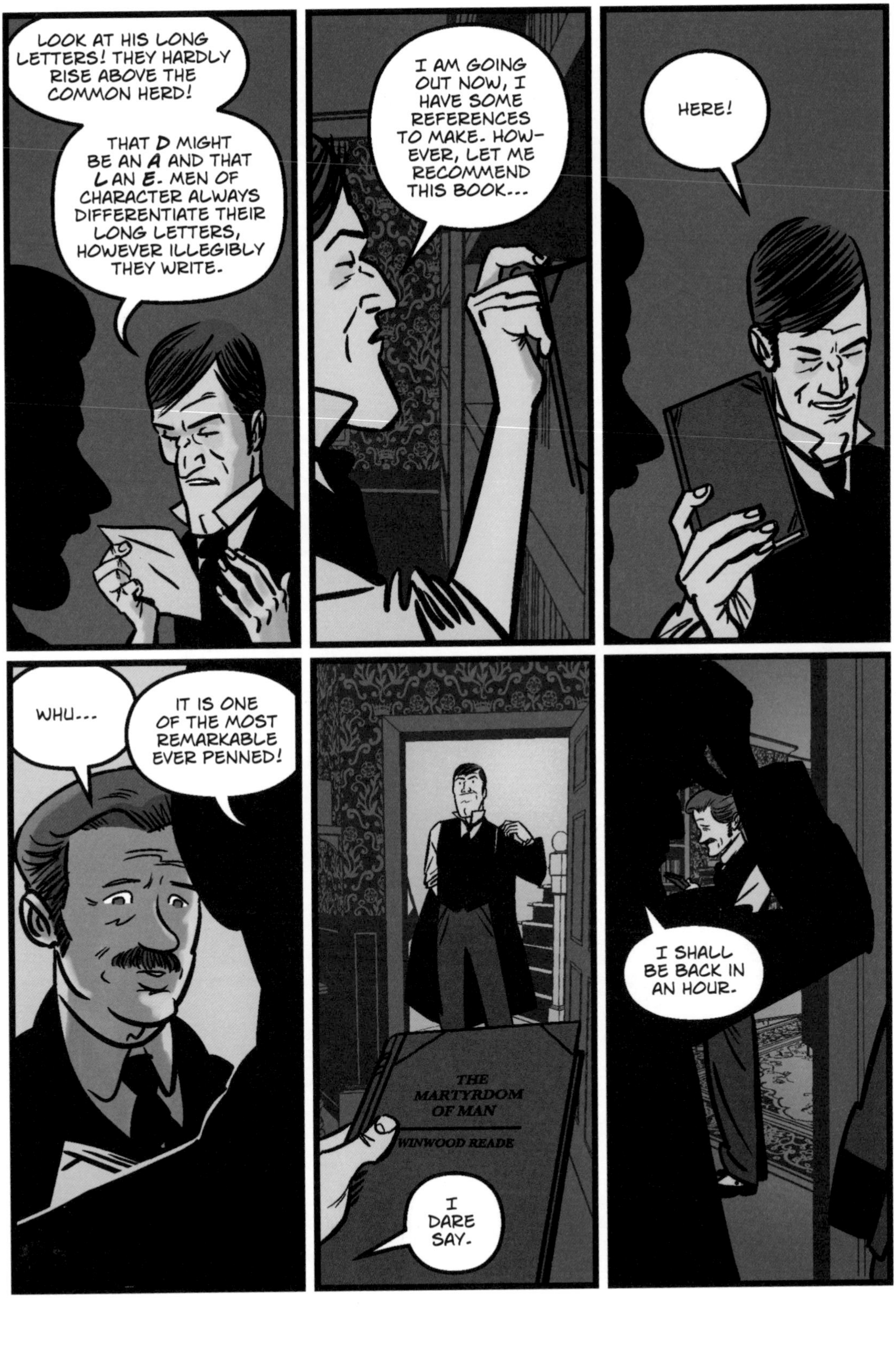
LOOK AT HIS LONG LETTERS! THEY HARDLY RISE ABOVE THE COMMON HERD!
THAT D MIGHT BE AN A AND THAT L AN E. MEN OF CHARACTER ALWAYS DIFFERENTIATE THEIR LONG LETTERS, HOWEVER ILLEGIBLY THEY WRITE.
I AM GOING OUT NOW, I HAVE SOME REFERENCES TO MAKE. HOW-EVER, LET ME RECOMMEND THIS BOOK...
HERE!
WHU...
IT IS ONE OF THE MOST REMARKABLE EVER PENNED!
THE MARTYRDOM OF MAN
WINWOOD READE
I DARE SAY.
I SHALL BE BACK IN AN HOUR.

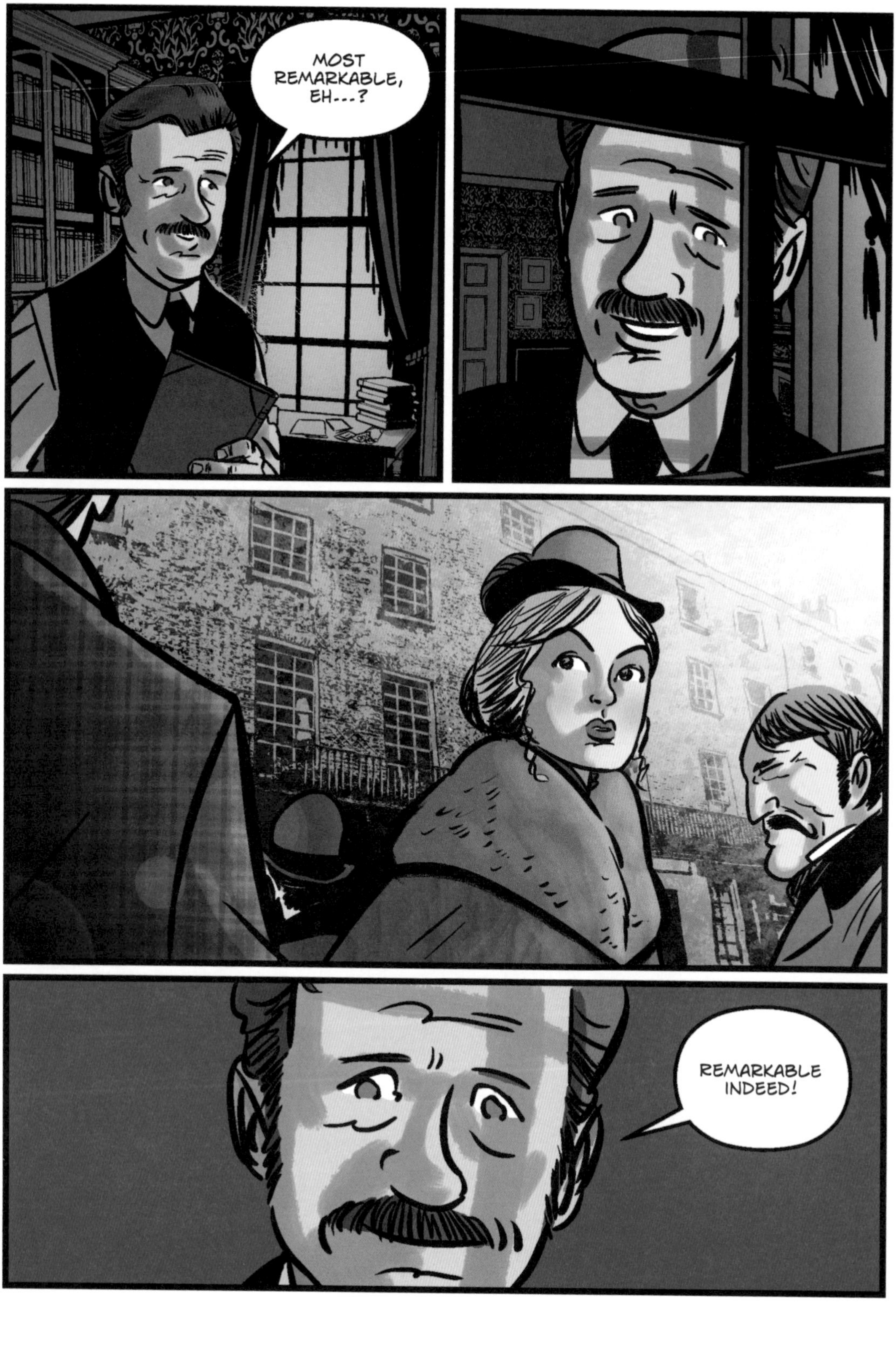
MOST REMARKABLE, EH...?
REMARKABLE INDEED!

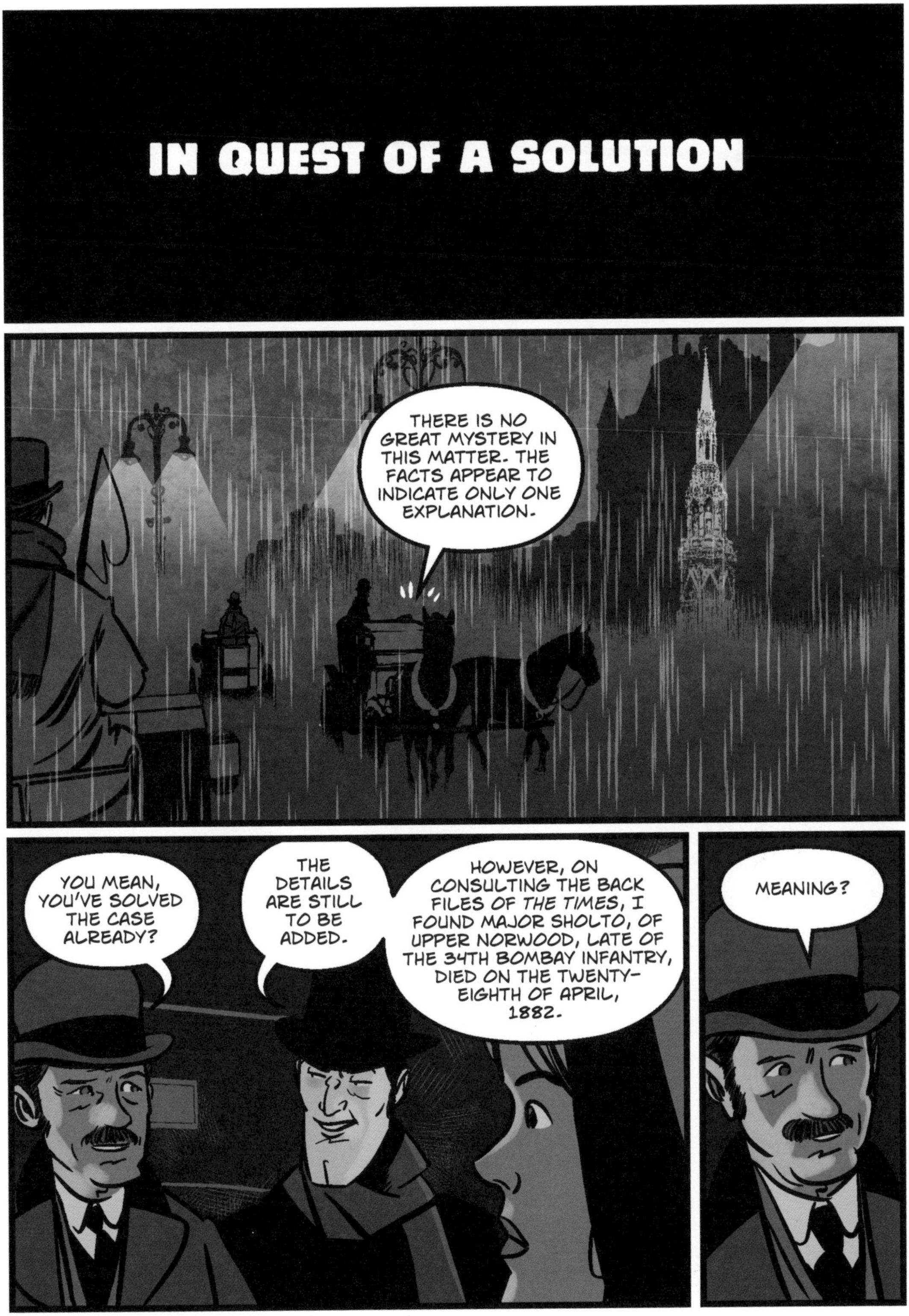
IN QUEST OF A SOLUTION
THERE IS NO GREAT MYSTERY IN THIS MATTER. THE FACTS APPEAR TO INDICATE ONLY ONE EXPLANATION.
YOU MEAN, YOU'VE SOLVED THE CASE ALREADY?
THE DETAILS ARE STILL TO BE ADDED.
HOWEVER, ON CONSULTING THE BACK FILES OF *THE TIMES*, I FOUND MAJOR SHOLTO, OF UPPER NORWOOD, LATE OF THE 34TH BOMBAY INFANTRY, DIED ON THE TWENTY-EIGHTH OF APRIL, 1882.
MEANING?

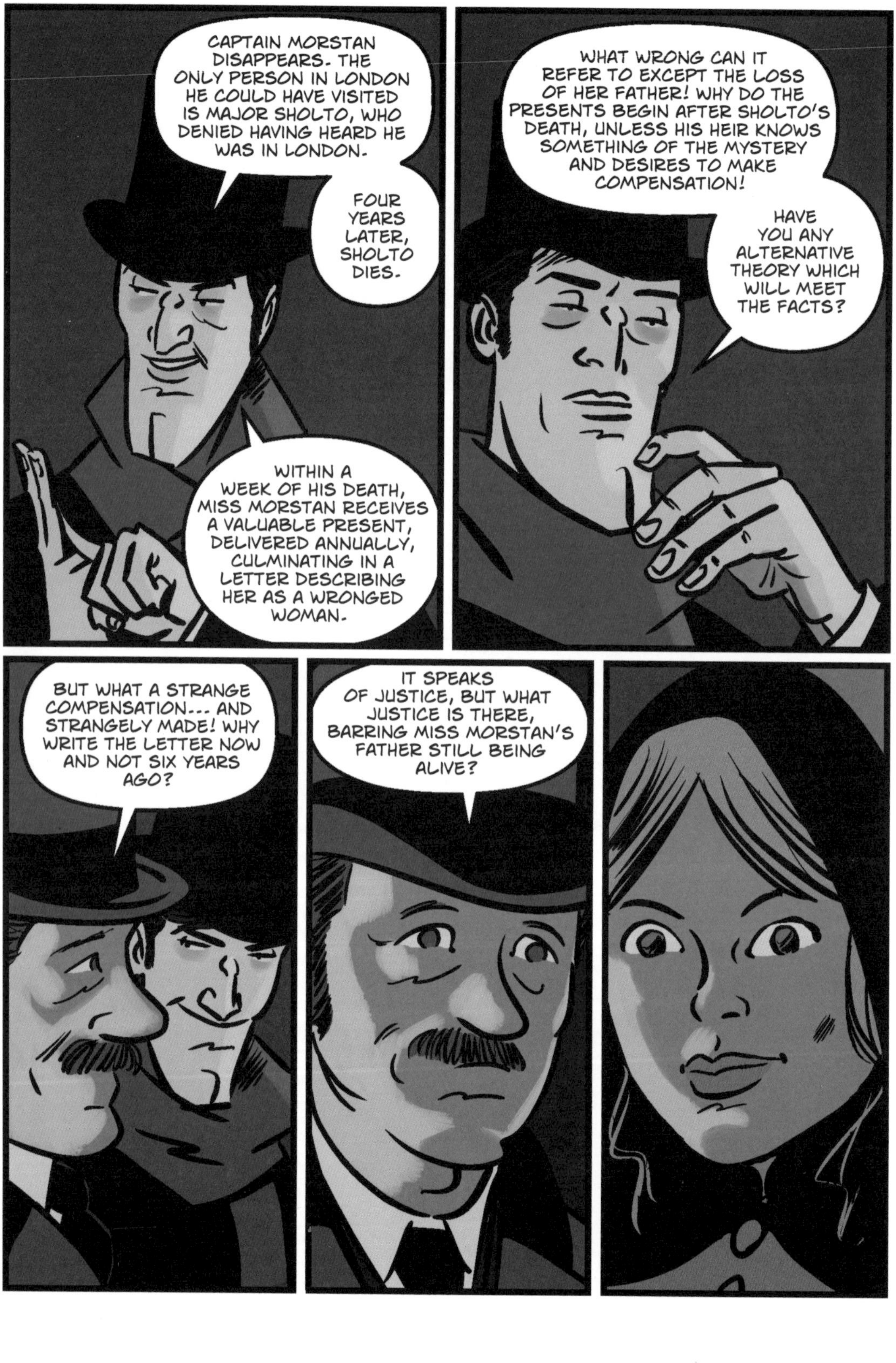
CAPTAIN MORSTAN DISAPPEARS. THE ONLY PERSON IN LONDON HE COULD HAVE VISITED IS MAJOR SHOLTO, WHO DENIED HAVING HEARD HE WAS IN LONDON.
FOUR YEARS LATER, SHOLTO DIES.
WITHIN A WEEK OF HIS DEATH, MISS MORSTAN RECEIVES A VALUABLE PRESENT, DELIVERED ANNUALLY, CULMINATING IN A LETTER DESCRIBING HER AS A WRONGED WOMAN.
WHAT WRONG CAN IT REFER TO EXCEPT THE LOSS OF HER FATHER! WHY DO THE PRESENTS BEGIN AFTER SHOLTO'S DEATH, UNLESS HIS HEIR KNOWS SOMETHING OF THE MYSTERY AND DESIRES TO MAKE COMPENSATION!
HAVE YOU ANY ALTERNATIVE THEORY WHICH WILL MEET THE FACTS?
BUT WHAT A STRANGE COMPENSATION... AND STRANGELY MADE! WHY WRITE THE LETTER NOW AND NOT SIX YEARS AGO?
IT SPEAKS OF JUSTICE, BUT WHAT JUSTICE IS THERE, BARRING MISS MORSTAN'S FATHER STILL BEING ALIVE?

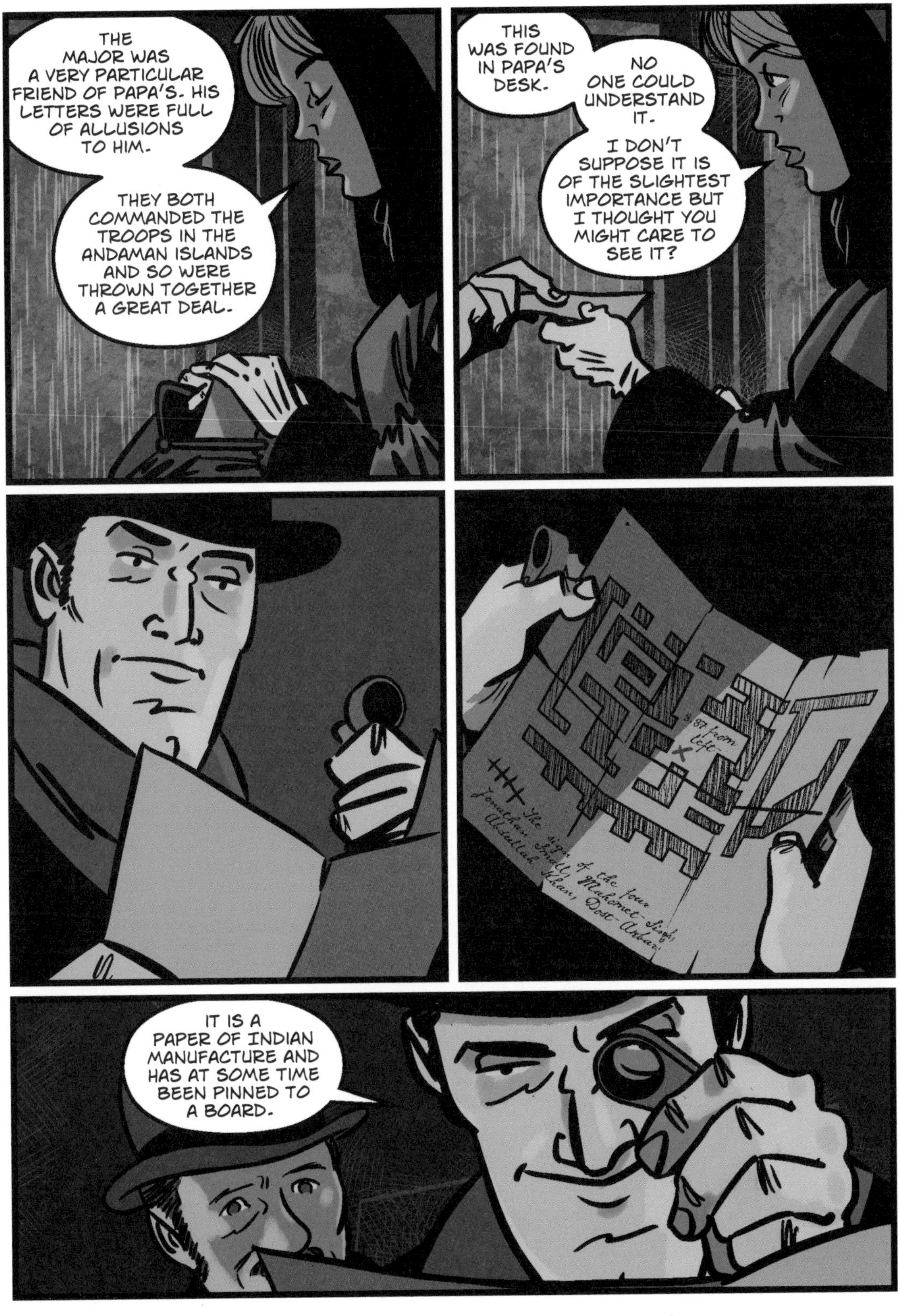
THE MAJOR WAS A VERY PARTICULAR FRIEND OF PAPA'S. HIS LETTERS WERE FULL OF ALLUSIONS TO HIM.
THEY BOTH COMMANDED THE TROOPS IN THE ANDAMAN ISLANDS AND SO WERE THROWN TOGETHER A GREAT DEAL.
THIS WAS FOUND IN PAPA'S DESK.
NO ONE COULD UNDERSTAND IT.
I DON'T SUPPOSE IT IS OF THE SLIGHTEST IMPORTANCE BUT I THOUGHT YOU MIGHT CARE TO SEE IT?
3.37 from left
The sign of the four
Jonathan Small, Mahomet Singh, Abdullah Khan, Dost Akbar
IT IS A PAPER OF INDIAN MANUFACTURE AND HAS AT SOME TIME BEEN PINNED TO A BOARD.

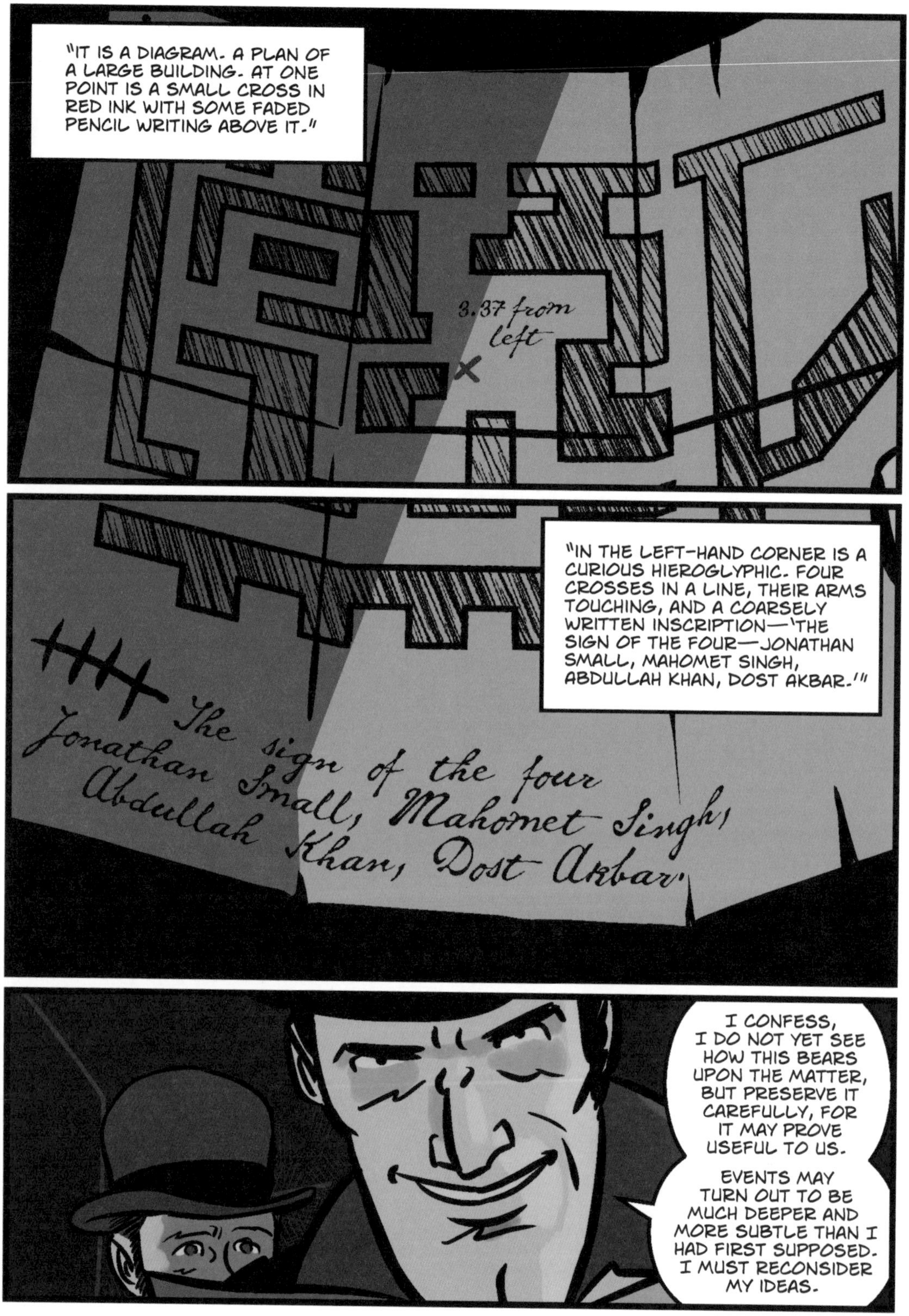
"IT IS A DIAGRAM. A PLAN OF A LARGE BUILDING. AT ONE POINT IS A SMALL CROSS IN RED INK WITH SOME FADED PENCIL WRITING ABOVE IT."
3.37 from left
"IN THE LEFT-HAND CORNER IS A CURIOUS HIEROGLYPHIC. FOUR CROSSES IN A LINE, THEIR ARMS TOUCHING, AND A COARSELY WRITTEN INSCRIPTION—'THE SIGN OF THE FOUR—JONATHAN SMALL, MAHOMET SINGH, ABDULLAH KHAN, DOST AKBAR.'"
The sign of the four
Jonathan Small, Mahomet Singh,
Abdullah Khan, Dost Akbar.
I CONFESS, I DO NOT YET SEE HOW THIS BEARS UPON THE MATTER, BUT PRESERVE IT CAREFULLY, FOR IT MAY PROVE USEFUL TO US.
EVENTS MAY TURN OUT TO BE MUCH DEEPER AND MORE SUBTLE THAN I HAD FIRST SUPPOSED. I MUST RECONSIDER MY IDEAS.

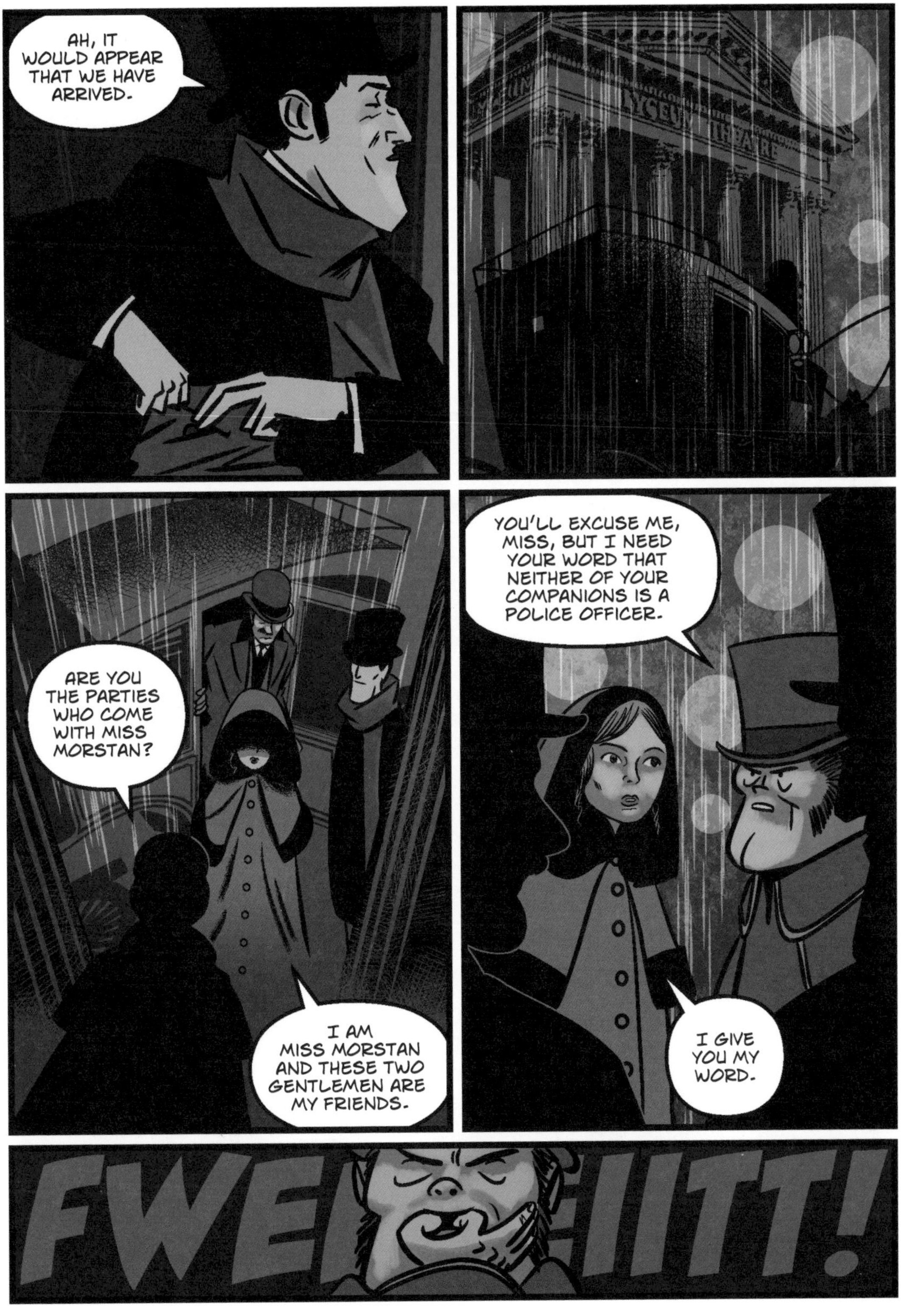
AH, IT WOULD APPEAR THAT WE HAVE ARRIVED.
LYCEUM THEATRE
ARE YOU THE PARTIES WHO COME WITH MISS MORSTAN?
I AM MISS MORSTAN AND THESE TWO GENTLEMEN ARE MY FRIENDS.
YOU'LL EXCUSE ME, MISS, BUT I NEED YOUR WORD THAT NEITHER OF YOUR COMPANIONS IS A POLICE OFFICER.
I GIVE YOU MY WORD.
FWE EIITT!

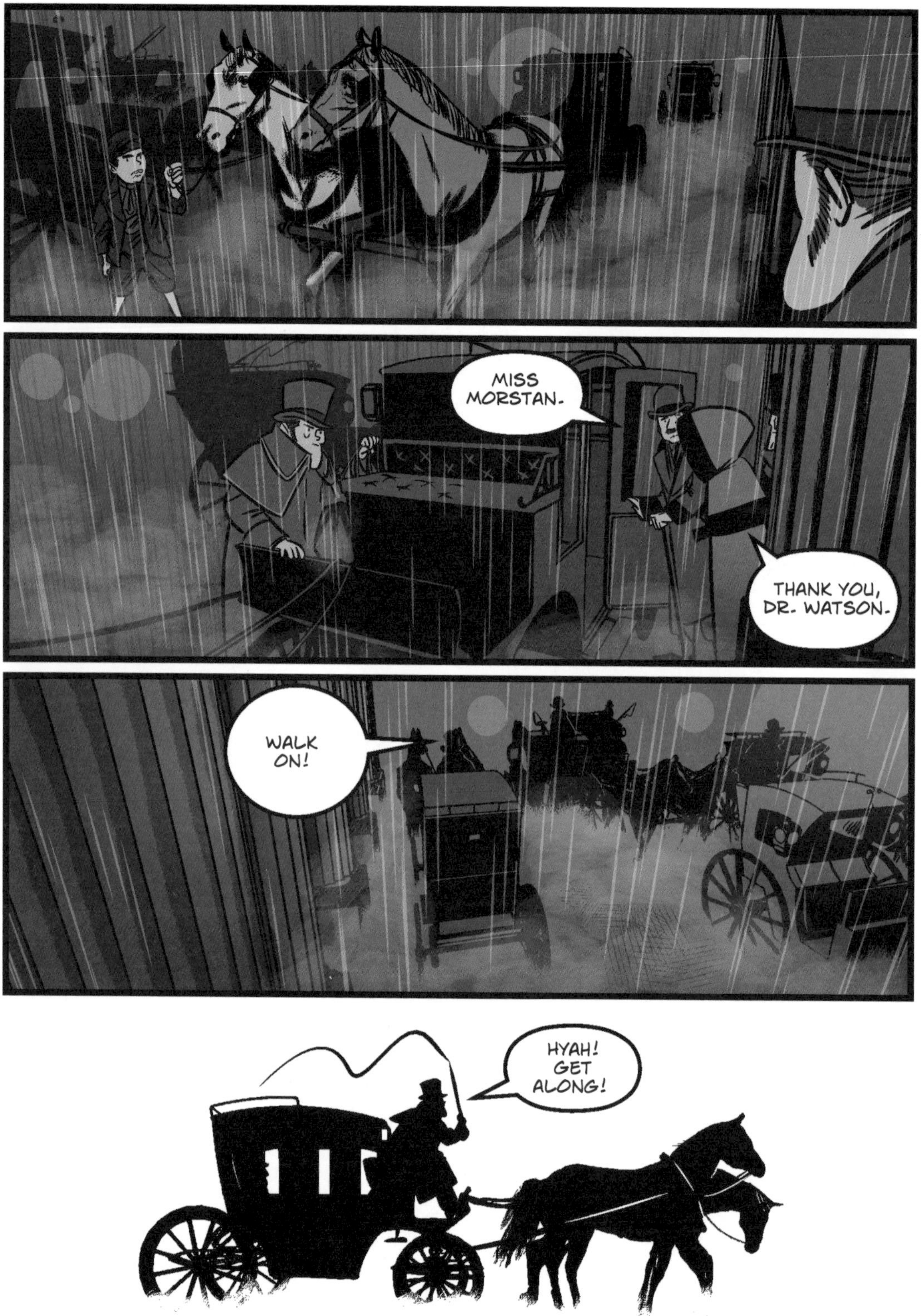
MISS MORSTAN.
THANK YOU, DR. WATSON.
WALK ON!
HYAH! GET ALONG!

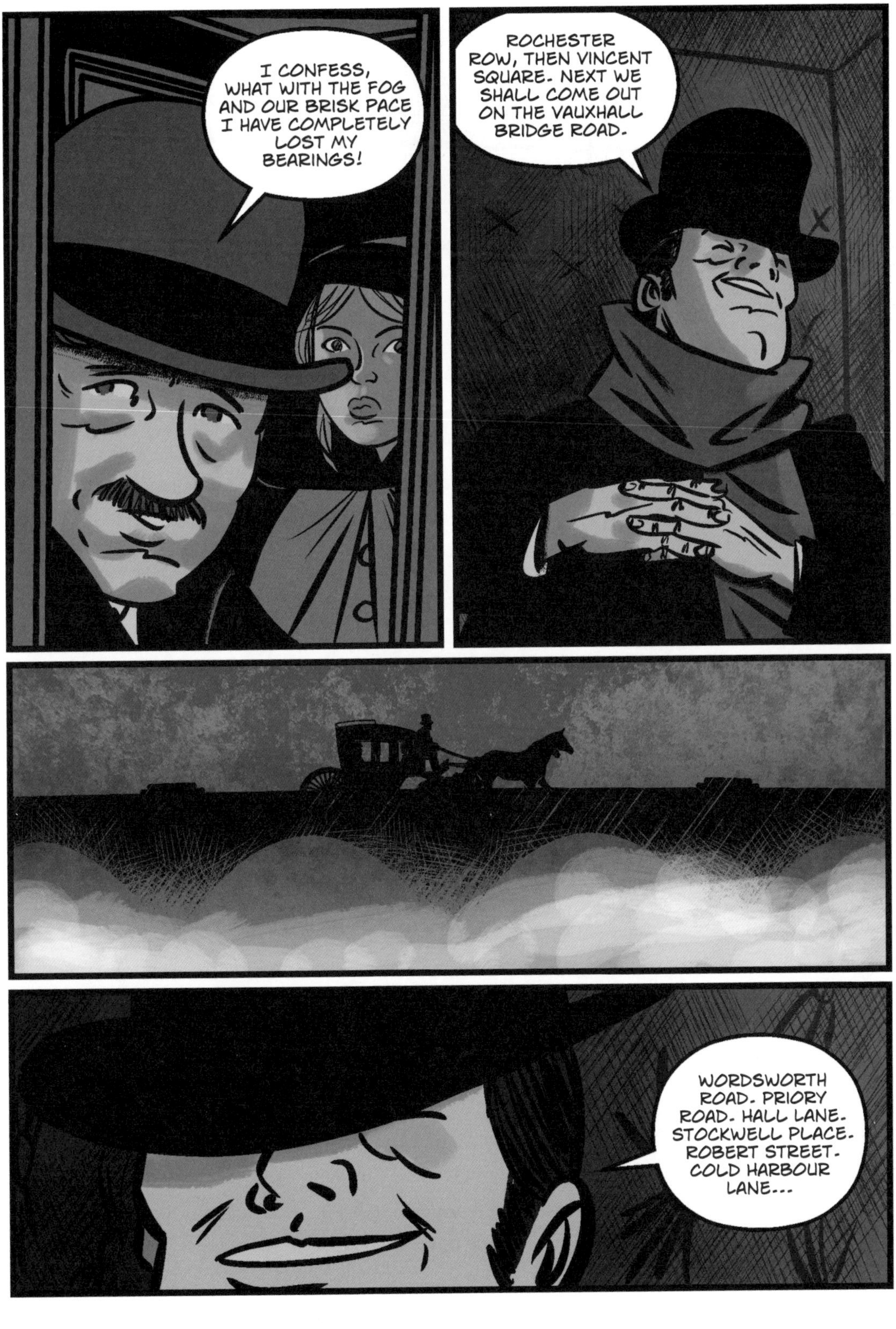
I CONFESS, WHAT WITH THE FOG AND OUR BRISK PACE I HAVE COMPLETELY LOST MY BEARINGS!
ROCHESTER ROW, THEN VINCENT SQUARE. NEXT WE SHALL COME OUT ON THE VAUXHALL BRIDGE ROAD.
WORDSWORTH ROAD. PRIORY ROAD. HALL LANE. STOCKWELL PLACE. ROBERT STREET. COLD HARBOUR LANE...

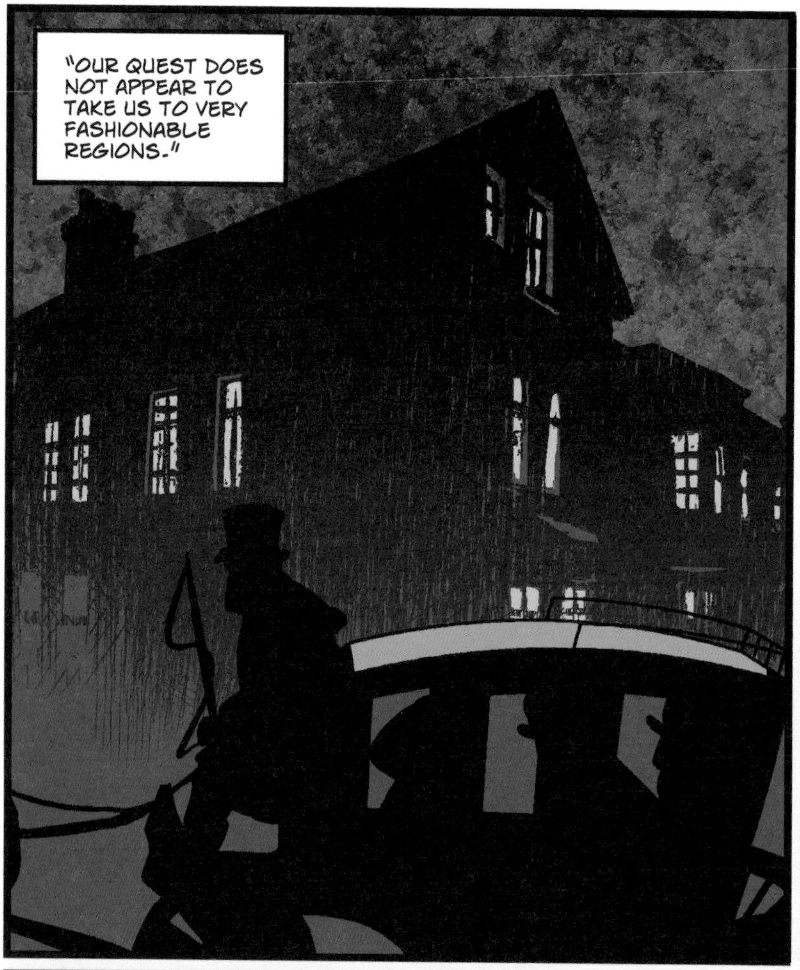
"OUR QUEST DOES NOT APPEAR TO TAKE US TO VERY FASHIONABLE REGIONS."

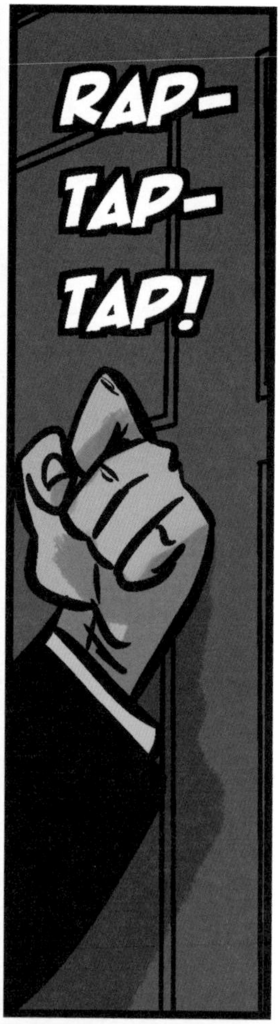
RAP-
TAP-
TAP!

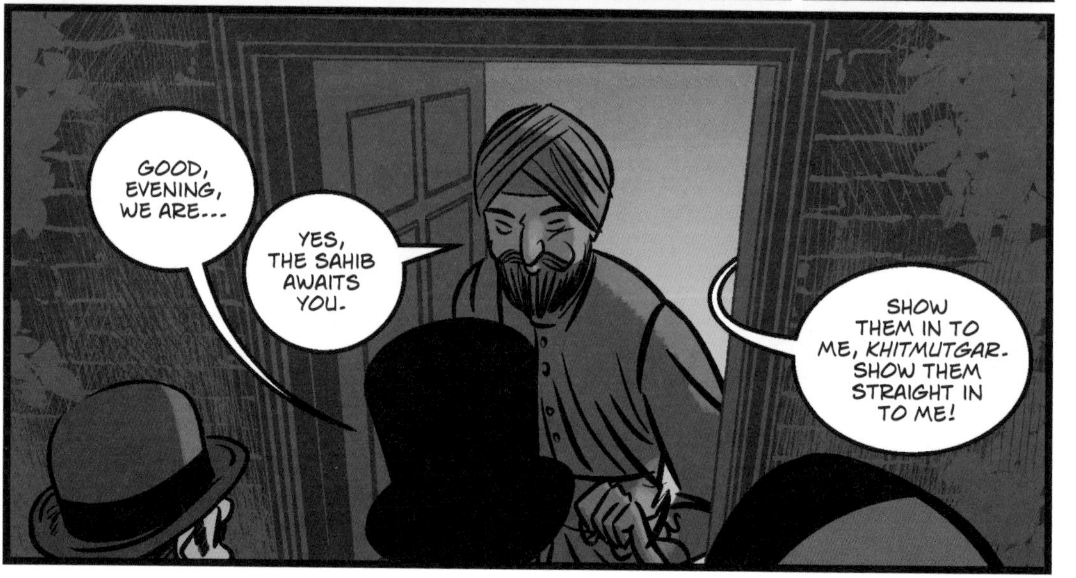
GOOD, EVENING, WE ARE...
YES, THE SAHIB AWAITS YOU.
SHOW THEM IN TO ME, KHITMUTGAR. SHOW THEM STRAIGHT IN TO ME!

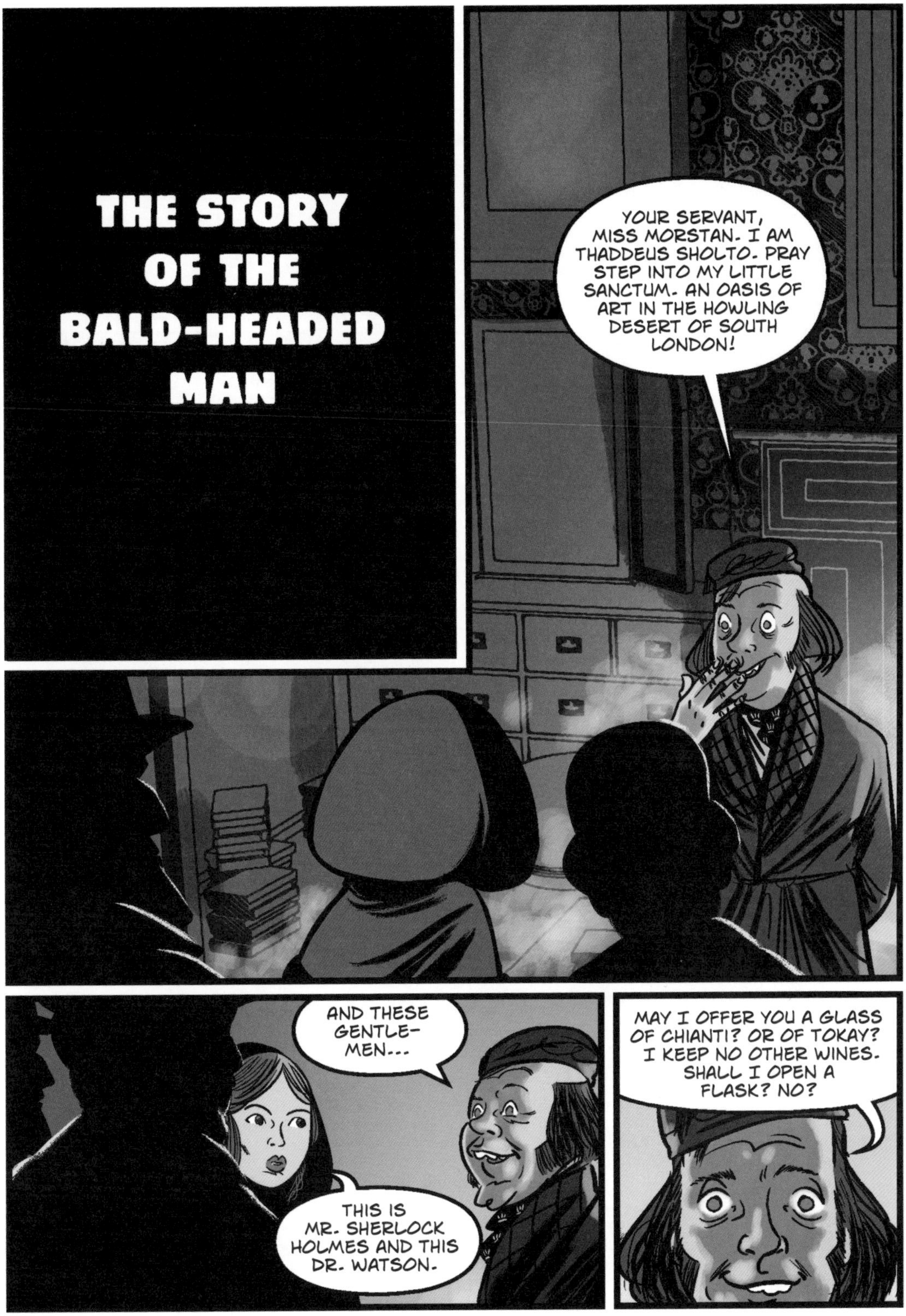
THE STORY OF THE BALD-HEADED MAN
YOUR SERVANT, MISS MORSTAN. I AM THADDEUS SHOLTO. PRAY STEP INTO MY LITTLE SANCTUM. AN OASIS OF ART IN THE HOWLING DESERT OF SOUTH LONDON!
AND THESE GENTLE-MEN...
THIS IS MR. SHERLOCK HOLMES AND THIS DR. WATSON.
MAY I OFFER YOU A GLASS OF CHIANTI? OR OF TOKAY? I KEEP NO OTHER WINES. SHALL I OPEN A FLASK? NO?

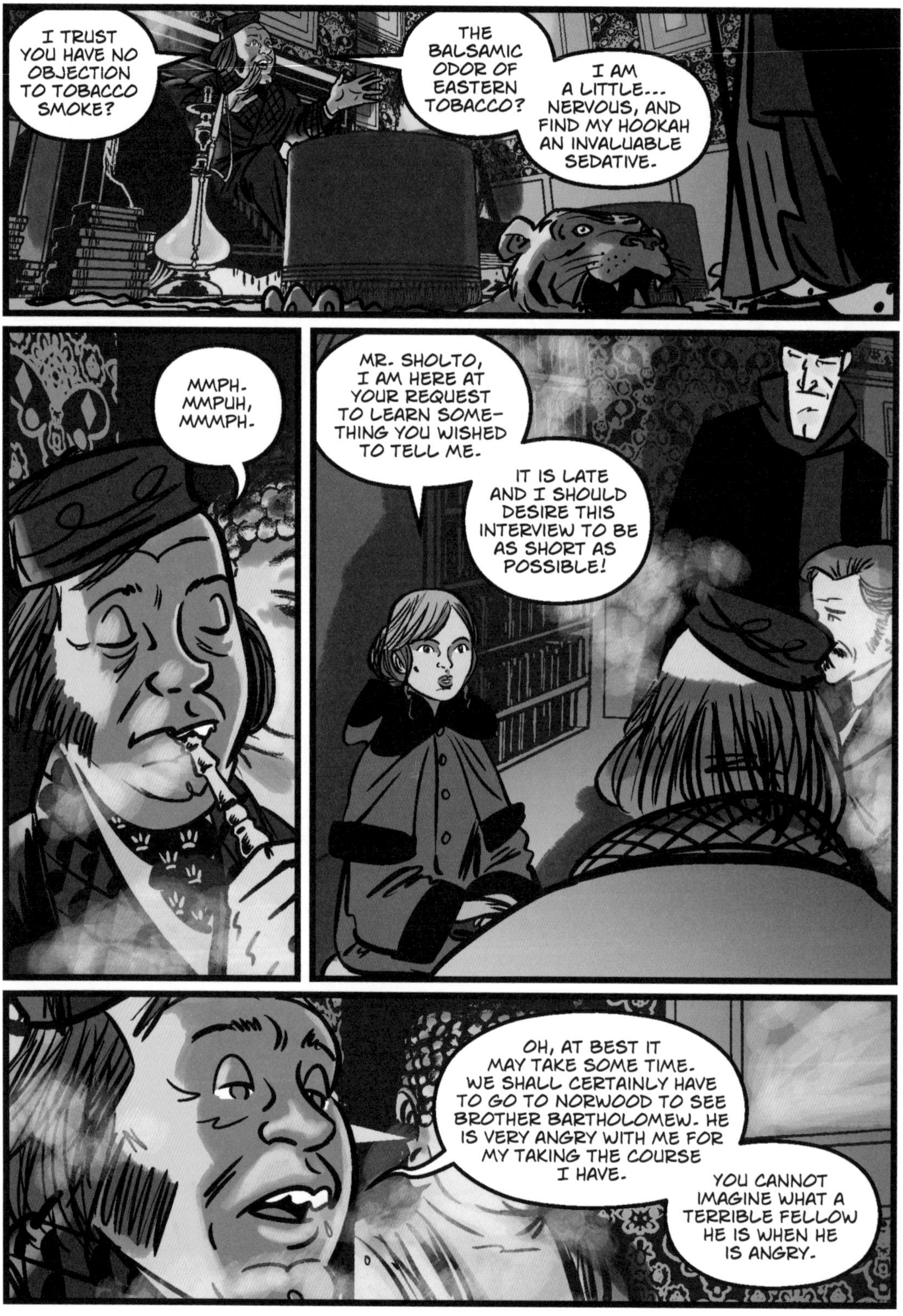
I TRUST YOU HAVE NO OBJECTION TO TOBACCO SMOKE?
THE BALSAMIC ODOR OF EASTERN TOBACCO?
I AM A LITTLE... NERVOUS, AND FIND MY HOOKAH AN INVALUABLE SEDATIVE.
MMPH. MMPUH, MMMPH.
MR. SHOLTO, I AM HERE AT YOUR REQUEST TO LEARN SOME-THING YOU WISHED TO TELL ME.
IT IS LATE AND I SHOULD DESIRE THIS INTERVIEW TO BE AS SHORT AS POSSIBLE!
OH, AT BEST IT MAY TAKE SOME TIME. WE SHALL CERTAINLY HAVE TO GO TO NORWOOD TO SEE BROTHER BARTHOLOMEW. HE IS VERY ANGRY WITH ME FOR MY TAKING THE COURSE I HAVE.
YOU CANNOT IMAGINE WHAT A TERRIBLE FELLOW HE IS WHEN HE IS ANGRY.

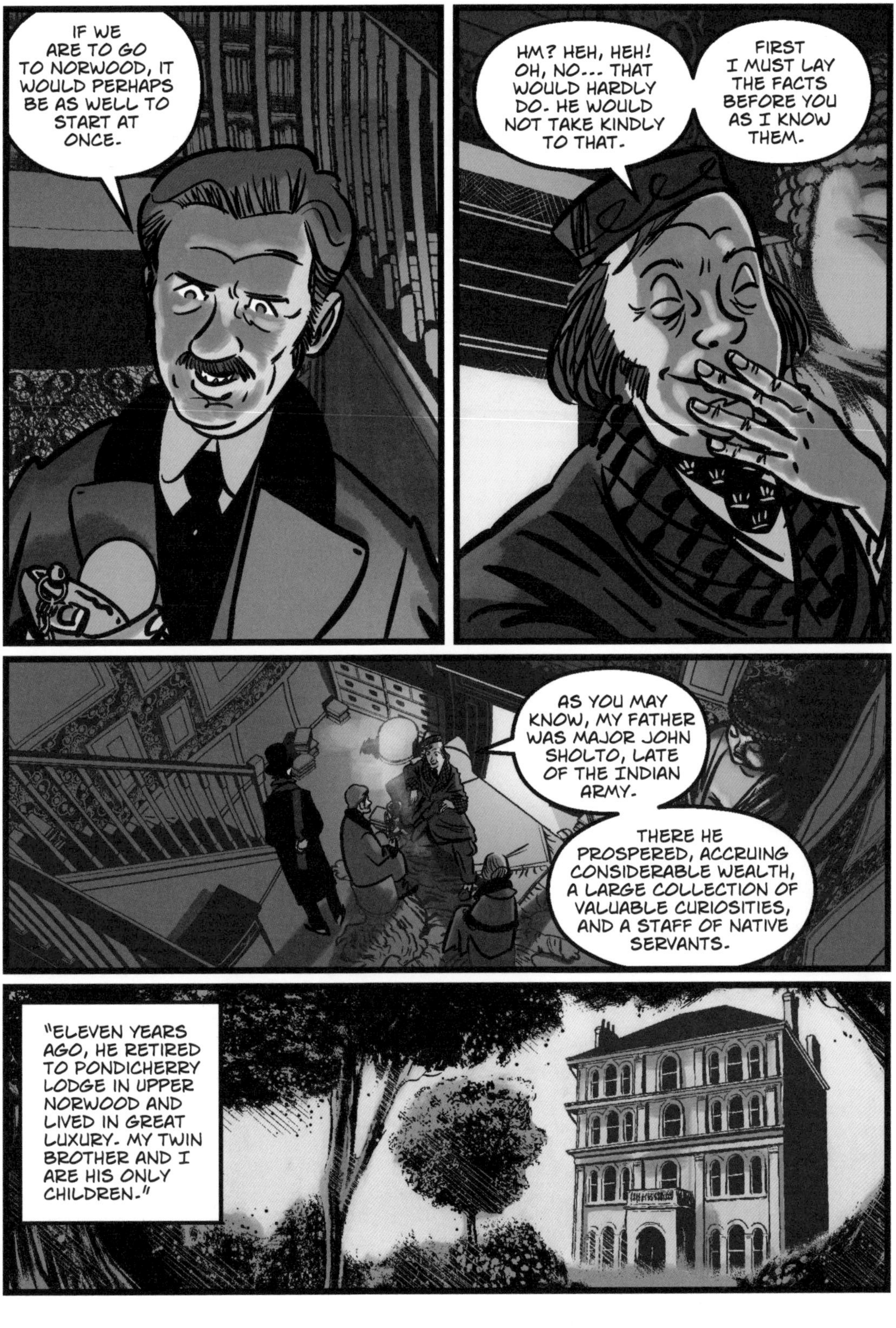
IF WE ARE TO GO TO NORWOOD, IT WOULD PERHAPS BE AS WELL TO START AT ONCE.
HM? HEH, HEH! OH, NO... THAT WOULD HARDLY DO. HE WOULD NOT TAKE KINDLY TO THAT.
FIRST I MUST LAY THE FACTS BEFORE YOU AS I KNOW THEM.
AS YOU MAY KNOW, MY FATHER WAS MAJOR JOHN SHOLTO, LATE OF THE INDIAN ARMY.
THERE HE PROSPERED, ACCRUING CONSIDERABLE WEALTH, A LARGE COLLECTION OF VALUABLE CURIOSITIES, AND A STAFF OF NATIVE SERVANTS.
"ELEVEN YEARS AGO, HE RETIRED TO PONDICHERRY LODGE IN UPPER NORWOOD AND LIVED IN GREAT LUXURY. MY TWIN BROTHER AND I ARE HIS ONLY CHILDREN."

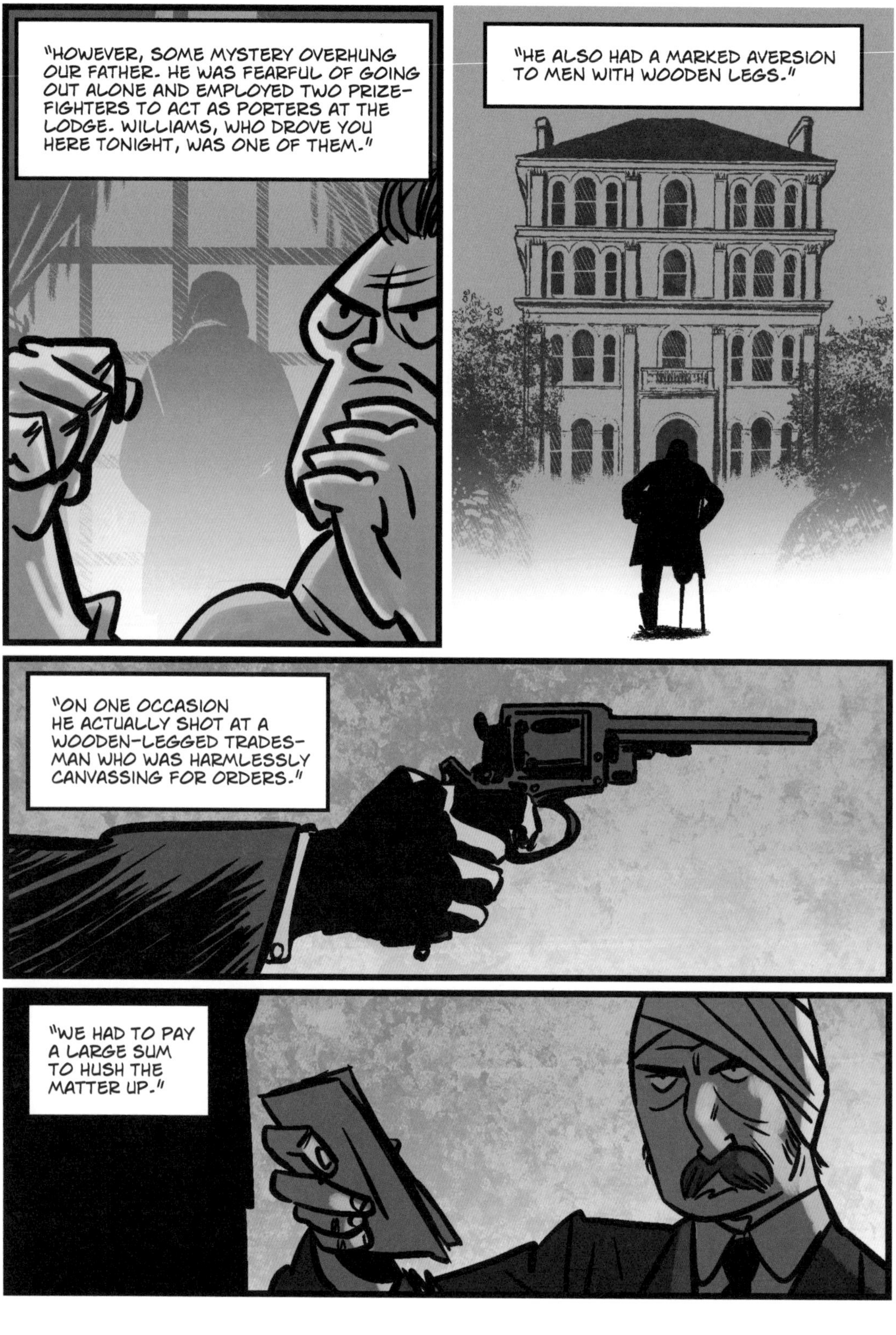
"HOWEVER, SOME MYSTERY OVERHUNG OUR FATHER. HE WAS FEARFUL OF GOING OUT ALONE AND EMPLOYED TWO PRIZE-FIGHTERS TO ACT AS PORTERS AT THE LODGE. WILLIAMS, WHO DROVE YOU HERE TONIGHT, WAS ONE OF THEM."
"HE ALSO HAD A MARKED AVERSION TO MEN WITH WOODEN LEGS."
"ON ONE OCCASION HE ACTUALLY SHOT AT A WOODEN-LEGGED TRADES-MAN WHO WAS HARMLESSLY CANVASSING FOR ORDERS."
"WE HAD TO PAY A LARGE SUM TO HUSH THE MATTER UP."

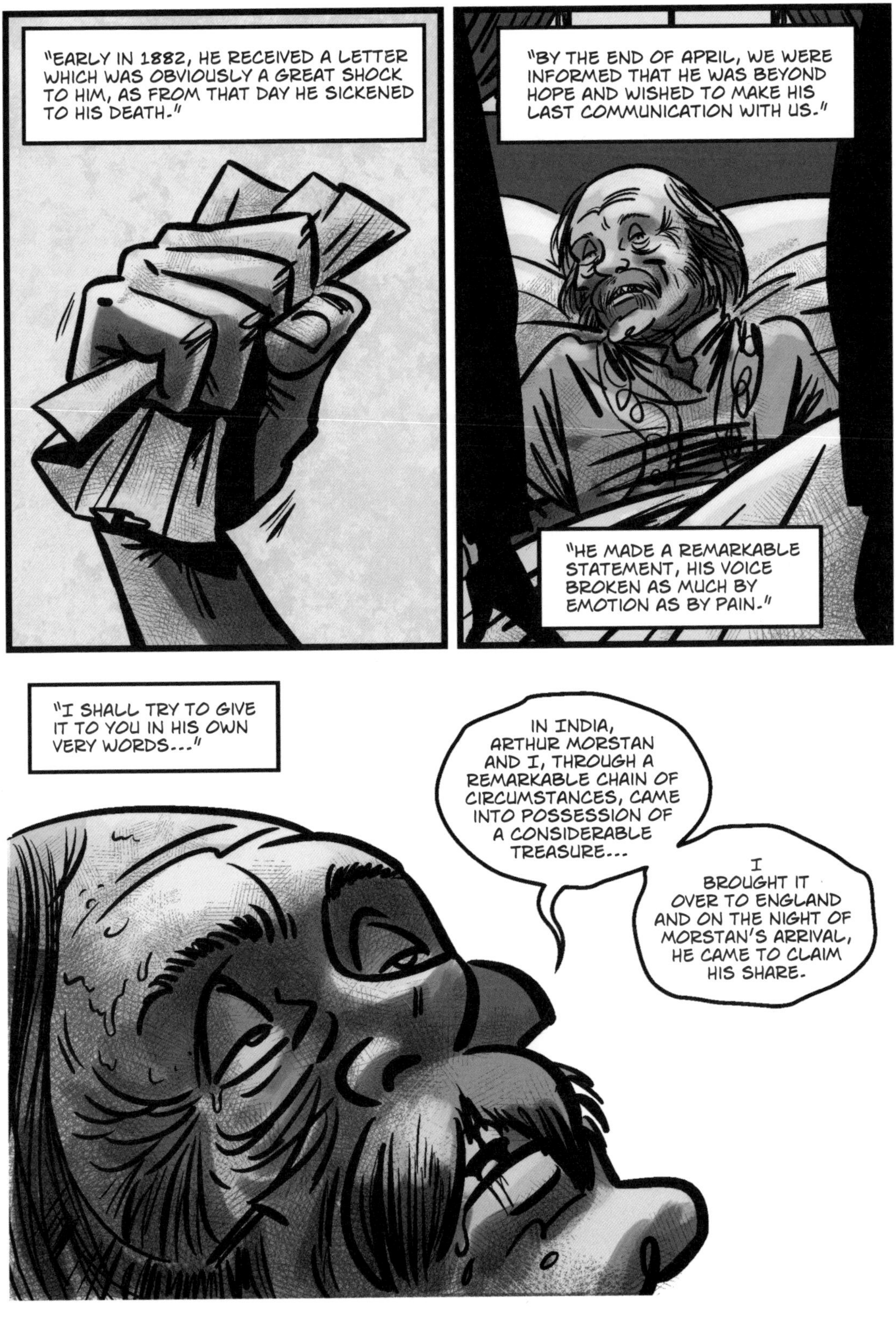
"EARLY IN 1882, HE RECEIVED A LETTER WHICH WAS OBVIOUSLY A GREAT SHOCK TO HIM, AS FROM THAT DAY HE SICKENED TO HIS DEATH."
"BY THE END OF APRIL, WE WERE INFORMED THAT HE WAS BEYOND HOPE AND WISHED TO MAKE HIS LAST COMMUNICATION WITH US."
"HE MADE A REMARKABLE STATEMENT, HIS VOICE BROKEN AS MUCH BY EMOTION AS BY PAIN."
"I SHALL TRY TO GIVE IT TO YOU IN HIS OWN VERY WORDS..."
IN INDIA, ARTHUR MORSTAN AND I, THROUGH A REMARKABLE CHAIN OF CIRCUMSTANCES, CAME INTO POSSESSION OF A CONSIDERABLE TREASURE...
I BROUGHT IT OVER TO ENGLAND AND ON THE NIGHT OF MORSTAN'S ARRIVAL, HE CAME TO CLAIM HIS SHARE.

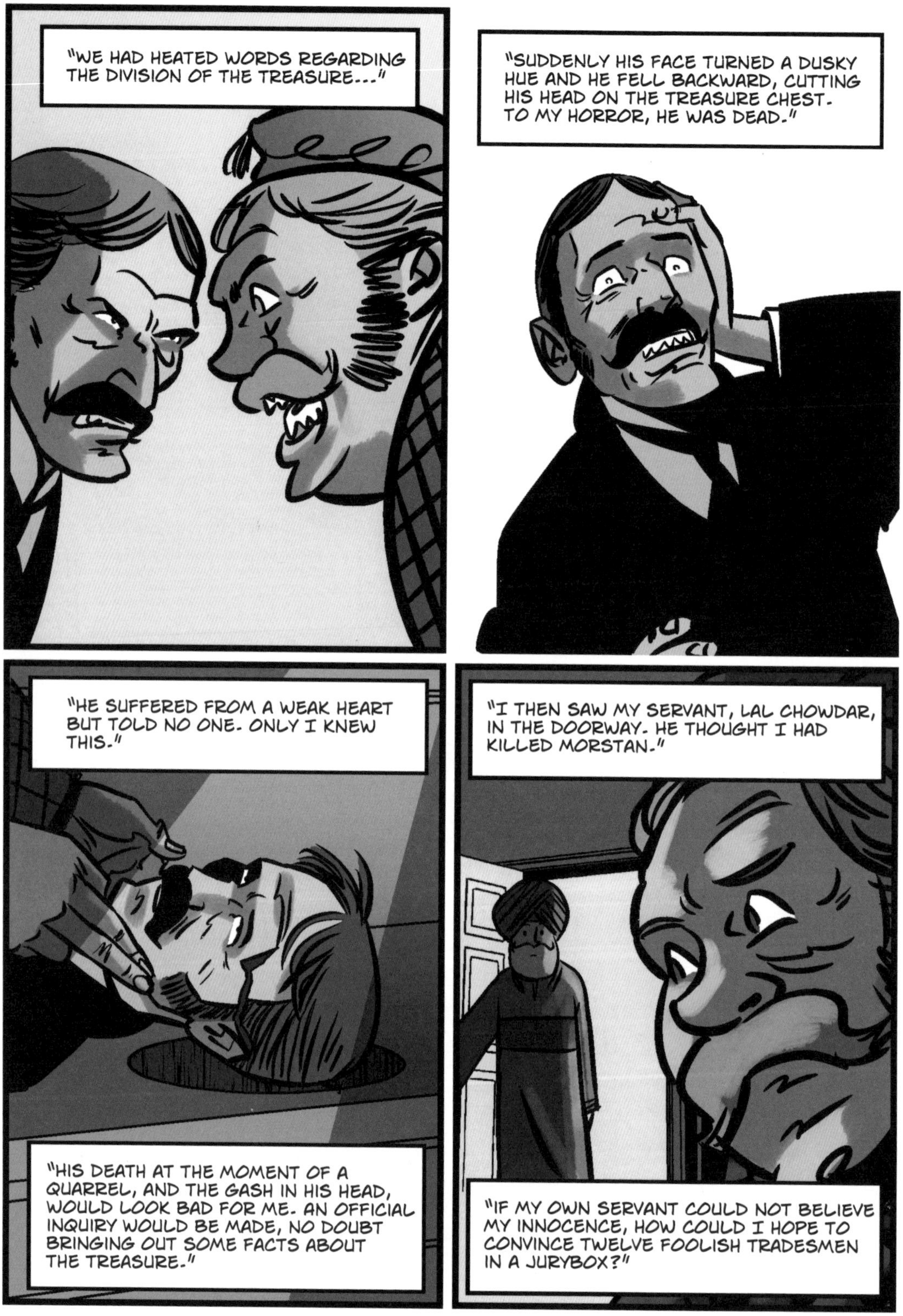
"WE HAD HEATED WORDS REGARDING THE DIVISION OF THE TREASURE..."
"SUDDENLY HIS FACE TURNED A DUSKY HUE AND HE FELL BACKWARD, CUTTING HIS HEAD ON THE TREASURE CHEST. TO MY HORROR, HE WAS DEAD."
"HE SUFFERED FROM A WEAK HEART BUT TOLD NO ONE. ONLY I KNEW THIS."
"HIS DEATH AT THE MOMENT OF A QUARREL, AND THE GASH IN HIS HEAD, WOULD LOOK BAD FOR ME. AN OFFICIAL INQUIRY WOULD BE MADE, NO DOUBT BRINGING OUT SOME FACTS ABOUT THE TREASURE."
"I THEN SAW MY SERVANT, LAL CHOWDAR, IN THE DOORWAY. HE THOUGHT I HAD KILLED MORSTAN."
"IF MY OWN SERVANT COULD NOT BELIEVE MY INNOCENCE, HOW COULD I HOPE TO CONVINCE TWELVE FOOLISH TRADESMEN IN A JURYBOX?"

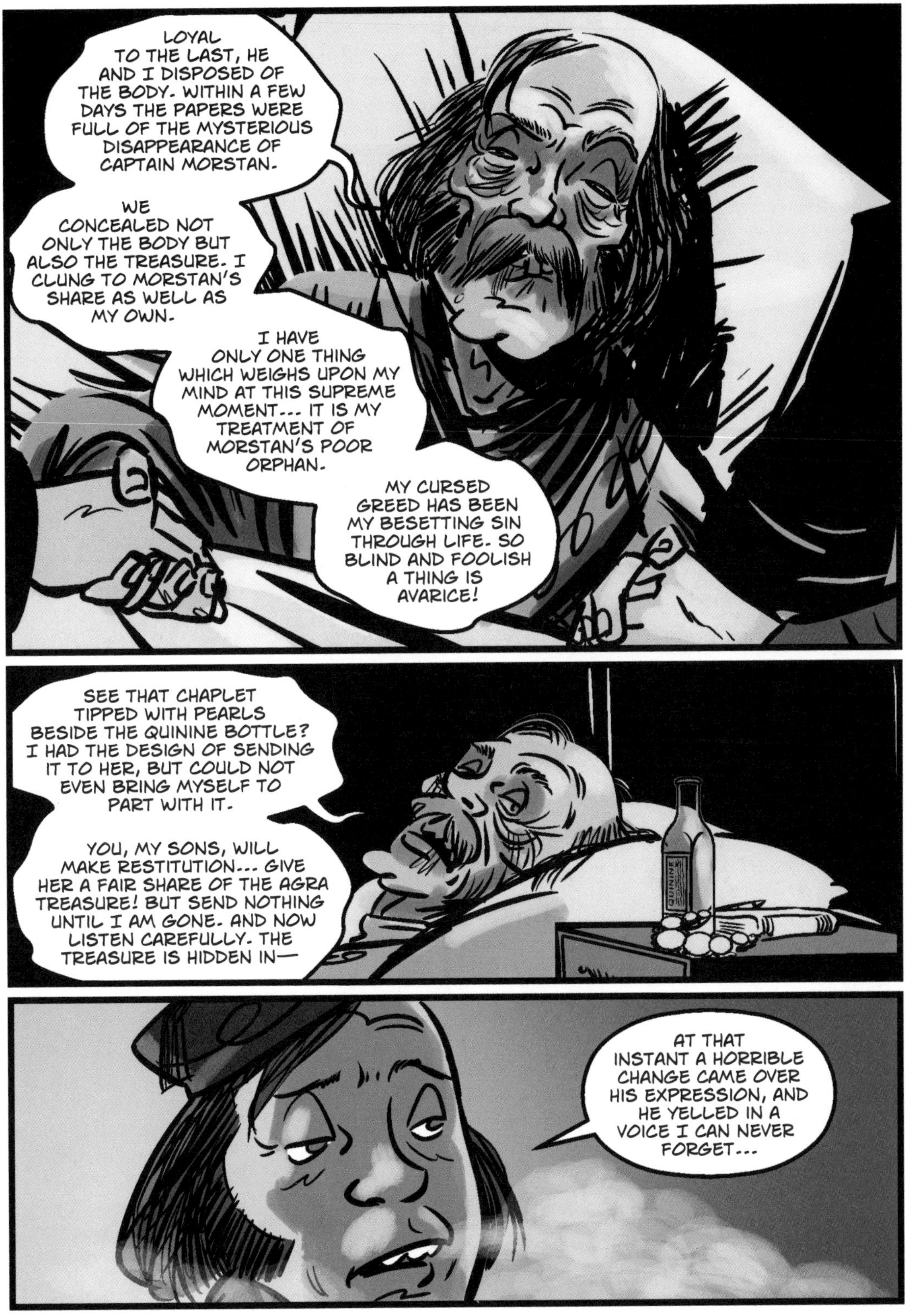
LOYAL TO THE LAST, HE AND I DISPOSED OF THE BODY. WITHIN A FEW DAYS THE PAPERS WERE FULL OF THE MYSTERIOUS DISAPPEARANCE OF CAPTAIN MORSTAN.
WE CONCEALED NOT ONLY THE BODY BUT ALSO THE TREASURE. I CLUNG TO MORSTAN'S SHARE AS WELL AS MY OWN.
I HAVE ONLY ONE THING WHICH WEIGHS UPON MY MIND AT THIS SUPREME MOMENT... IT IS MY TREATMENT OF MORSTAN'S POOR ORPHAN.
MY CURSED GREED HAS BEEN MY BESETTING SIN THROUGH LIFE. SO BLIND AND FOOLISH A THING IS AVARICE!
SEE THAT CHAPLET TIPPED WITH PEARLS BESIDE THE QUININE BOTTLE? I HAD THE DESIGN OF SENDING IT TO HER, BUT COULD NOT EVEN BRING MYSELF TO PART WITH IT.
YOU, MY SONS, WILL MAKE RESTITUTION... GIVE HER A FAIR SHARE OF THE AGRA TREASURE! BUT SEND NOTHING UNTIL I AM GONE. AND NOW LISTEN CAREFULLY. THE TREASURE IS HIDDEN IN—
QUININE
AT THAT INSTANT A HORRIBLE CHANGE CAME OVER HIS EXPRESSION, AND HE YELLED IN A VOICE I CAN NEVER FORGET...

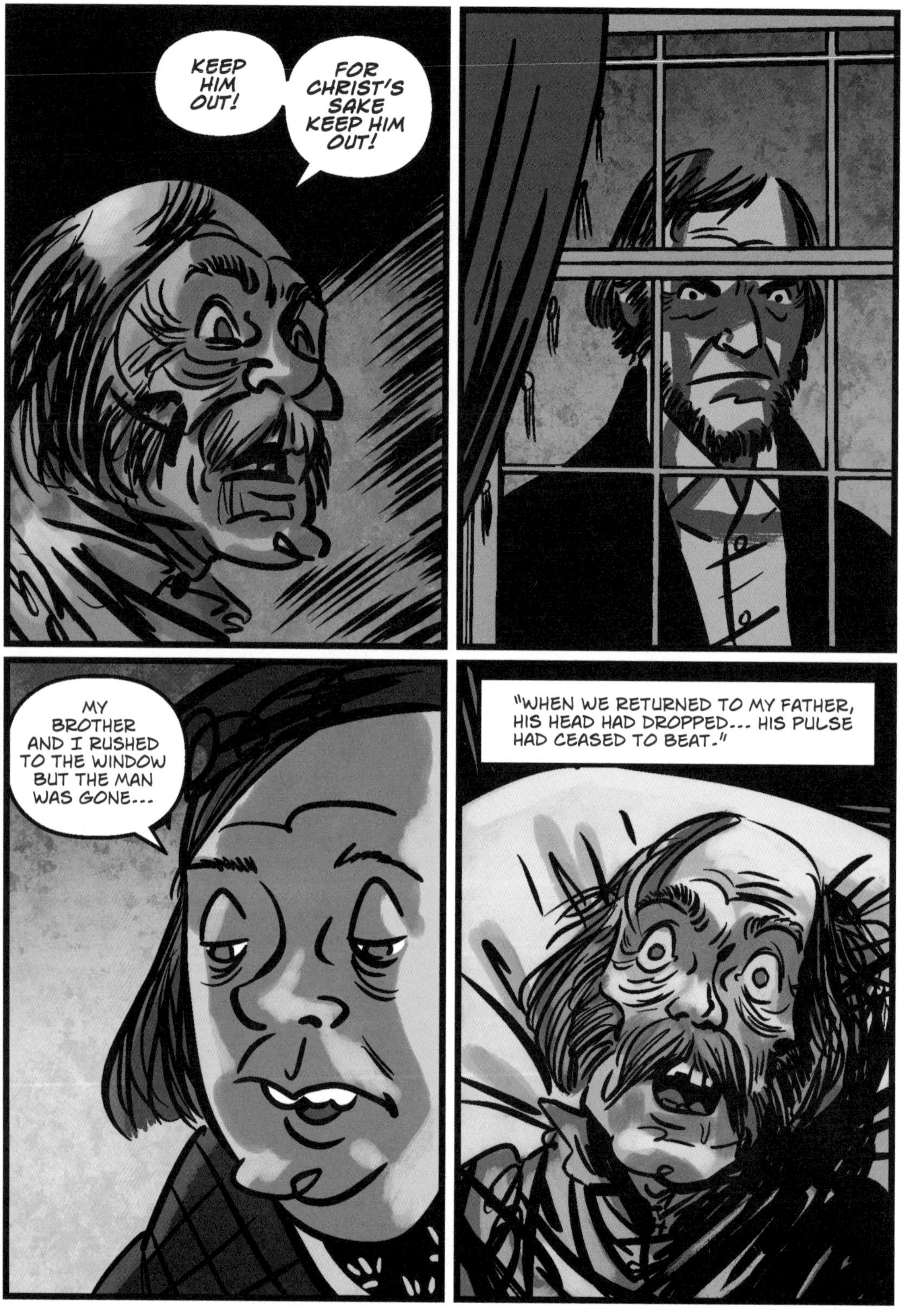
KEEP HIM OUT!
FOR CHRIST'S SAKE KEEP HIM OUT!
MY BROTHER AND I RUSHED TO THE WINDOW BUT THE MAN WAS GONE...
"WHEN WE RETURNED TO MY FATHER, HIS HEAD HAD DROPPED... HIS PULSE HAD CEASED TO BEAT."

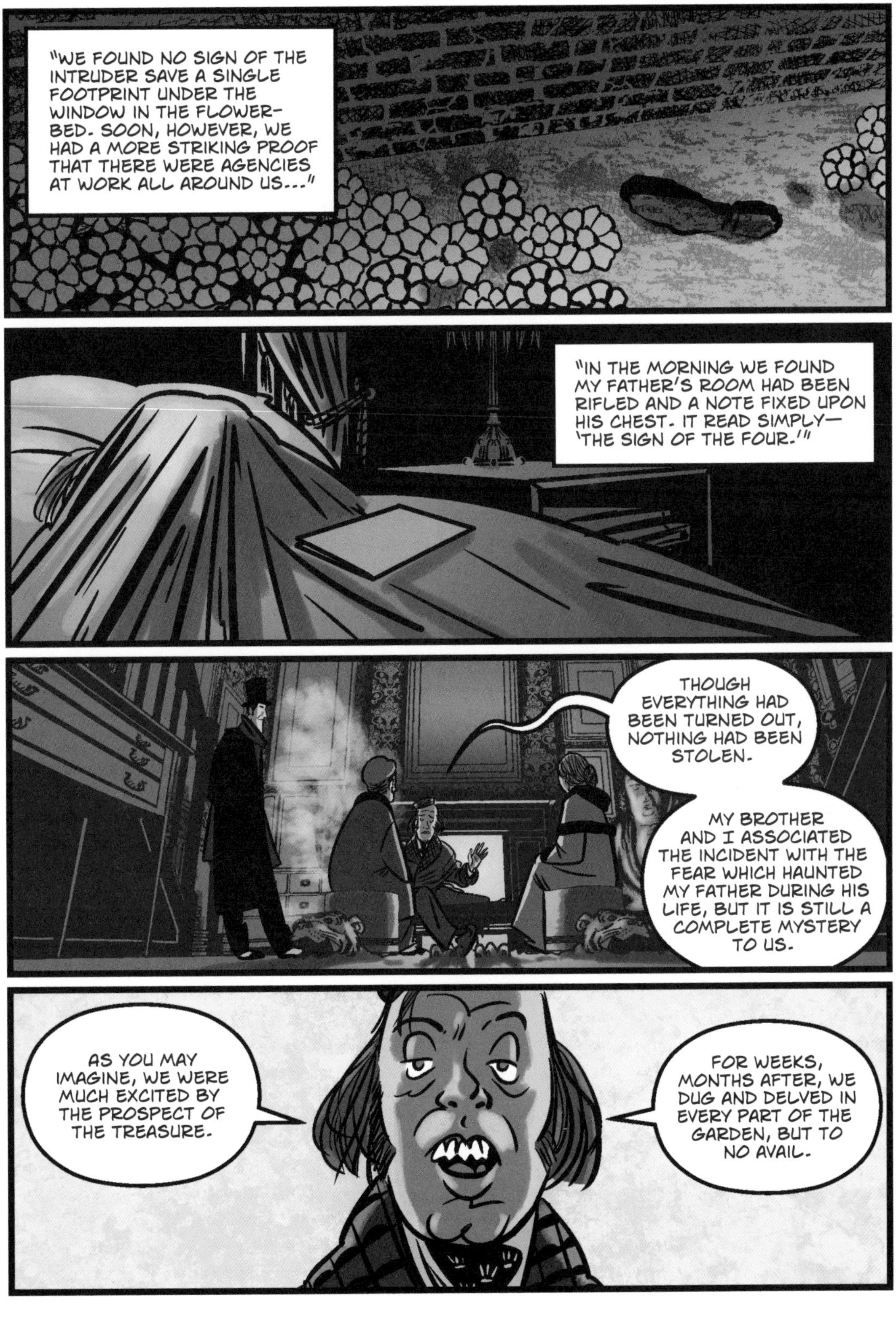
"WE FOUND NO SIGN OF THE INTRUDER SAVE A SINGLE FOOTPRINT UNDER THE WINDOW IN THE FLOWER-BED. SOON, HOWEVER, WE HAD A MORE STRIKING PROOF THAT THERE WERE AGENCIES AT WORK ALL AROUND US..."
"IN THE MORNING WE FOUND MY FATHER'S ROOM HAD BEEN RIFLED AND A NOTE FIXED UPON HIS CHEST. IT READ SIMPLY— 'THE SIGN OF THE FOUR.'"
THOUGH EVERYTHING HAD BEEN TURNED OUT, NOTHING HAD BEEN STOLEN.
MY BROTHER AND I ASSOCIATED THE INCIDENT WITH THE FEAR WHICH HAUNTED MY FATHER DURING HIS LIFE, BUT IT IS STILL A COMPLETE MYSTERY TO US.
AS YOU MAY IMAGINE, WE WERE MUCH EXCITED BY THE PROSPECT OF THE TREASURE.
FOR WEEKS, MONTHS AFTER, WE DUG AND DELVED IN EVERY PART OF THE GARDEN, BUT TO NO AVAIL.

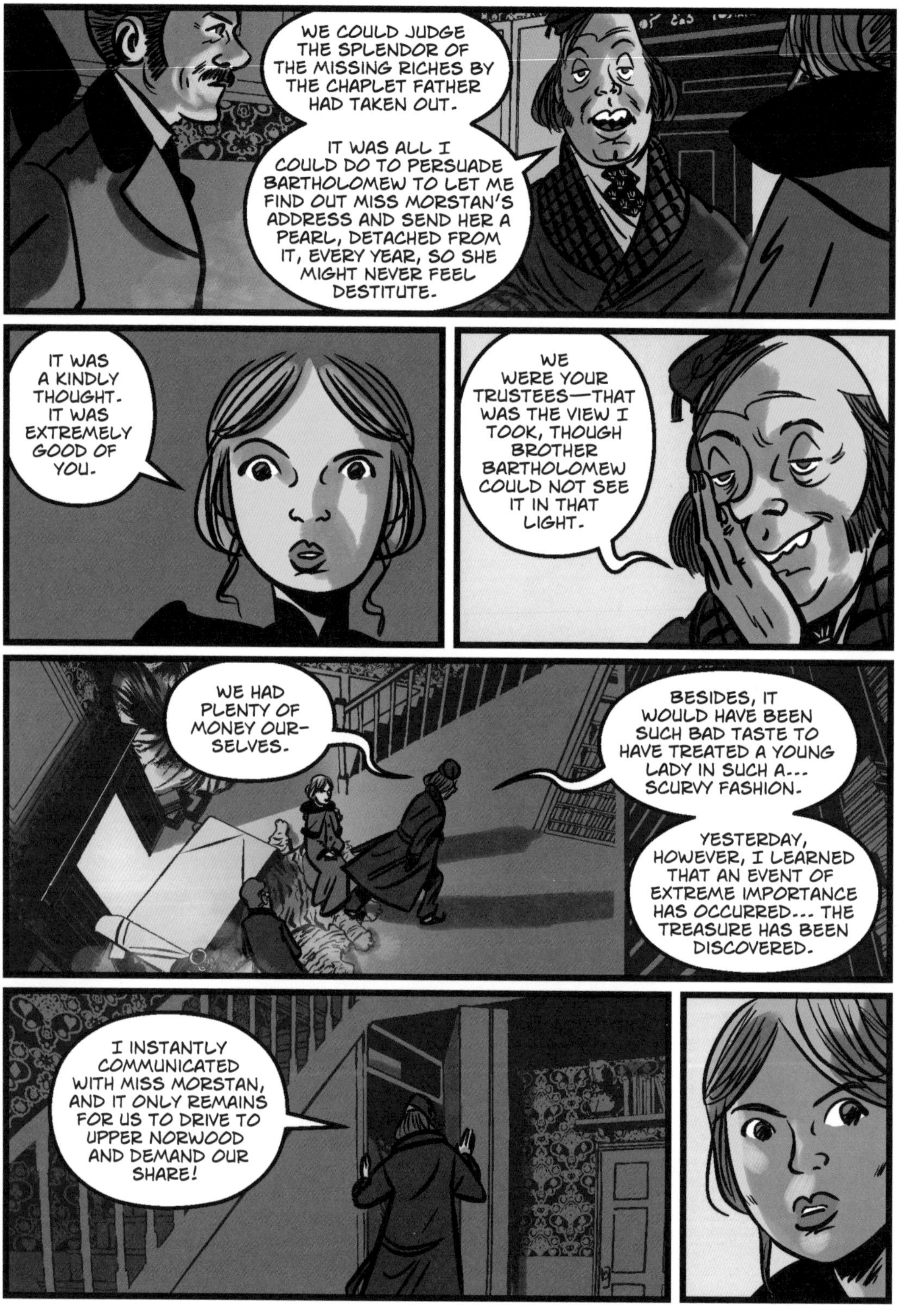
WE COULD JUDGE THE SPLENDOR OF THE MISSING RICHES BY THE CHAPLET FATHER HAD TAKEN OUT.
IT WAS ALL I COULD DO TO PERSUADE BARTHOLOMEW TO LET ME FIND OUT MISS MORSTAN'S ADDRESS AND SEND HER A PEARL, DETACHED FROM IT, EVERY YEAR, SO SHE MIGHT NEVER FEEL DESTITUTE.
IT WAS A KINDLY THOUGHT. IT WAS EXTREMELY GOOD OF YOU.
WE WERE YOUR TRUSTEES—THAT WAS THE VIEW I TOOK, THOUGH BROTHER BARTHOLOMEW COULD NOT SEE IT IN THAT LIGHT.
WE HAD PLENTY OF MONEY OUR-SELVES.
BESIDES, IT WOULD HAVE BEEN SUCH BAD TASTE TO HAVE TREATED A YOUNG LADY IN SUCH A... SCURVY FASHION.
YESTERDAY, HOWEVER, I LEARNED THAT AN EVENT OF EXTREME IMPORTANCE HAS OCCURRED... THE TREASURE HAS BEEN DISCOVERED.
I INSTANTLY COMMUNICATED WITH MISS MORSTAN, AND IT ONLY REMAINS FOR US TO DRIVE TO UPPER NORWOOD AND DEMAND OUR SHARE!

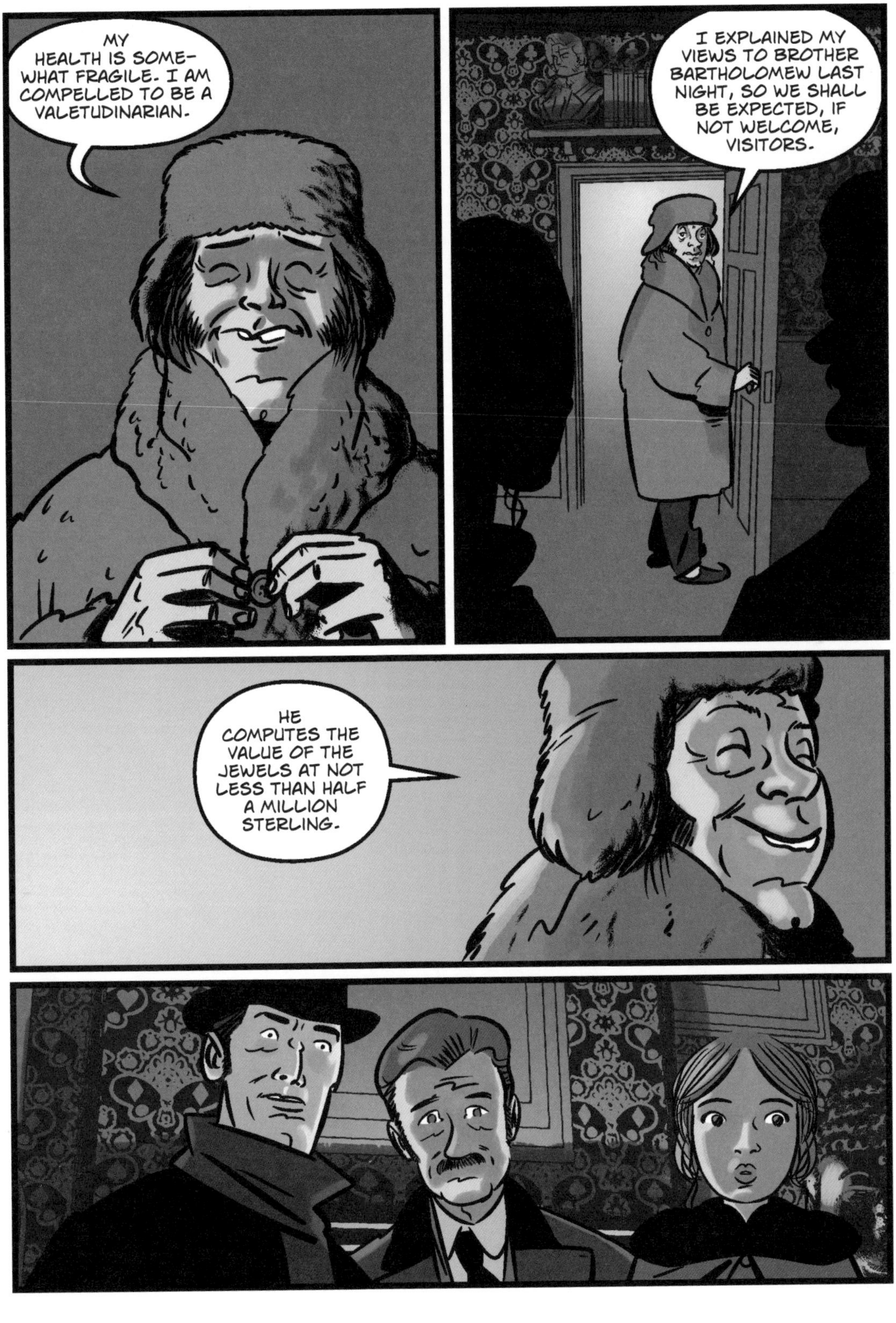
MY HEALTH IS SOME-WHAT FRAGILE. I AM COMPELLED TO BE A VALETUDINARIAN.
I EXPLAINED MY VIEWS TO BROTHER BARTHOLOMEW LAST NIGHT, SO WE SHALL BE EXPECTED, IF NOT WELCOME, VISITORS.
HE COMPUTES THE VALUE OF THE JEWELS AT NOT LESS THAN HALF A MILLION STERLING.

THE TRAGEDY OF PONDICHERRY LODGE

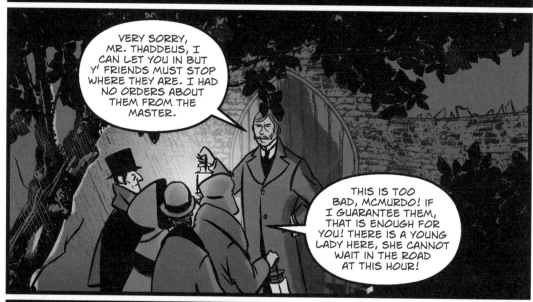

VERY SORRY, MR. THADDEUS, I CAN LET YOU IN BUT Y' FRIENDS MUST STOP WHERE THEY ARE. I HAD NO ORDERS ABOUT THEM FROM THE MASTER.

THIS IS TOO BAD, MCMURDO! IF I GUARANTEE THEM, THAT IS ENOUGH FOR YOU! THERE IS A YOUNG LADY HERE, SHE CANNOT WAIT IN THE ROAD AT THIS HOUR!

THESE FOLK MAY BE FRIENDS O' YOURS AND YET NO FRIEND O' THE MASTER'S.

I DON'T KNOW NONE OF THEM.

OH, YES YOU DO, MCMURDO!

DON'T YOU REMEMBER THAT AMATEUR WHO FOUGHT THREE ROUNDS WITH YOU AT ALLISON'S ROOMS ON THE NIGHT OF YOUR BENEFIT FOUR YEARS BACK?

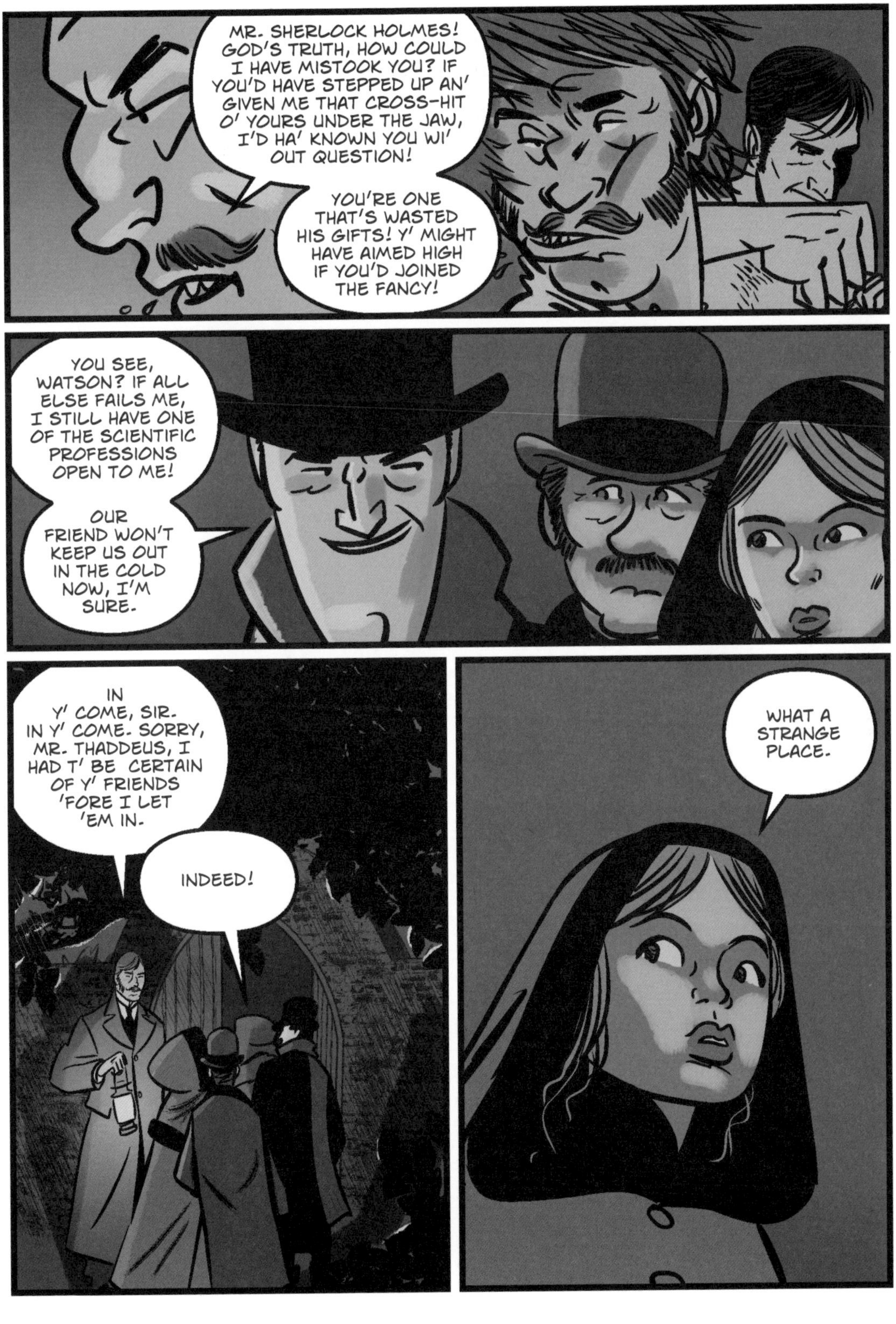
MR. SHERLOCK HOLMES! GOD'S TRUTH, HOW COULD I HAVE MISTOOK YOU? IF YOU'D HAVE STEPPED UP AN' GIVEN ME THAT CROSS-HIT O' YOURS UNDER THE JAW, I'D HA' KNOWN YOU WI' OUT QUESTION!
YOU'RE ONE THAT'S WASTED HIS GIFTS! Y' MIGHT HAVE AIMED HIGH IF YOU'D JOINED THE FANCY!
YOU SEE, WATSON? IF ALL ELSE FAILS ME, I STILL HAVE ONE OF THE SCIENTIFIC PROFESSIONS OPEN TO ME!
OUR FRIEND WON'T KEEP US OUT IN THE COLD NOW, I'M SURE.
IN Y' COME, SIR. IN Y' COME. SORRY, MR. THADDEUS, I HAD T' BE CERTAIN OF Y' FRIENDS 'FORE I LET 'EM IN.
INDEED!
WHAT A STRANGE PLACE.

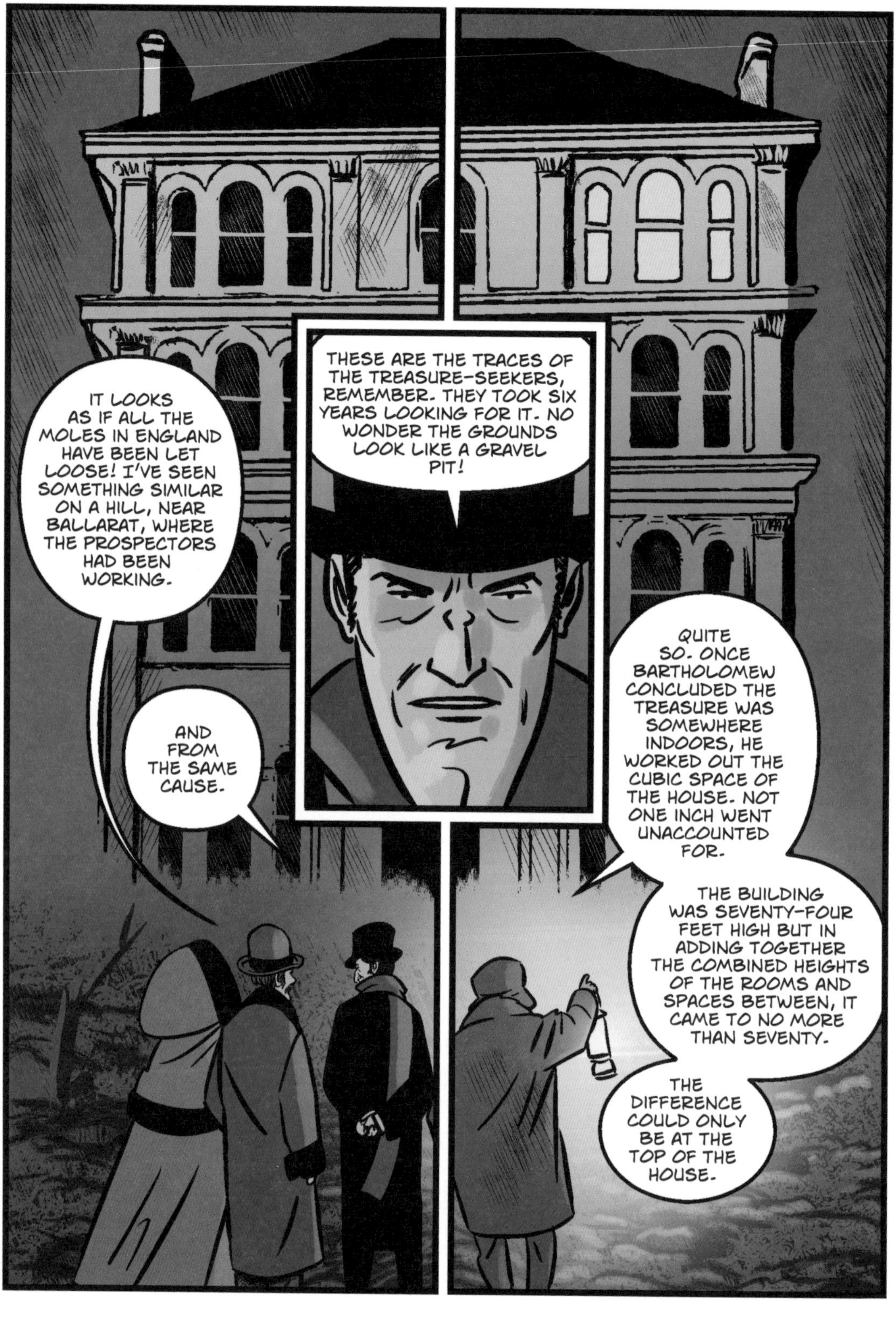
IT LOOKS AS IF ALL THE MOLES IN ENGLAND HAVE BEEN LET LOOSE! I'VE SEEN SOMETHING SIMILAR ON A HILL, NEAR BALLARAT, WHERE THE PROSPECTORS HAD BEEN WORKING.
AND FROM THE SAME CAUSE.
THESE ARE THE TRACES OF THE TREASURE-SEEKERS, REMEMBER. THEY TOOK SIX YEARS LOOKING FOR IT. NO WONDER THE GROUNDS LOOK LIKE A GRAVEL PIT!
QUITE SO. ONCE BARTHOLOMEW CONCLUDED THE TREASURE WAS SOMEWHERE INDOORS, HE WORKED OUT THE CUBIC SPACE OF THE HOUSE. NOT ONE INCH WENT UNACCOUNTED FOR.
THE BUILDING WAS SEVENTY-FOUR FEET HIGH BUT IN ADDING TOGETHER THE COMBINED HEIGHTS OF THE ROOMS AND SPACES BETWEEN, IT CAME TO NO MORE THAN SEVENTY.
THE DIFFERENCE COULD ONLY BE AT THE TOP OF THE HOUSE.

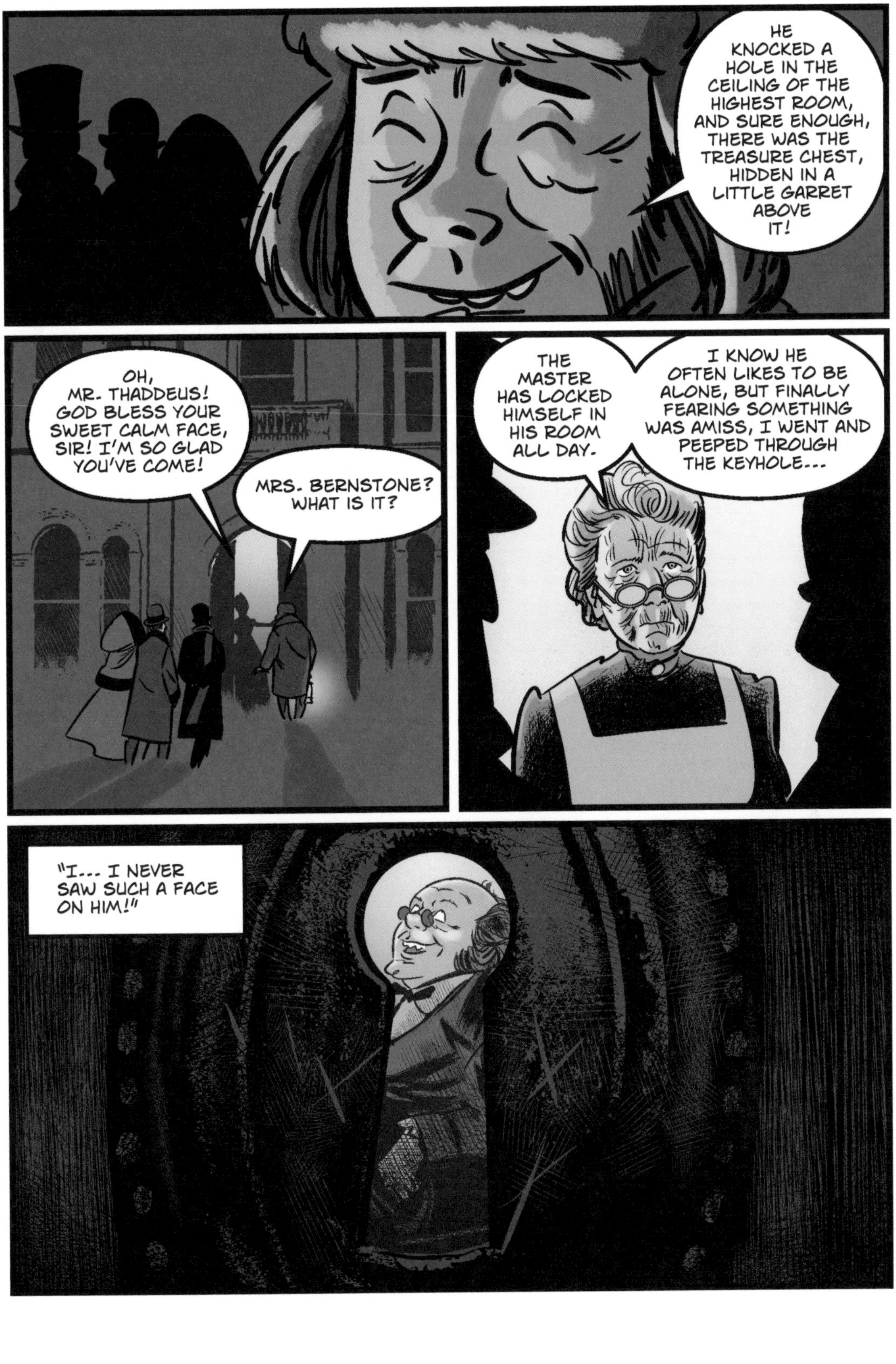
HE KNOCKED A HOLE IN THE CEILING OF THE HIGHEST ROOM, AND SURE ENOUGH, THERE WAS THE TREASURE CHEST, HIDDEN IN A LITTLE GARRET ABOVE IT!
OH, MR. THADDEUS! GOD BLESS YOUR SWEET CALM FACE, SIR! I'M SO GLAD YOU'VE COME!
MRS. BERNSTONE? WHAT IS IT?
THE MASTER HAS LOCKED HIMSELF IN HIS ROOM ALL DAY.
I KNOW HE OFTEN LIKES TO BE ALONE, BUT FINALLY FEARING SOMETHING WAS AMISS, I WENT AND PEEPED THROUGH THE KEYHOLE...
"I... I NEVER SAW SUCH A FACE ON HIM!"

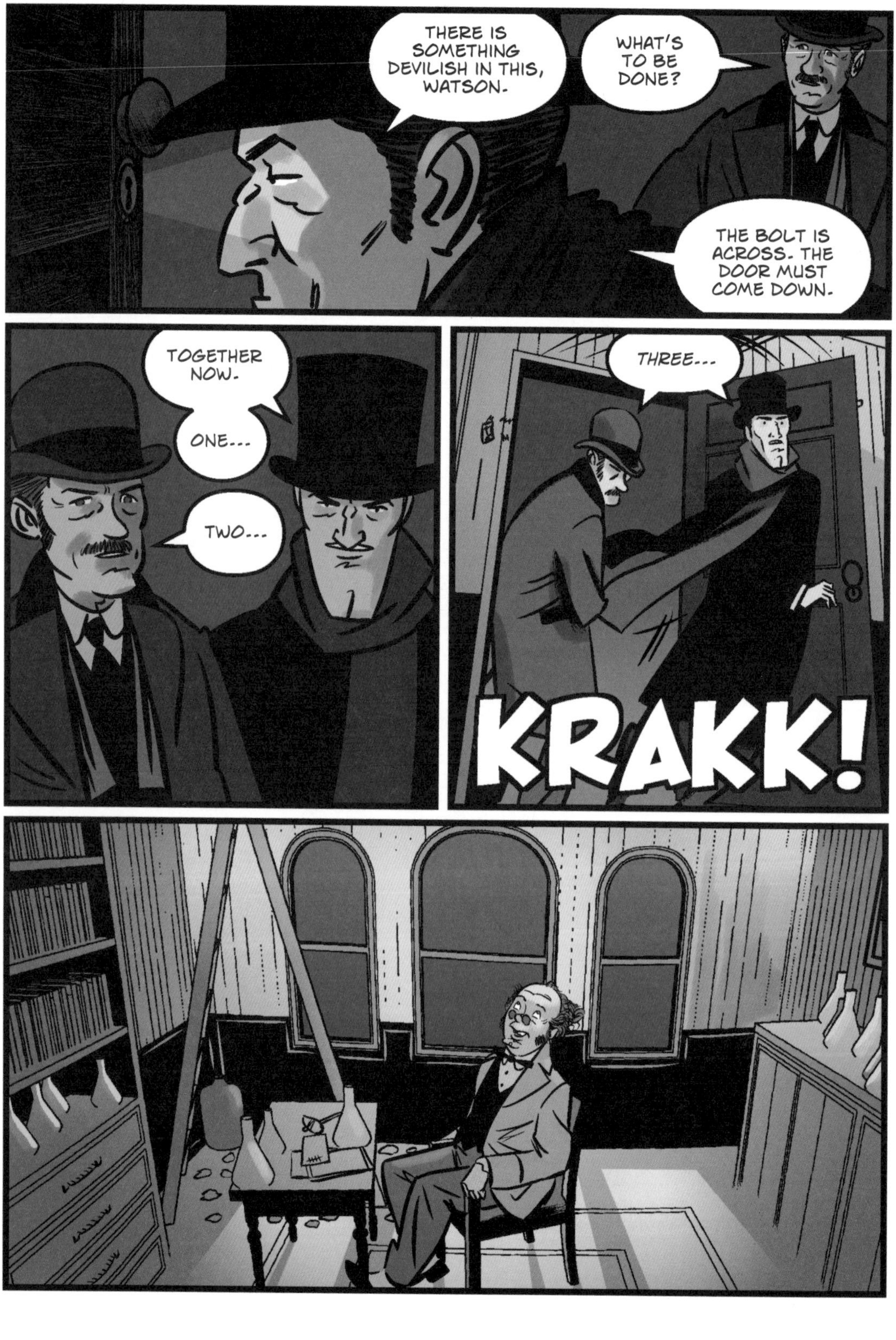
THERE IS SOMETHING DEVILISH IN THIS, WATSON.
WHAT'S TO BE DONE?
THE BOLT IS ACROSS. THE DOOR MUST COME DOWN.
TOGETHER NOW.
ONE...
TWO...
THREE...
KRAKK!

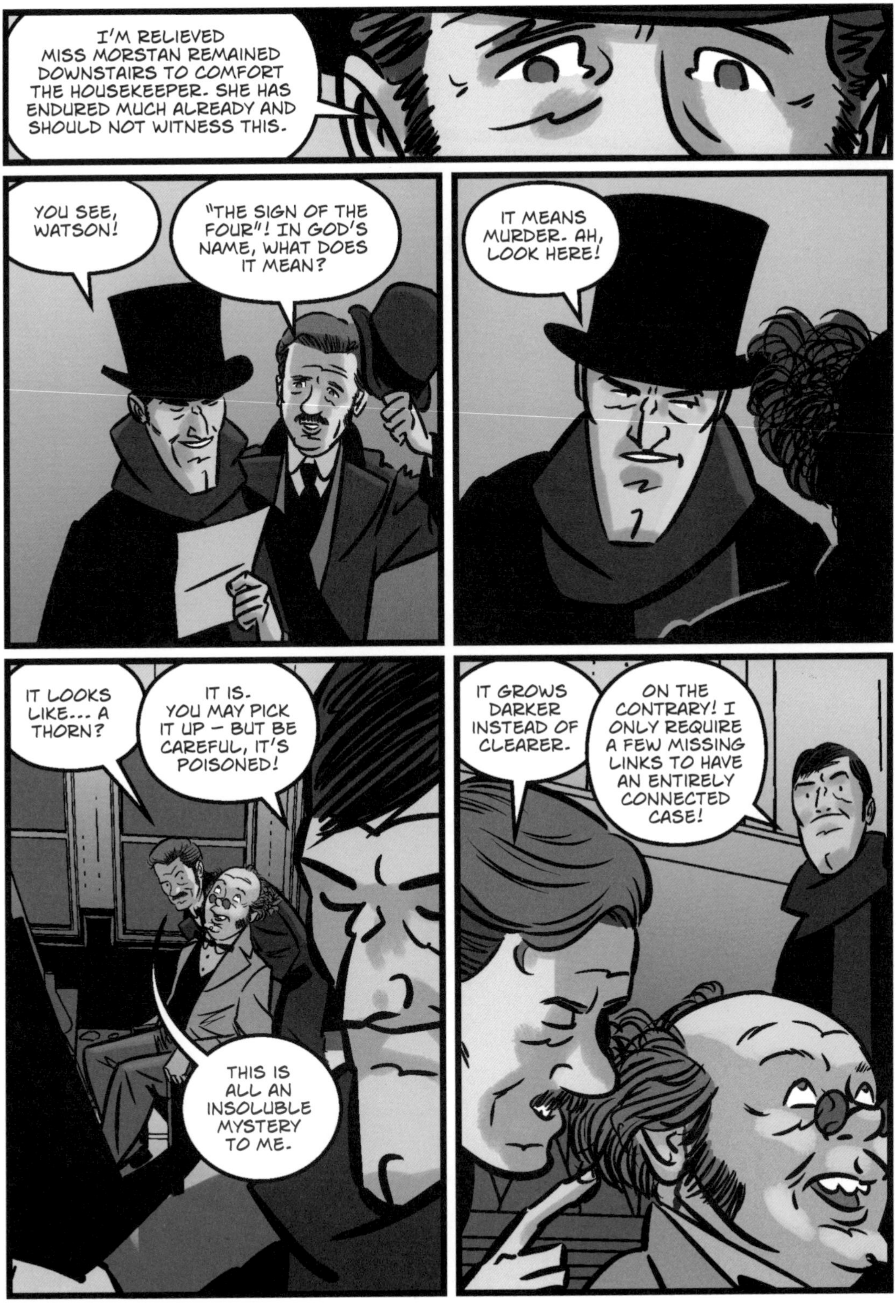
I'M RELIEVED MISS MORSTAN REMAINED DOWNSTAIRS TO COMFORT THE HOUSEKEEPER. SHE HAS ENDURED MUCH ALREADY AND SHOULD NOT WITNESS THIS.
YOU SEE, WATSON!
"THE SIGN OF THE FOUR"! IN GOD'S NAME, WHAT DOES IT MEAN?
IT MEANS MURDER. AH, LOOK HERE!
IT LOOKS LIKE... A THORN?
IT IS. YOU MAY PICK IT UP – BUT BE CAREFUL, IT'S POISONED!
THIS IS ALL AN INSOLUBLE MYSTERY TO ME.
IT GROWS DARKER INSTEAD OF CLEARER.
ON THE CONTRARY! I ONLY REQUIRE A FEW MISSING LINKS TO HAVE AN ENTIRELY CONNECTED CASE!

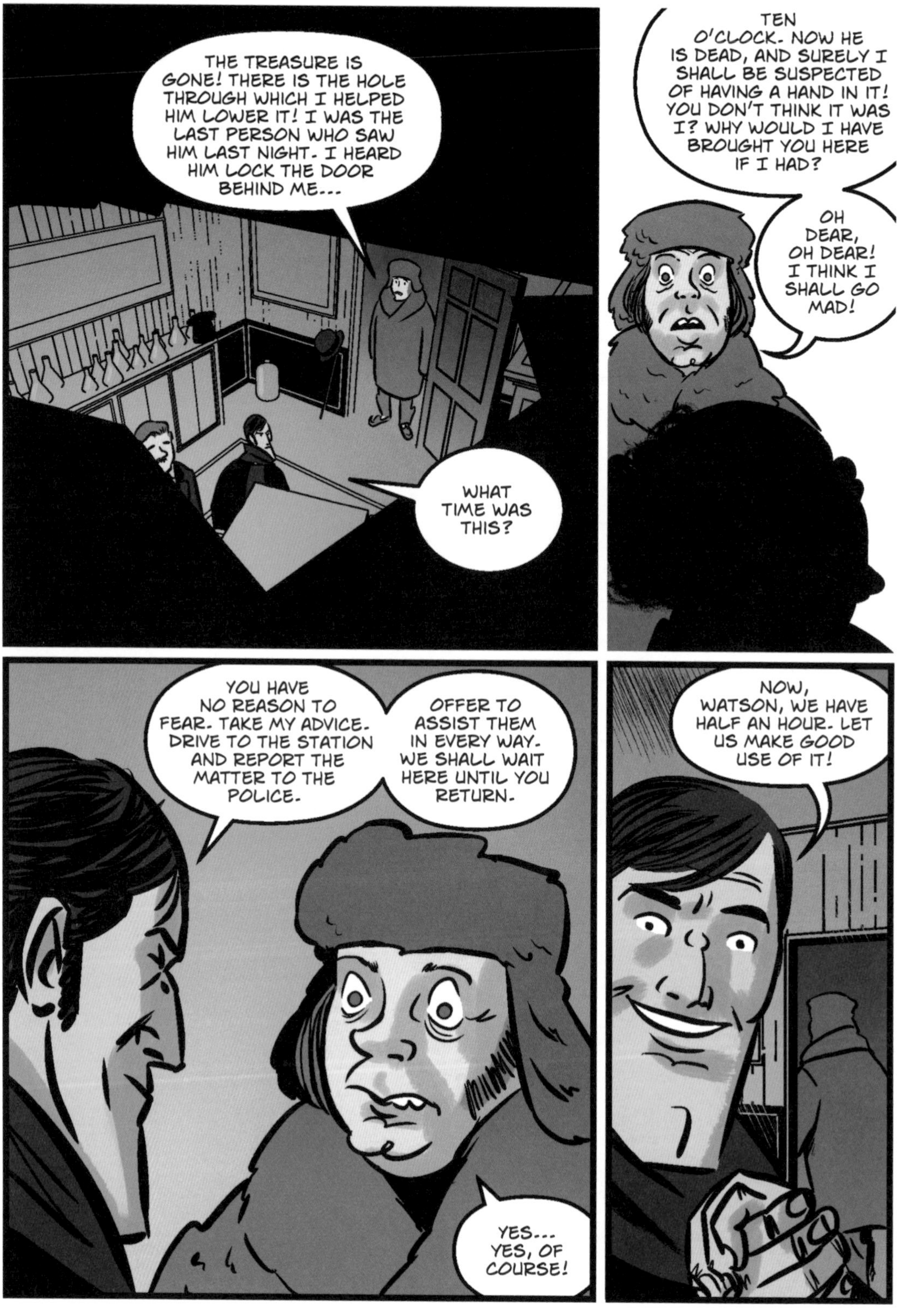
THE TREASURE IS GONE! THERE IS THE HOLE THROUGH WHICH I HELPED HIM LOWER IT! I WAS THE LAST PERSON WHO SAW HIM LAST NIGHT. I HEARD HIM LOCK THE DOOR BEHIND ME...
WHAT TIME WAS THIS?
TEN O'CLOCK. NOW HE IS DEAD, AND SURELY I SHALL BE SUSPECTED OF HAVING A HAND IN IT! YOU DON'T THINK IT WAS I? WHY WOULD I HAVE BROUGHT YOU HERE IF I HAD?
OH DEAR, OH DEAR! I THINK I SHALL GO MAD!
YOU HAVE NO REASON TO FEAR. TAKE MY ADVICE. DRIVE TO THE STATION AND REPORT THE MATTER TO THE POLICE.
OFFER TO ASSIST THEM IN EVERY WAY. WE SHALL WAIT HERE UNTIL YOU RETURN.
YES... YES, OF COURSE!
NOW, WATSON, WE HAVE HALF AN HOUR. LET US MAKE GOOD USE OF IT!

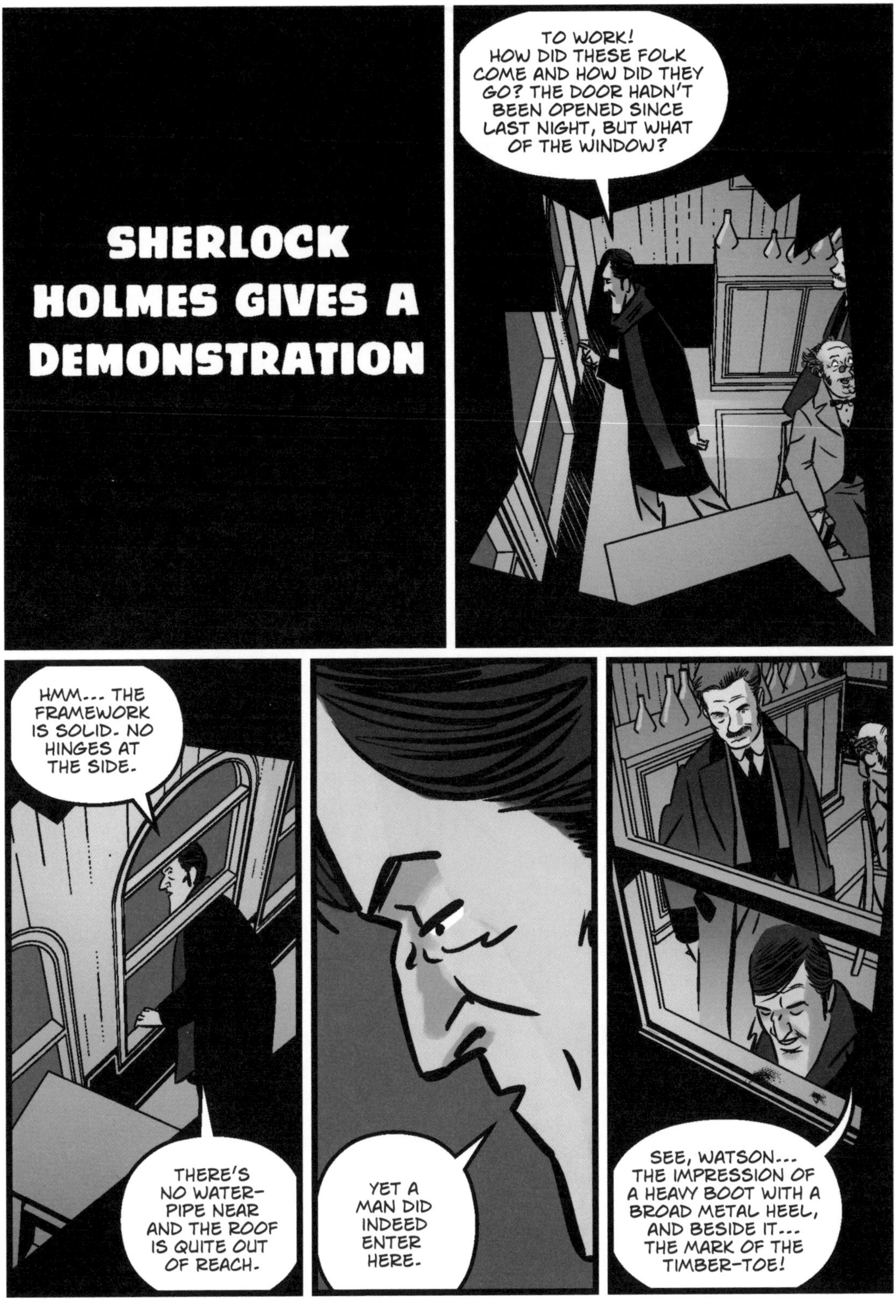
SHERLOCK HOLMES GIVES A DEMONSTRATION
TO WORK! HOW DID THESE FOLK COME AND HOW DID THEY GO? THE DOOR HADN'T BEEN OPENED SINCE LAST NIGHT, BUT WHAT OF THE WINDOW?
HMM... THE FRAMEWORK IS SOLID. NO HINGES AT THE SIDE.
THERE'S NO WATER-PIPE NEAR AND THE ROOF IS QUITE OUT OF REACH.
YET A MAN DID INDEED ENTER HERE.
SEE, WATSON... THE IMPRESSION OF A HEAVY BOOT WITH A BROAD METAL HEEL, AND BESIDE IT... THE MARK OF THE TIMBER-TOE!

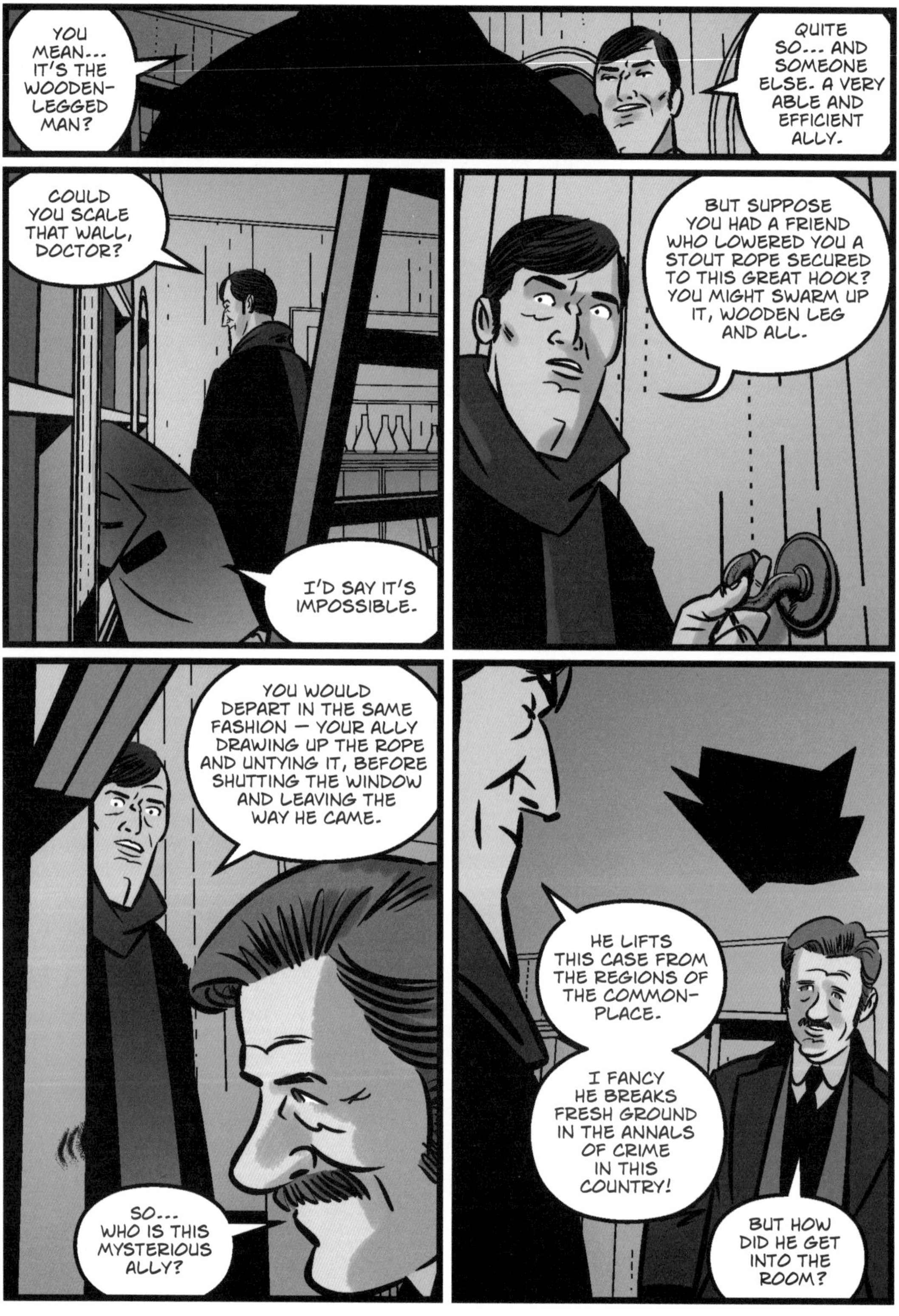
YOU MEAN... IT'S THE WOODEN-LEGGED MAN?
QUITE SO... AND SOMEONE ELSE. A VERY ABLE AND EFFICIENT ALLY.
COULD YOU SCALE THAT WALL, DOCTOR?
I'D SAY IT'S IMPOSSIBLE.
BUT SUPPOSE YOU HAD A FRIEND WHO LOWERED YOU A STOUT ROPE SECURED TO THIS GREAT HOOK? YOU MIGHT SWARM UP IT, WOODEN LEG AND ALL.
YOU WOULD DEPART IN THE SAME FASHION — YOUR ALLY DRAWING UP THE ROPE AND UNTYING IT, BEFORE SHUTTING THE WINDOW AND LEAVING THE WAY HE CAME.
SO... WHO IS THIS MYSTERIOUS ALLY?
HE LIFTS THIS CASE FROM THE REGIONS OF THE COMMON-PLACE.
I FANCY HE BREAKS FRESH GROUND IN THE ANNALS OF CRIME IN THIS COUNTRY!
BUT HOW DID HE GET INTO THE ROOM?

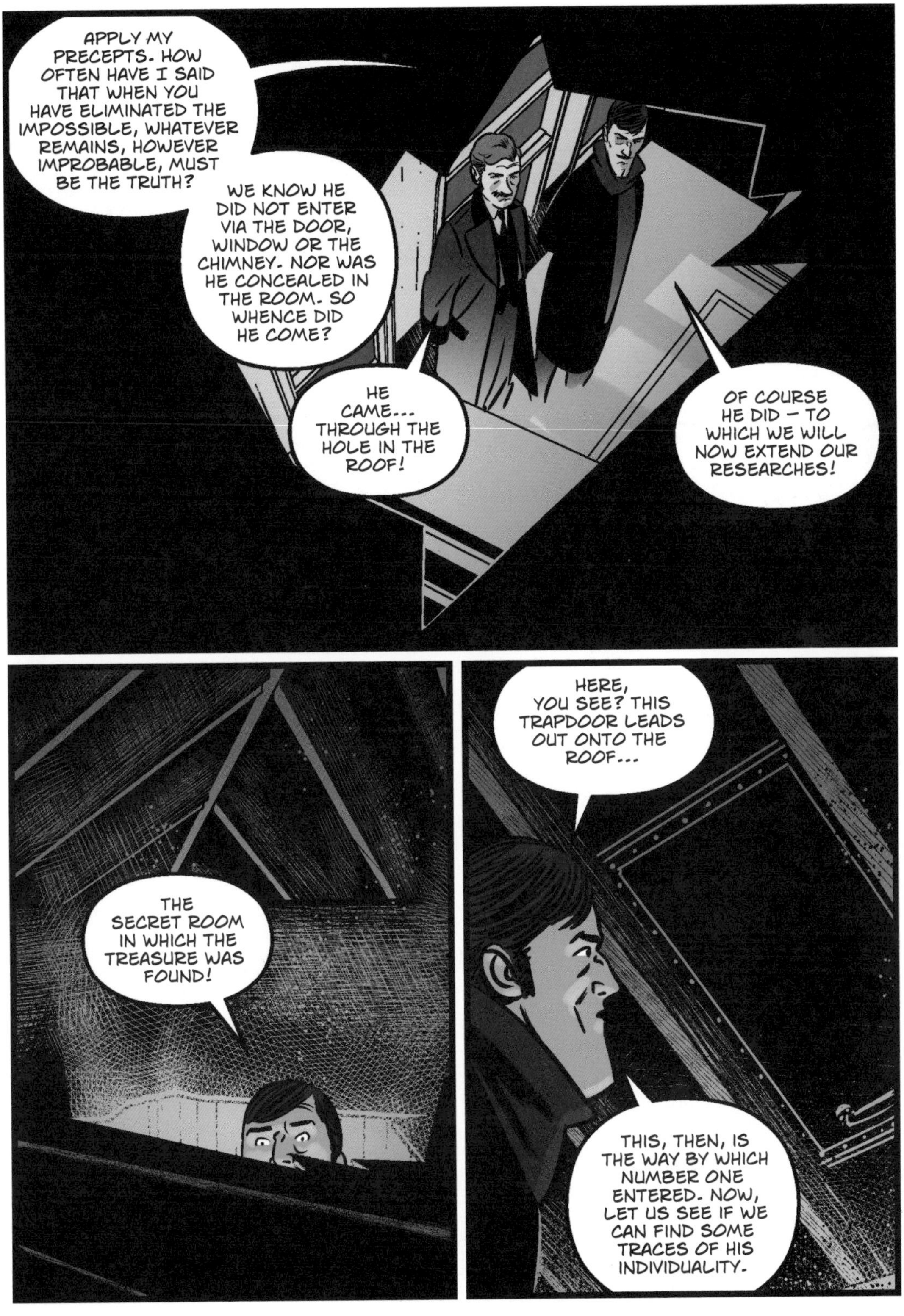
APPLY MY PRECEPTS. HOW OFTEN HAVE I SAID THAT WHEN YOU HAVE ELIMINATED THE IMPOSSIBLE, WHATEVER REMAINS, HOWEVER IMPROBABLE, MUST BE THE TRUTH?
WE KNOW HE DID NOT ENTER VIA THE DOOR, WINDOW OR THE CHIMNEY. NOR WAS HE CONCEALED IN THE ROOM. SO WHENCE DID HE COME?
HE CAME... THROUGH THE HOLE IN THE ROOF!
OF COURSE HE DID — TO WHICH WE WILL NOW EXTEND OUR RESEARCHES!
THE SECRET ROOM IN WHICH THE TREASURE WAS FOUND!
HERE, YOU SEE? THIS TRAPDOOR LEADS OUT ONTO THE ROOF...
THIS, THEN, IS THE WAY BY WHICH NUMBER ONE ENTERED. NOW, LET US SEE IF WE CAN FIND SOME TRACES OF HIS INDIVIDUALITY.

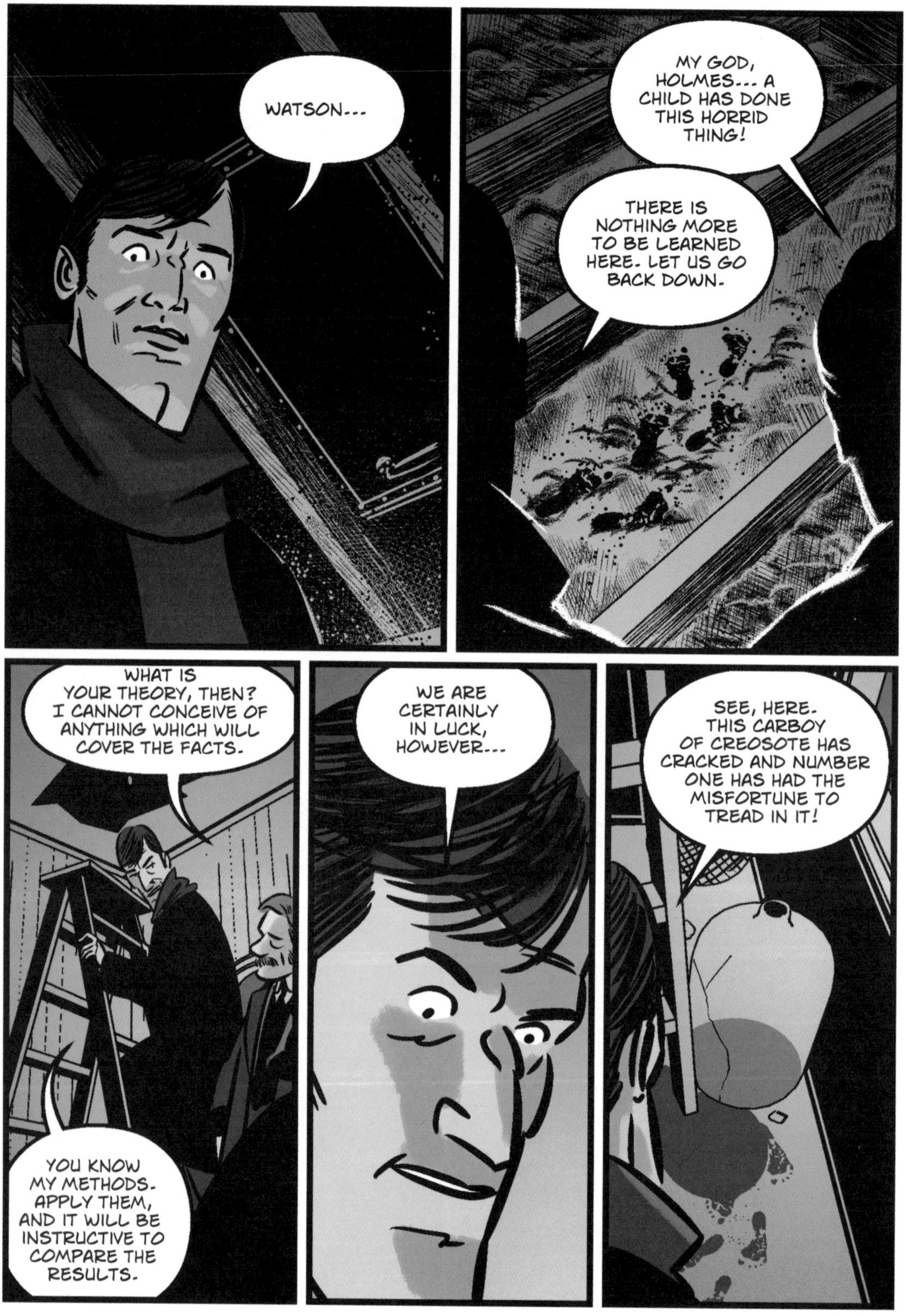
WATSON...
MY GOD, HOLMES... A CHILD HAS DONE THIS HORRID THING!
THERE IS NOTHING MORE TO BE LEARNED HERE. LET US GO BACK DOWN.
WHAT IS YOUR THEORY, THEN? I CANNOT CONCEIVE OF ANYTHING WHICH WILL COVER THE FACTS.
YOU KNOW MY METHODS. APPLY THEM, AND IT WILL BE INSTRUCTIVE TO COMPARE THE RESULTS.
WE ARE CERTAINLY IN LUCK, HOWEVER...
SEE, HERE. THIS CARBOY OF CREOSOTE HAS CRACKED AND NUMBER ONE HAS HAD THE MISFORTUNE TO TREAD IN IT!

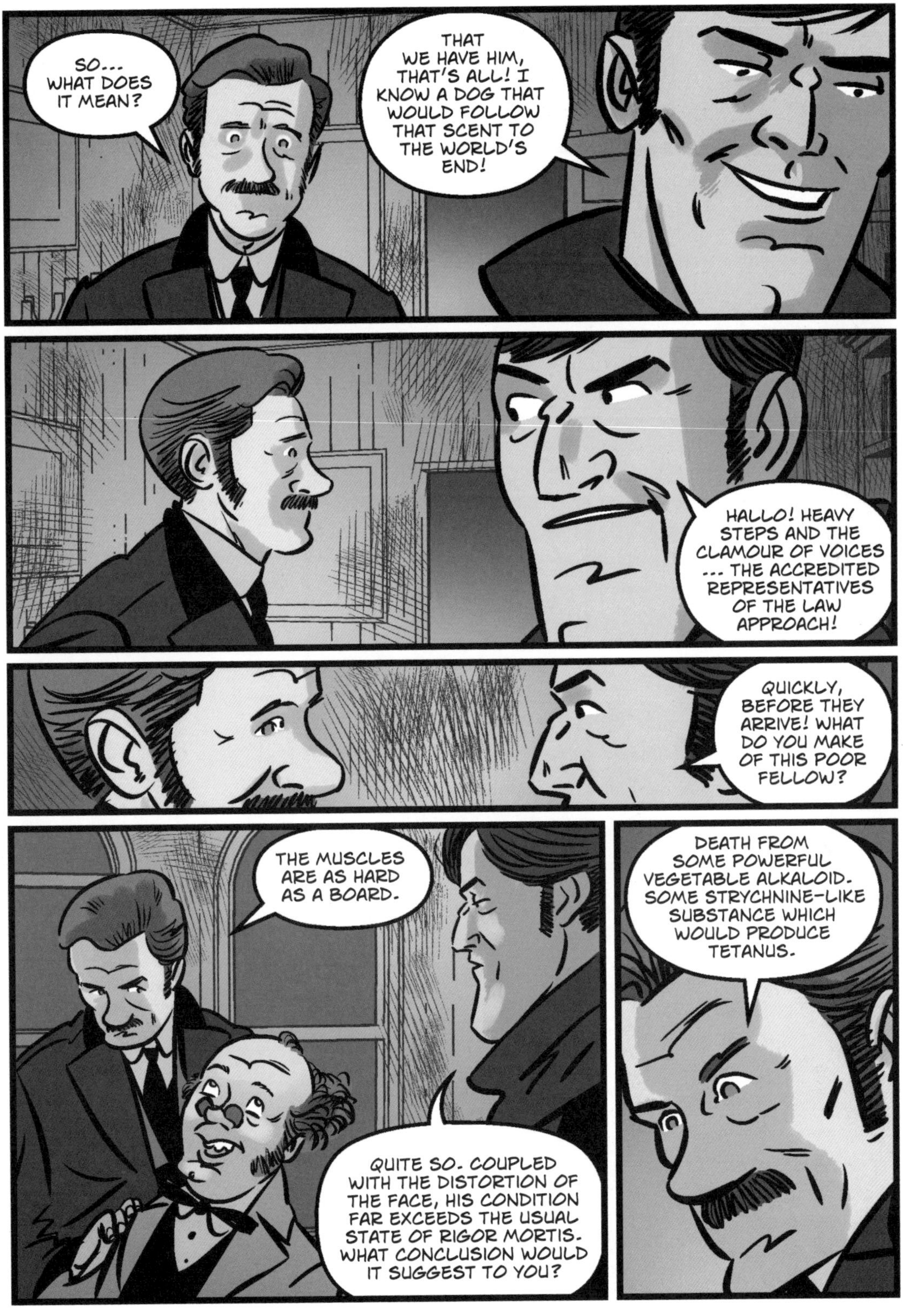
SO... WHAT DOES IT MEAN?
THAT WE HAVE HIM, THAT'S ALL! I KNOW A DOG THAT WOULD FOLLOW THAT SCENT TO THE WORLD'S END!
HALLO! HEAVY STEPS AND THE CLAMOUR OF VOICES --- THE ACCREDITED REPRESENTATIVES OF THE LAW APPROACH!
QUICKLY, BEFORE THEY ARRIVE! WHAT DO YOU MAKE OF THIS POOR FELLOW?
THE MUSCLES ARE AS HARD AS A BOARD.
QUITE SO. COUPLED WITH THE DISTORTION OF THE FACE, HIS CONDITION FAR EXCEEDS THE USUAL STATE OF RIGOR MORTIS. WHAT CONCLUSION WOULD IT SUGGEST TO YOU?
DEATH FROM SOME POWERFUL VEGETABLE ALKALOID. SOME STRYCHNINE-LIKE SUBSTANCE WHICH WOULD PRODUCE TETANUS.

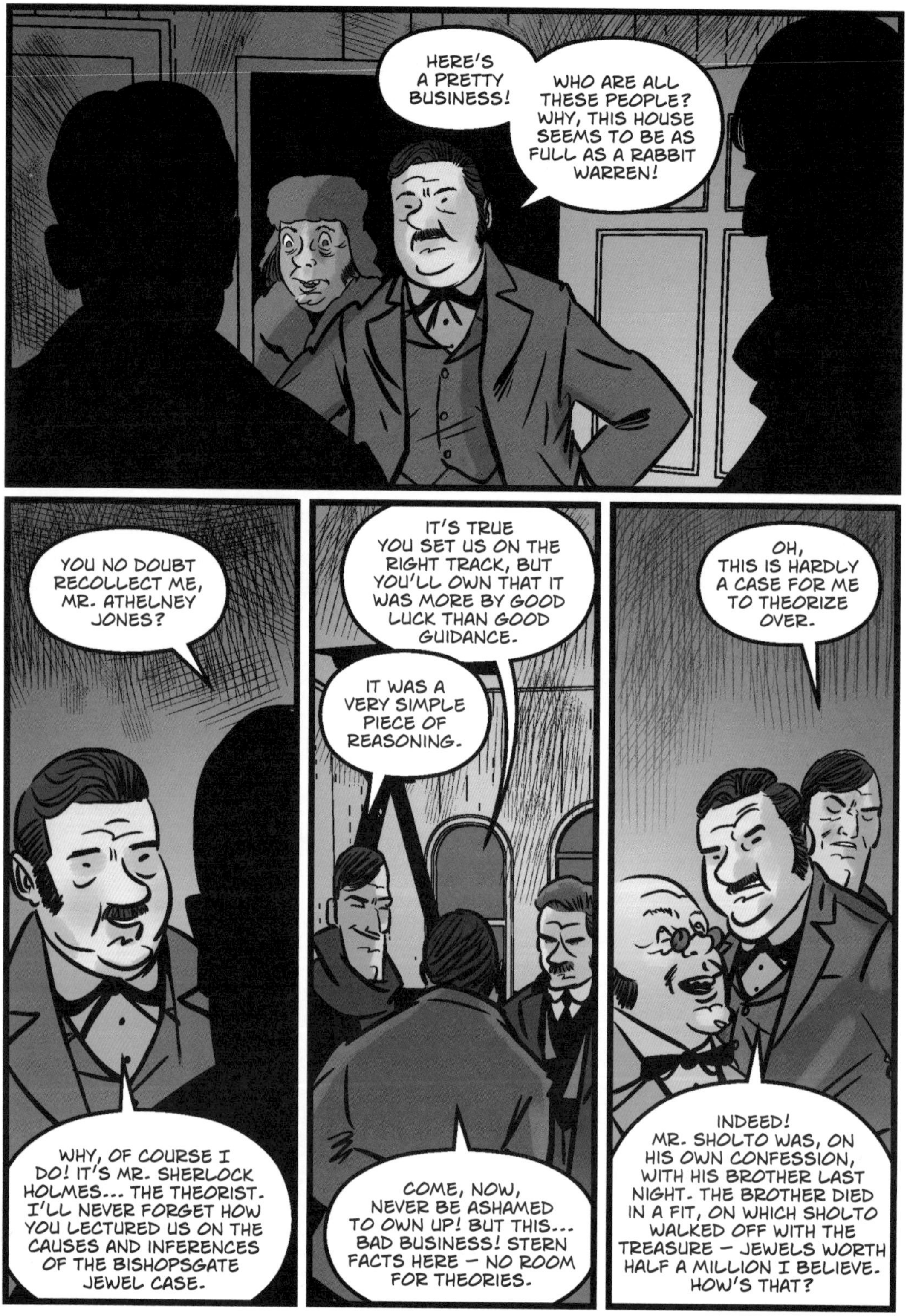
HERE'S A PRETTY BUSINESS!
WHO ARE ALL THESE PEOPLE? WHY, THIS HOUSE SEEMS TO BE AS FULL AS A RABBIT WARREN!
YOU NO DOUBT RECOLLECT ME, MR. ATHELNEY JONES?
WHY, OF COURSE I DO! IT'S MR. SHERLOCK HOLMES... THE THEORIST. I'LL NEVER FORGET HOW YOU LECTURED US ON THE CAUSES AND INFERENCES OF THE BISHOPSGATE JEWEL CASE.
IT'S TRUE YOU SET US ON THE RIGHT TRACK, BUT YOU'LL OWN THAT IT WAS MORE BY GOOD LUCK THAN GOOD GUIDANCE.
IT WAS A VERY SIMPLE PIECE OF REASONING.
COME, NOW, NEVER BE ASHAMED TO OWN UP! BUT THIS... BAD BUSINESS! STERN FACTS HERE — NO ROOM FOR THEORIES.
OH, THIS IS HARDLY A CASE FOR ME TO THEORIZE OVER.
INDEED! MR. SHOLTO WAS, ON HIS OWN CONFESSION, WITH HIS BROTHER LAST NIGHT. THE BROTHER DIED IN A FIT, ON WHICH SHOLTO WALKED OFF WITH THE TREASURE — JEWELS WORTH HALF A MILLION I BELIEVE. HOW'S THAT?

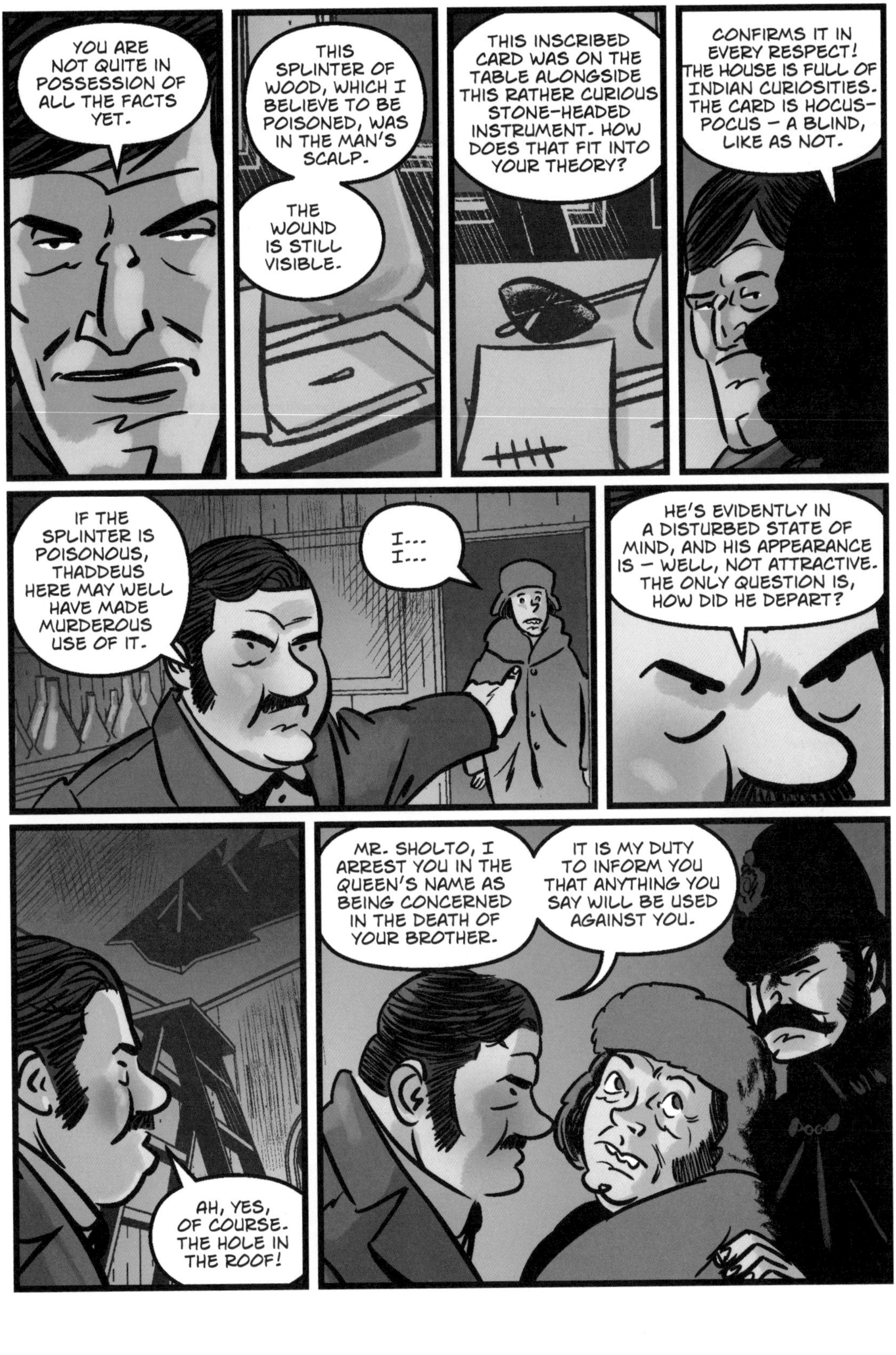
YOU ARE NOT QUITE IN POSSESSION OF ALL THE FACTS YET.
THIS SPLINTER OF WOOD, WHICH I BELIEVE TO BE POISONED, WAS IN THE MAN'S SCALP.
THE WOUND IS STILL VISIBLE.
THIS INSCRIBED CARD WAS ON THE TABLE ALONGSIDE THIS RATHER CURIOUS STONE-HEADED INSTRUMENT. HOW DOES THAT FIT INTO YOUR THEORY?
CONFIRMS IT IN EVERY RESPECT! THE HOUSE IS FULL OF INDIAN CURIOSITIES. THE CARD IS HOCUS-POCUS – A BLIND, LIKE AS NOT.
IF THE SPLINTER IS POISONOUS, THADDEUS HERE MAY WELL HAVE MADE MURDEROUS USE OF IT.
I... I...
HE'S EVIDENTLY IN A DISTURBED STATE OF MIND, AND HIS APPEARANCE IS – WELL, NOT ATTRACTIVE. THE ONLY QUESTION IS, HOW DID HE DEPART?
AH, YES, OF COURSE. THE HOLE IN THE ROOF!
MR. SHOLTO, I ARREST YOU IN THE QUEEN'S NAME AS BEING CONCERNED IN THE DEATH OF YOUR BROTHER.
IT IS MY DUTY TO INFORM YOU THAT ANYTHING YOU SAY WILL BE USED AGAINST YOU.

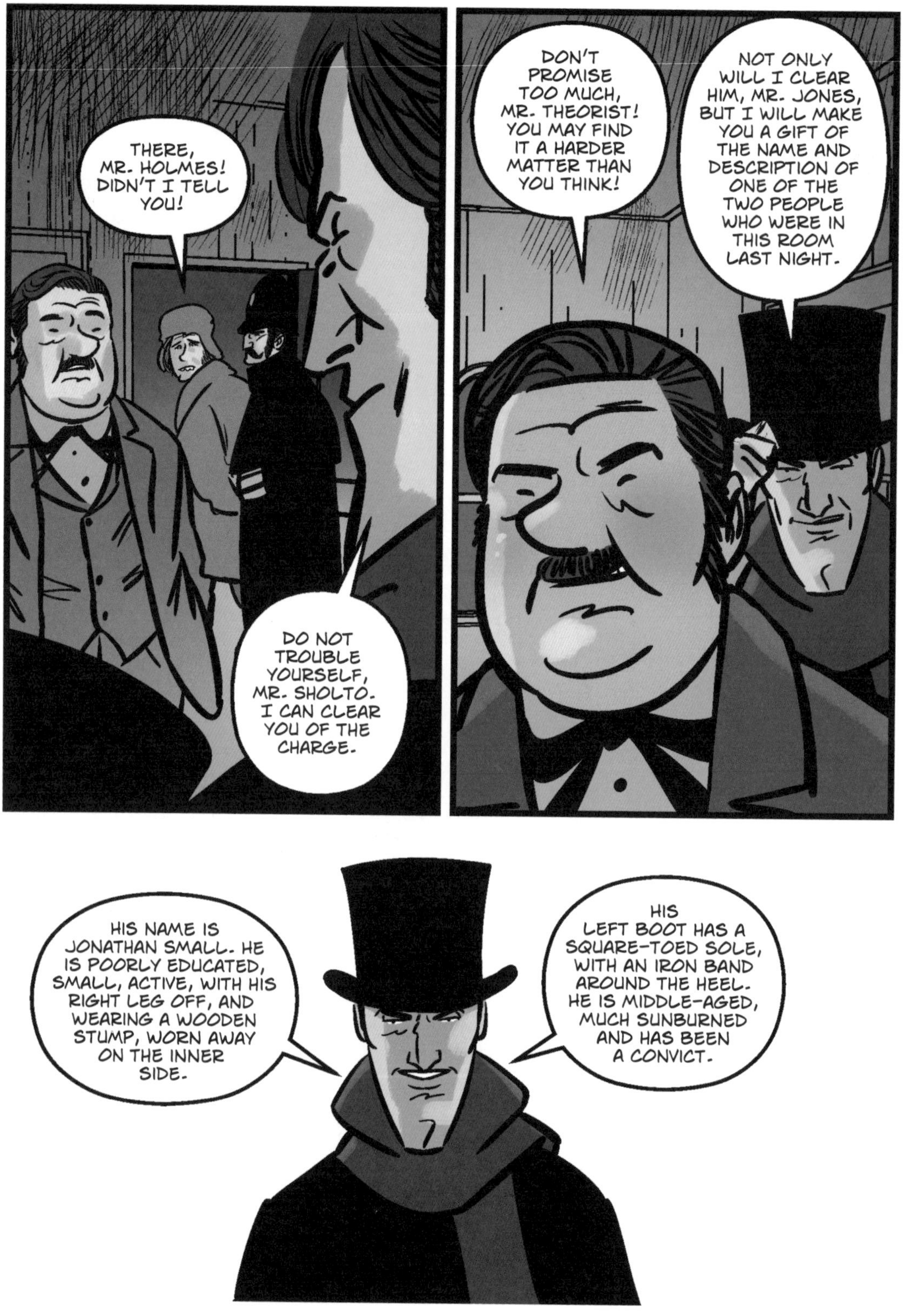
THERE, MR. HOLMES! DIDN'T I TELL YOU!
DO NOT TROUBLE YOURSELF, MR. SHOLTO. I CAN CLEAR YOU OF THE CHARGE.
DON'T PROMISE TOO MUCH, MR. THEORIST! YOU MAY FIND IT A HARDER MATTER THAN YOU THINK!
NOT ONLY WILL I CLEAR HIM, MR. JONES, BUT I WILL MAKE YOU A GIFT OF THE NAME AND DESCRIPTION OF ONE OF THE TWO PEOPLE WHO WERE IN THIS ROOM LAST NIGHT.
HIS NAME IS JONATHAN SMALL. HE IS POORLY EDUCATED, SMALL, ACTIVE, WITH HIS RIGHT LEG OFF, AND WEARING A WOODEN STUMP, WORN AWAY ON THE INNER SIDE.
HIS LEFT BOOT HAS A SQUARE-TOED SOLE, WITH AN IRON BAND AROUND THE HEEL. HE IS MIDDLE-AGED, MUCH SUNBURNED AND HAS BEEN A CONVICT.

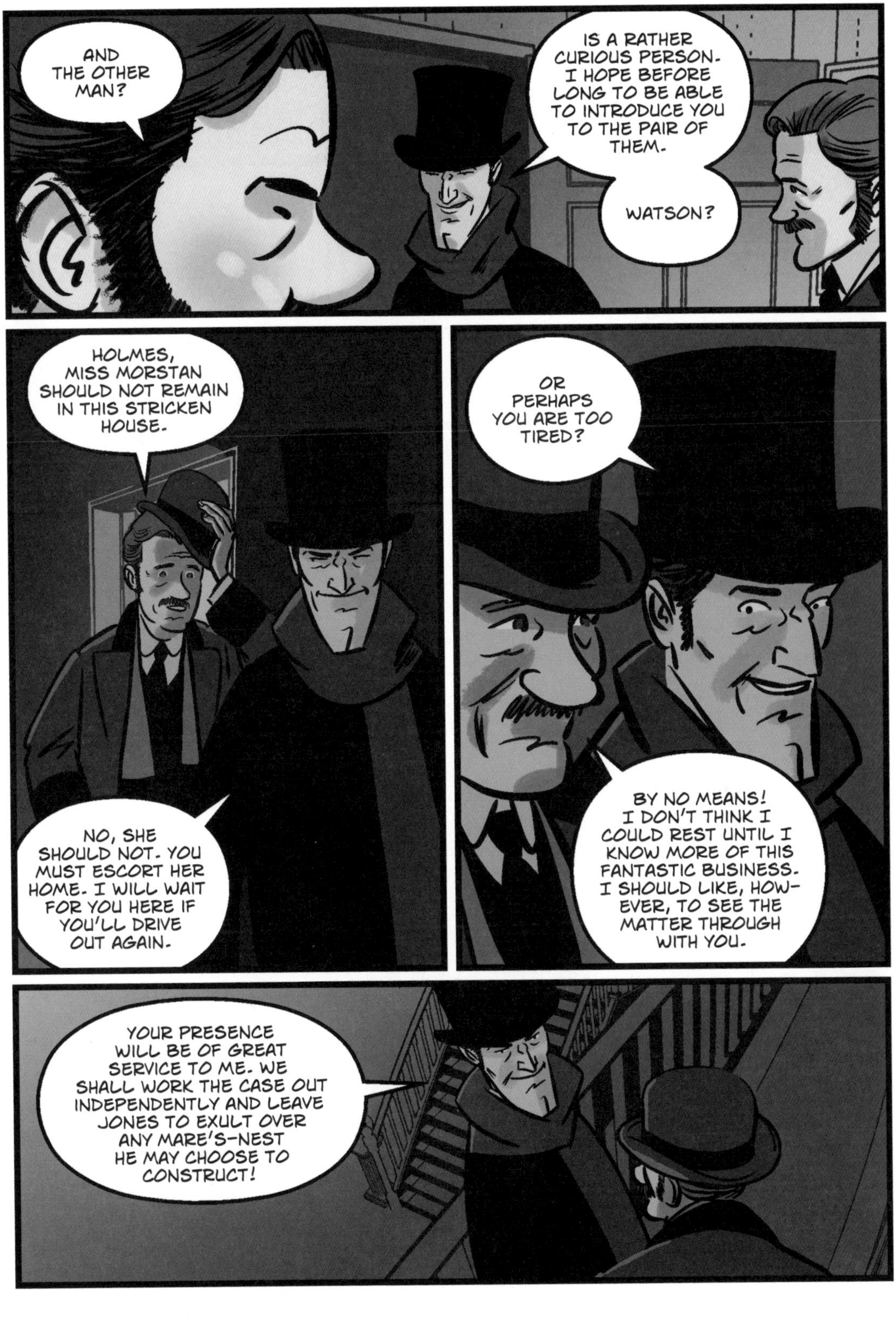
AND THE OTHER MAN?
IS A RATHER CURIOUS PERSON. I HOPE BEFORE LONG TO BE ABLE TO INTRODUCE YOU TO THE PAIR OF THEM.
WATSON?
HOLMES, MISS MORSTAN SHOULD NOT REMAIN IN THIS STRICKEN HOUSE.
NO, SHE SHOULD NOT. YOU MUST ESCORT HER HOME. I WILL WAIT FOR YOU HERE IF YOU'LL DRIVE OUT AGAIN.
OR PERHAPS YOU ARE TOO TIRED?
BY NO MEANS! I DON'T THINK I COULD REST UNTIL I KNOW MORE OF THIS FANTASTIC BUSINESS. I SHOULD LIKE, HOW-EVER, TO SEE THE MATTER THROUGH WITH YOU.
YOUR PRESENCE WILL BE OF GREAT SERVICE TO ME. WE SHALL WORK THE CASE OUT INDEPENDENTLY AND LEAVE JONES TO EXULT OVER ANY MARE'S-NEST HE MAY CHOOSE TO CONSTRUCT!

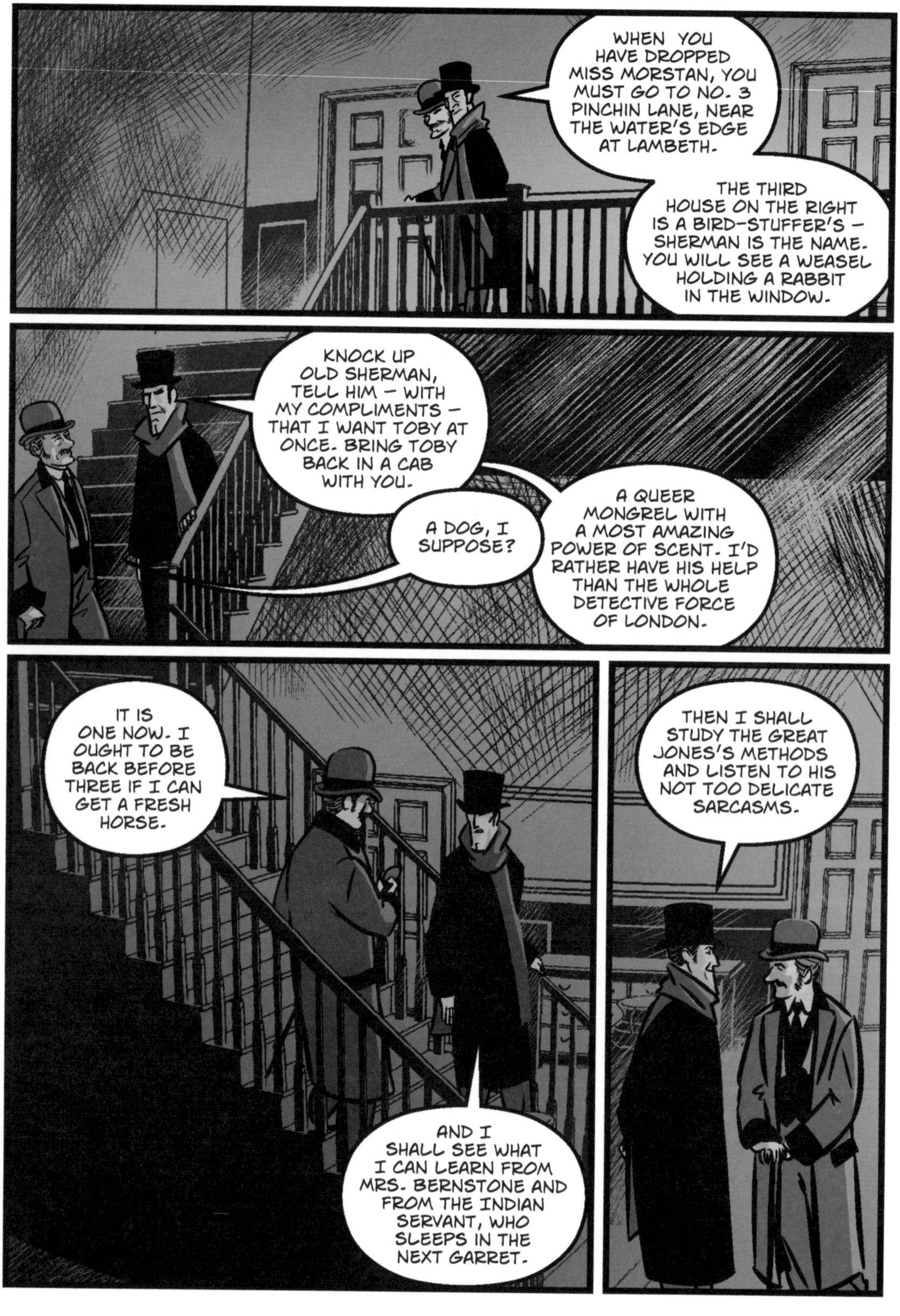
WHEN YOU HAVE DROPPED MISS MORSTAN, YOU MUST GO TO NO. 3 PINCHIN LANE, NEAR THE WATER'S EDGE AT LAMBETH.
THE THIRD HOUSE ON THE RIGHT IS A BIRD-STUFFER'S — SHERMAN IS THE NAME. YOU WILL SEE A WEASEL HOLDING A RABBIT IN THE WINDOW.
KNOCK UP OLD SHERMAN, TELL HIM — WITH MY COMPLIMENTS — THAT I WANT TOBY AT ONCE. BRING TOBY BACK IN A CAB WITH YOU.
A DOG, I SUPPOSE?
A QUEER MONGREL WITH A MOST AMAZING POWER OF SCENT. I'D RATHER HAVE HIS HELP THAN THE WHOLE DETECTIVE FORCE OF LONDON.
IT IS ONE NOW. I OUGHT TO BE BACK BEFORE THREE IF I CAN GET A FRESH HORSE.
AND I SHALL SEE WHAT I CAN LEARN FROM MRS. BERNSTONE AND FROM THE INDIAN SERVANT, WHO SLEEPS IN THE NEXT GARRET.
THEN I SHALL STUDY THE GREAT JONES'S METHODS AND LISTEN TO HIS NOT TOO DELICATE SARCASMS.

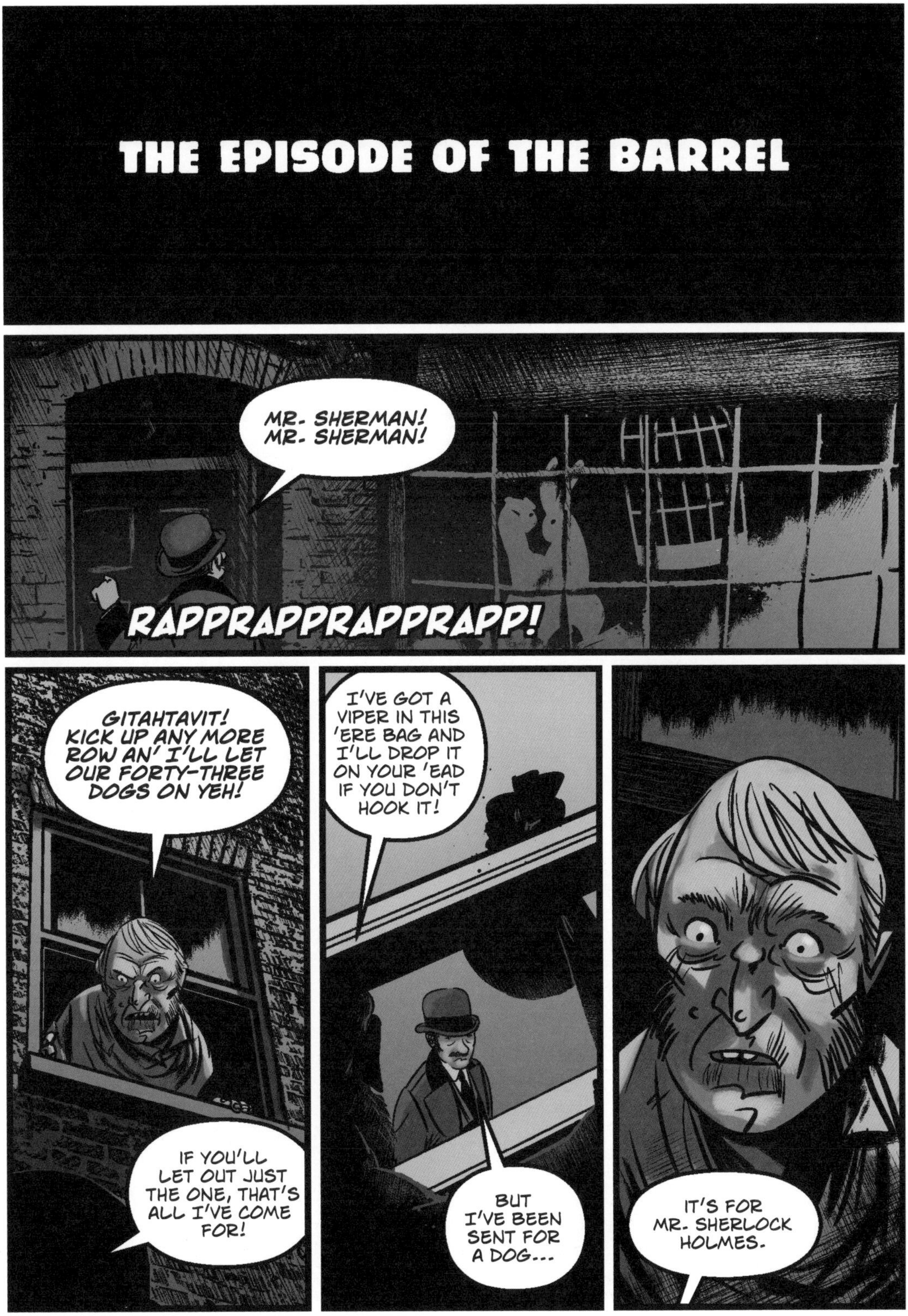
THE EPISODE OF THE BARREL
MR. SHERMAN! MR. SHERMAN!
RAPPRAPPRAPPRAPP!
GITAHTAVIT! KICK UP ANY MORE ROW AN' I'LL LET OUR FORTY-THREE DOGS ON YEH!
IF YOU'LL LET OUT JUST THE ONE, THAT'S ALL I'VE COME FOR!
I'VE GOT A VIPER IN THIS 'ERE BAG AND I'LL DROP IT ON YOUR 'EAD IF YOU DON'T HOOK IT!
BUT I'VE BEEN SENT FOR A DOG...
IT'S FOR MR. SHERLOCK HOLMES.

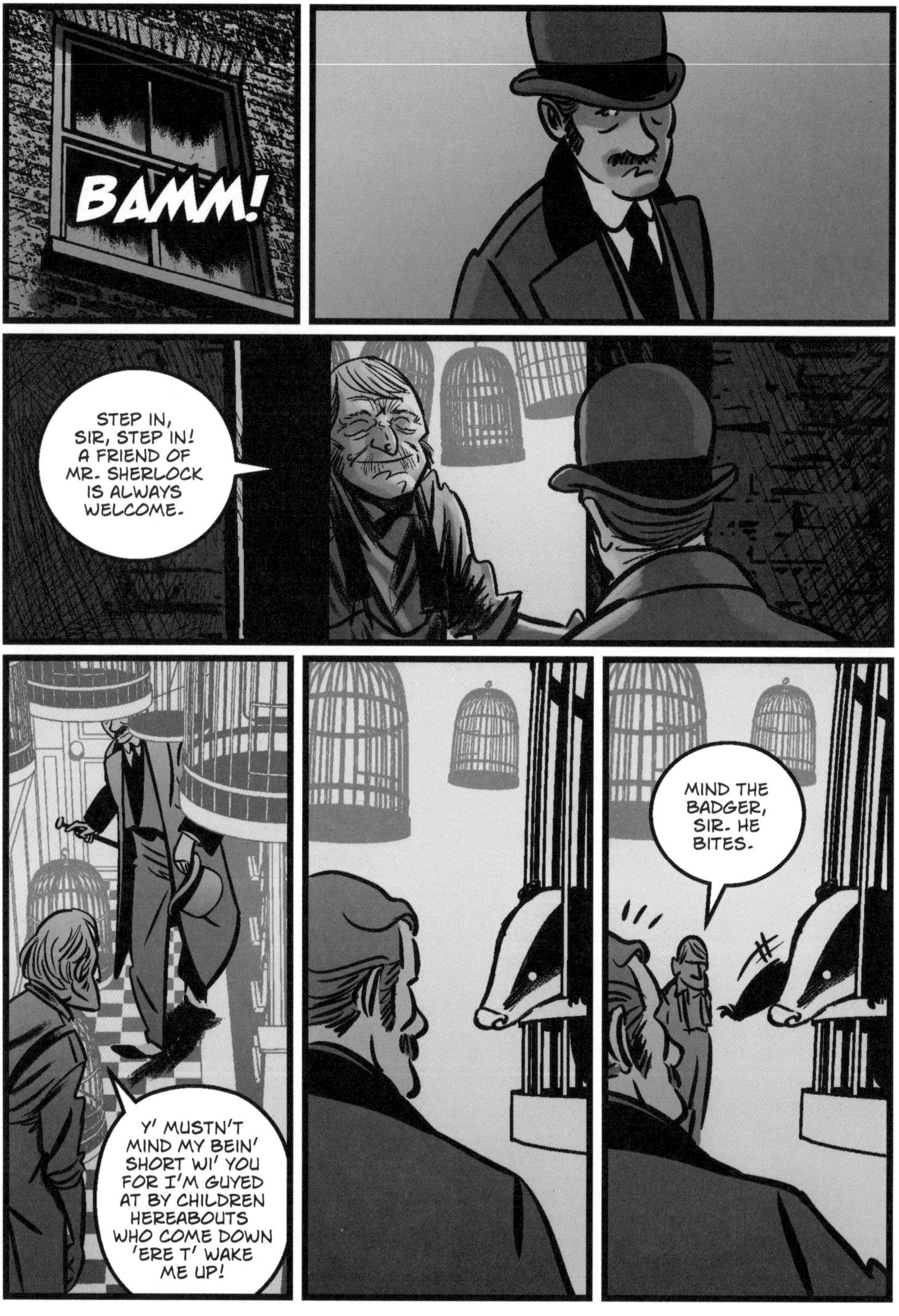
BAMM!
STEP IN, SIR, STEP IN! A FRIEND OF MR. SHERLOCK IS ALWAYS WELCOME.
Y' MUSTN'T MIND MY BEIN' SHORT WI' YOU FOR I'M GUYED AT BY CHILDREN HEREABOUTS WHO COME DOWN 'ERE T' WAKE ME UP!
MIND THE BADGER, SIR. HE BITES.

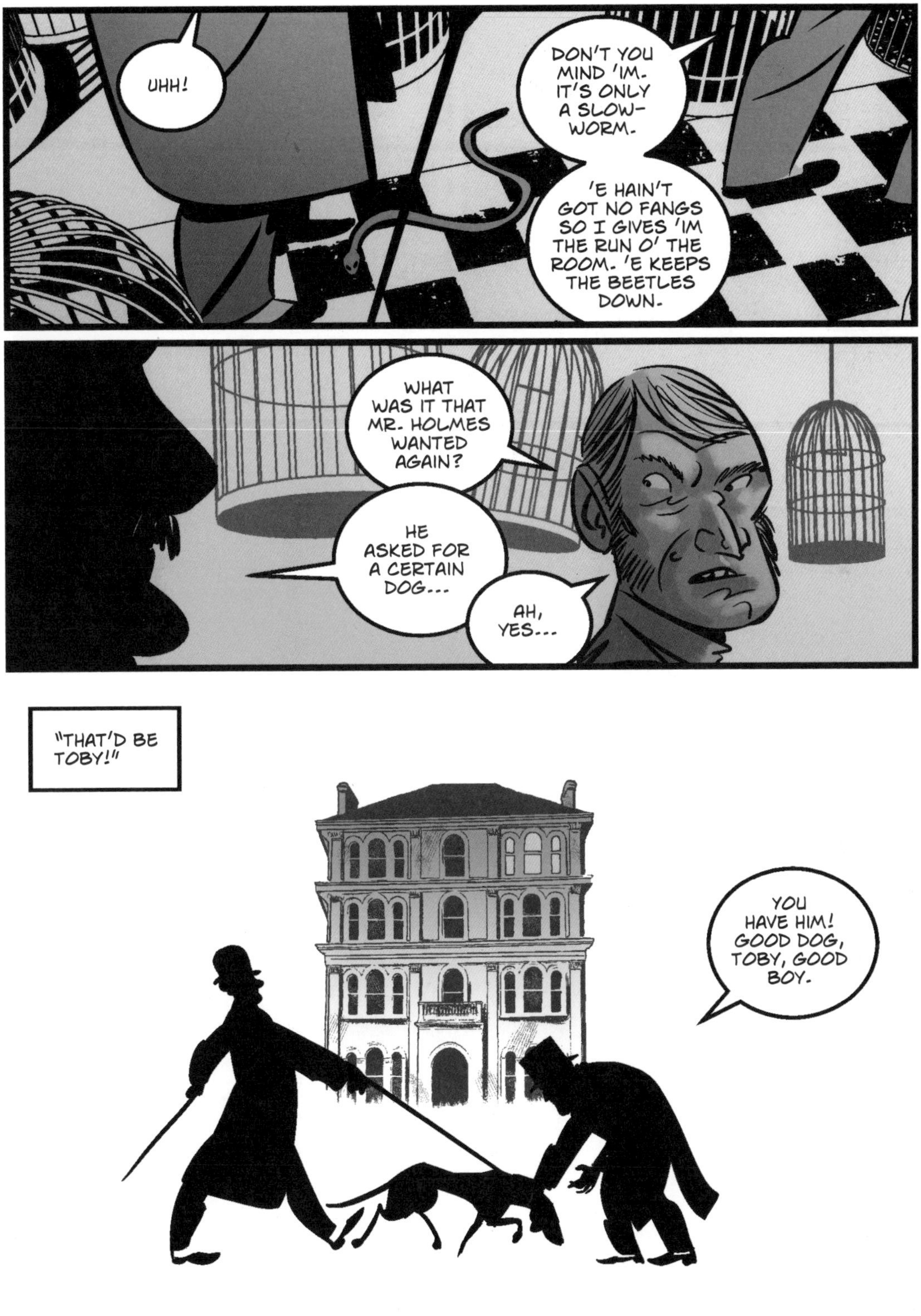
UHH!
DON'T YOU MIND 'IM. IT'S ONLY A SLOW-WORM.
'E HAIN'T GOT NO FANGS SO I GIVES 'IM THE RUN O' THE ROOM. 'E KEEPS THE BEETLES DOWN.
WHAT WAS IT THAT MR. HOLMES WANTED AGAIN?
HE ASKED FOR A CERTAIN DOG...
AH, YES...
"THAT'D BE TOBY!"
YOU HAVE HIM! GOOD DOG, TOBY, GOOD BOY.

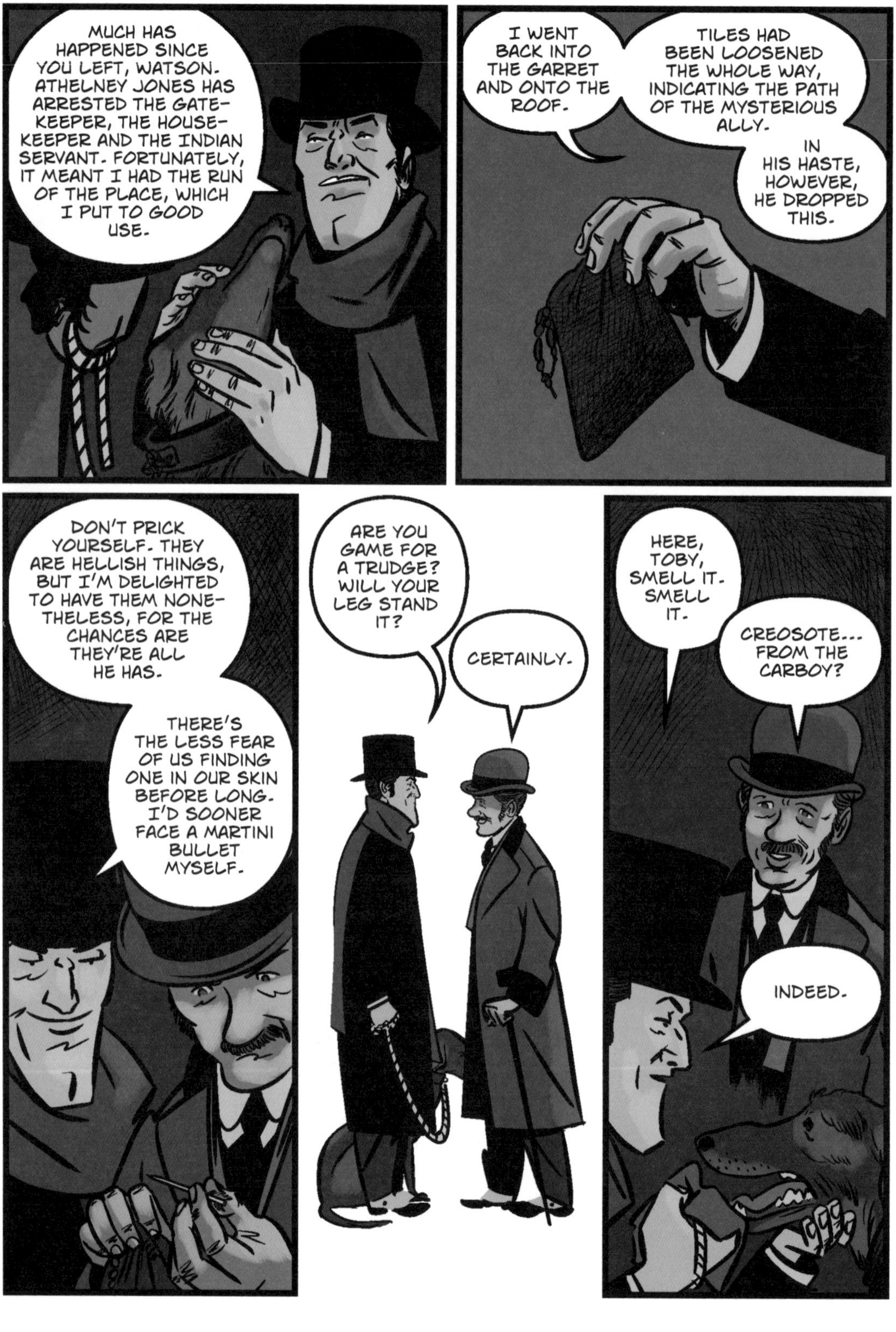
MUCH HAS HAPPENED SINCE YOU LEFT, WATSON. ATHELNEY JONES HAS ARRESTED THE GATE-KEEPER, THE HOUSE-KEEPER AND THE INDIAN SERVANT. FORTUNATELY, IT MEANT I HAD THE RUN OF THE PLACE, WHICH I PUT TO GOOD USE.
I WENT BACK INTO THE GARRET AND ONTO THE ROOF.
TILES HAD BEEN LOOSENED THE WHOLE WAY, INDICATING THE PATH OF THE MYSTERIOUS ALLY.
IN HIS HASTE, HOWEVER, HE DROPPED THIS.
DON'T PRICK YOURSELF. THEY ARE HELLISH THINGS, BUT I'M DELIGHTED TO HAVE THEM NONE-THELESS, FOR THE CHANCES ARE THEY'RE ALL HE HAS.
THERE'S THE LESS FEAR OF US FINDING ONE IN OUR SKIN BEFORE LONG. I'D SOONER FACE A MARTINI BULLET MYSELF.
ARE YOU GAME FOR A TRUDGE? WILL YOUR LEG STAND IT?
CERTAINLY.
HERE, TOBY, SMELL IT. SMELL IT.
CREOSOTE... FROM THE CARBOY?
INDEED.

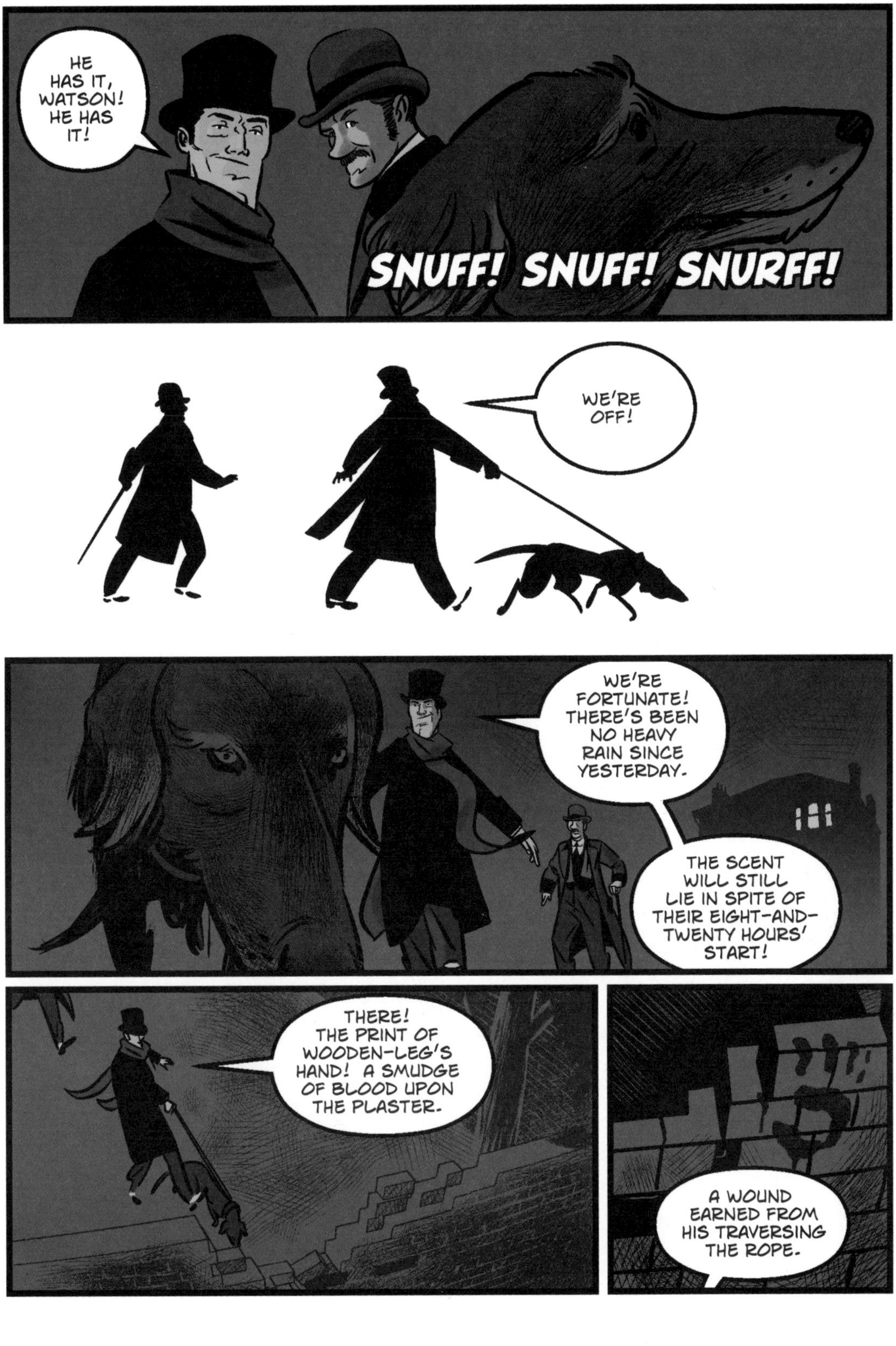
HE HAS IT, WATSON! HE HAS IT!
SNUFF! SNUFF! SNURFF!
WE'RE OFF!
WE'RE FORTUNATE! THERE'S BEEN NO HEAVY RAIN SINCE YESTERDAY.
THE SCENT WILL STILL LIE IN SPITE OF THEIR EIGHT-AND-TWENTY HOURS' START!
THERE! THE PRINT OF WOODEN-LEG'S HAND! A SMUDGE OF BLOOD UPON THE PLASTER.
A WOUND EARNED FROM HIS TRAVERSING THE ROPE.

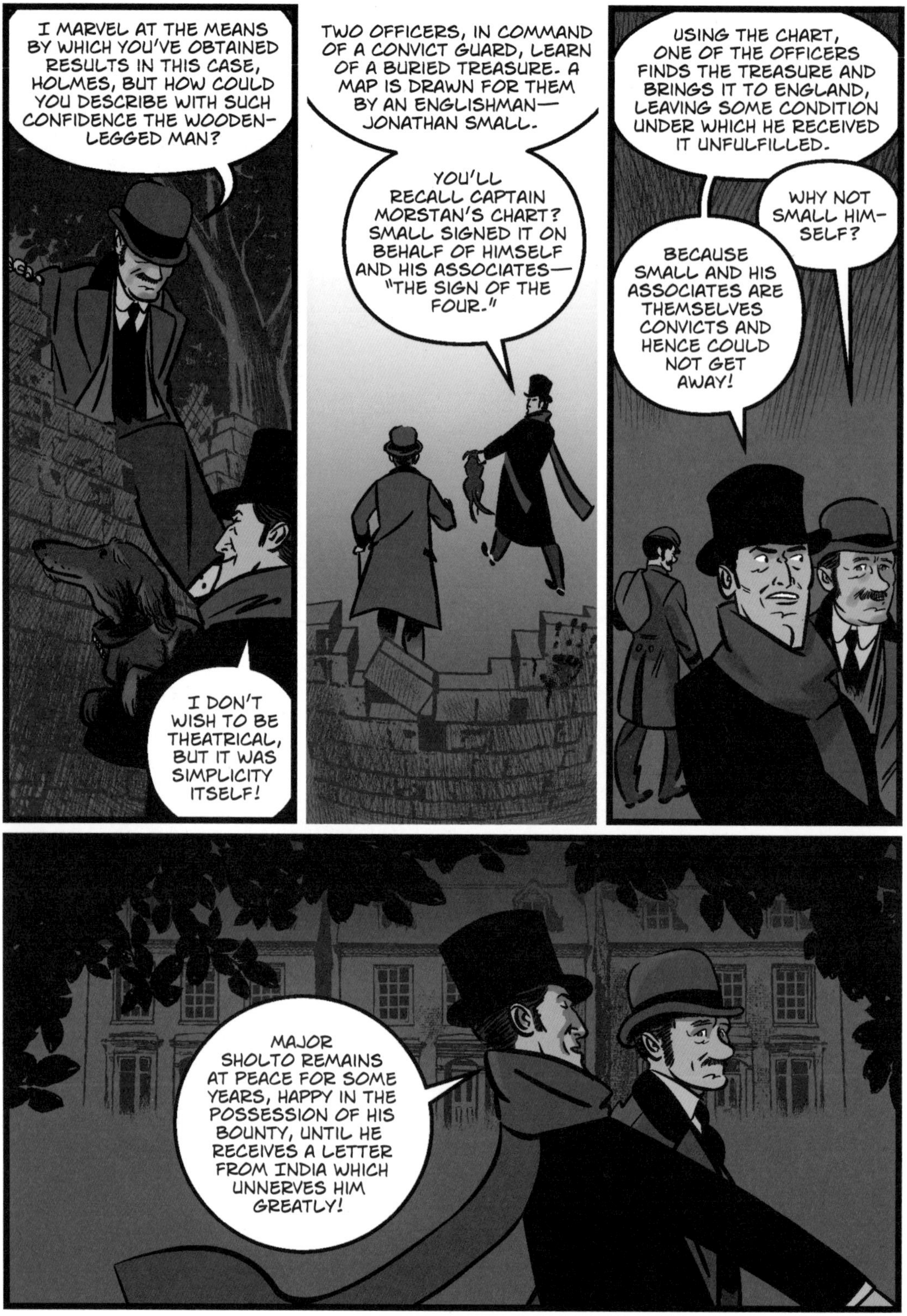
I MARVEL AT THE MEANS BY WHICH YOU'VE OBTAINED RESULTS IN THIS CASE, HOLMES, BUT HOW COULD YOU DESCRIBE WITH SUCH CONFIDENCE THE WOODEN-LEGGED MAN?
I DON'T WISH TO BE THEATRICAL, BUT IT WAS SIMPLICITY ITSELF!
TWO OFFICERS, IN COMMAND OF A CONVICT GUARD, LEARN OF A BURIED TREASURE. A MAP IS DRAWN FOR THEM BY AN ENGLISHMAN— JONATHAN SMALL.
YOU'LL RECALL CAPTAIN MORSTAN'S CHART? SMALL SIGNED IT ON BEHALF OF HIMSELF AND HIS ASSOCIATES— "THE SIGN OF THE FOUR."
USING THE CHART, ONE OF THE OFFICERS FINDS THE TREASURE AND BRINGS IT TO ENGLAND, LEAVING SOME CONDITION UNDER WHICH HE RECEIVED IT UNFULFILLED.
WHY NOT SMALL HIM-SELF?
BECAUSE SMALL AND HIS ASSOCIATES ARE THEMSELVES CONVICTS AND HENCE COULD NOT GET AWAY!
MAJOR SHOLTO REMAINS AT PEACE FOR SOME YEARS, HAPPY IN THE POSSESSION OF HIS BOUNTY, UNTIL HE RECEIVES A LETTER FROM INDIA WHICH UNNERVES HIM GREATLY!

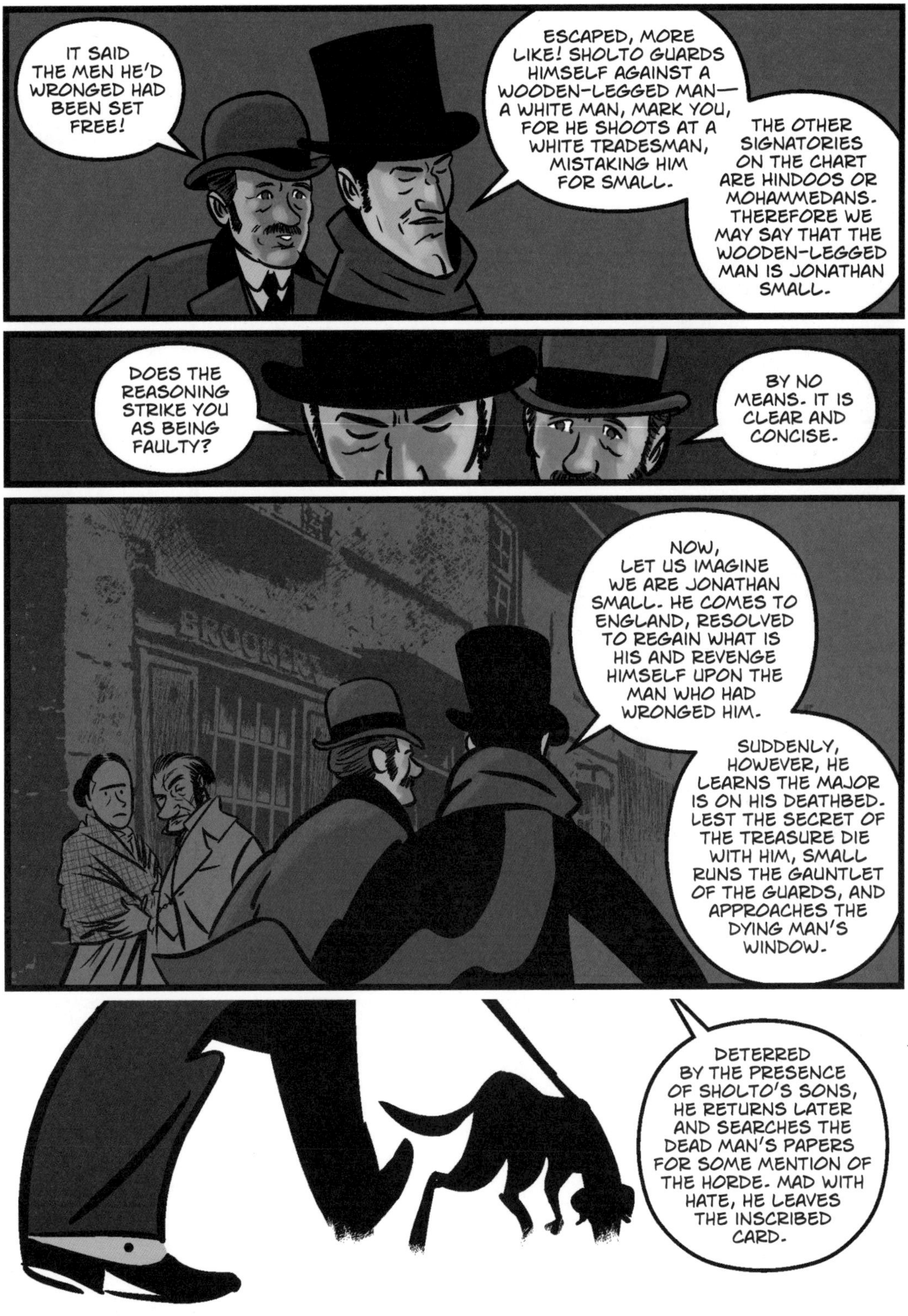
IT SAID THE MEN HE'D WRONGED HAD BEEN SET FREE!
ESCAPED, MORE LIKE! SHOLTO GUARDS HIMSELF AGAINST A WOODEN-LEGGED MAN— A WHITE MAN, MARK YOU, FOR HE SHOOTS AT A WHITE TRADESMAN, MISTAKING HIM FOR SMALL.
THE OTHER SIGNATORIES ON THE CHART ARE HINDOOS OR MOHAMMEDANS. THEREFORE WE MAY SAY THAT THE WOODEN-LEGGED MAN IS JONATHAN SMALL.
DOES THE REASONING STRIKE YOU AS BEING FAULTY?
BY NO MEANS. IT IS CLEAR AND CONCISE.
BROOKE
NOW, LET US IMAGINE WE ARE JONATHAN SMALL. HE COMES TO ENGLAND, RESOLVED TO REGAIN WHAT IS HIS AND REVENGE HIMSELF UPON THE MAN WHO HAD WRONGED HIM.
SUDDENLY, HOWEVER, HE LEARNS THE MAJOR IS ON HIS DEATHBED. LEST THE SECRET OF THE TREASURE DIE WITH HIM, SMALL RUNS THE GAUNTLET OF THE GUARDS, AND APPROACHES THE DYING MAN'S WINDOW.
DETERRED BY THE PRESENCE OF SHOLTO'S SONS, HE RETURNS LATER AND SEARCHES THE DEAD MAN'S PAPERS FOR SOME MENTION OF THE HORDE. MAD WITH HATE, HE LEAVES THE INSCRIBED CARD.

HE'D DOUBTLESS PLANNED BEFOREHAND TO SLAY THE MAJOR, AND LEAVE IT AS A RECORD UPON THE BODY—AS A SIGN TO SHOW IT WAS NOT A COMMON MURDER BUT AN ACT OF JUSTICE.

SMALL CAN DO NOTHING BUT KEEP A WATCH ON THE EFFORTS TO FIND THE TREASURE. HE POSSIBLY LEAVES ENGLAND, RETURNING WHEN INFORMED OF THE DISCOVERY IN THE GARRET.

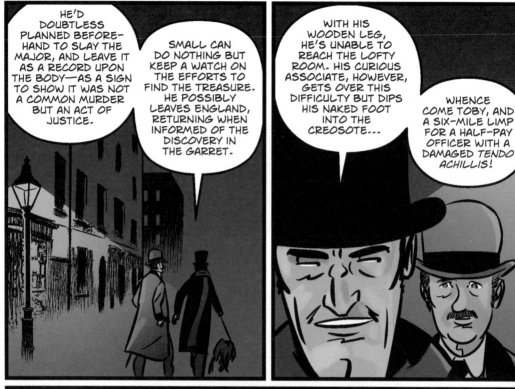

WITH HIS WOODEN LEG, HE'S UNABLE TO REACH THE LOFTY ROOM. HIS CURIOUS ASSOCIATE, HOWEVER, GETS OVER THIS DIFFICULTY BUT DIPS HIS NAKED FOOT INTO THE CREOSOTE...

WHENCE COME TOBY, AND A SIX-MILE LIMP FOR A HALF-PAY OFFICER WITH A DAMAGED TENDO ACHILLIS!

BUT IT WAS THE ASSOCIATE, NOT SMALL, WHO COMMITTED THE CRIME.

QUITE SO— MUCH TO SMALL'S DISGUST, BY THE WAY HE STAMPED AROUND WHEN HE REACHED THE ROOM.

HE BORE NO GRUDGE AGAINST BARTHOLOMEW SHOLTO, BUT THE SAVAGE INSTINCTS OF HIS COMPANION HAD BROKEN OUT.

SMALL THEN LEFT HIS RECORD, LOWERED THE TREASURE-BOX TO THE GROUND, AND FOLLOWED IT HIMSELF. THAT IS THE TRAIN OF EVENTS AS FAR AS I CAN DECIPHER THEM.

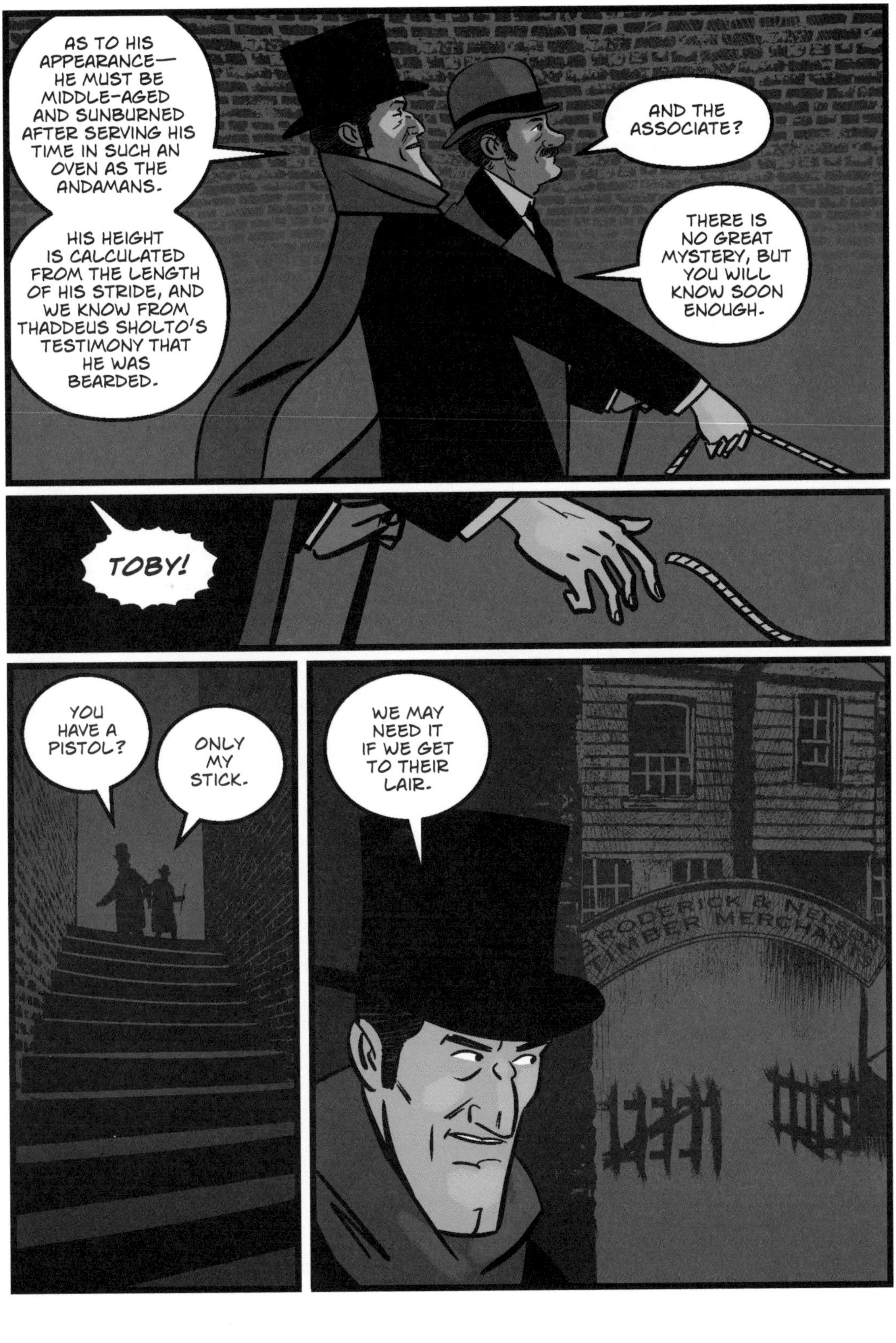
AS TO HIS APPEARANCE—HE MUST BE MIDDLE-AGED AND SUNBURNED AFTER SERVING HIS TIME IN SUCH AN OVEN AS THE ANDAMANS.
HIS HEIGHT IS CALCULATED FROM THE LENGTH OF HIS STRIDE, AND WE KNOW FROM THADDEUS SHOLTO'S TESTIMONY THAT HE WAS BEARDED.
AND THE ASSOCIATE?
THERE IS NO GREAT MYSTERY, BUT YOU WILL KNOW SOON ENOUGH.
TOBY!
YOU HAVE A PISTOL?
ONLY MY STICK.
WE MAY NEED IT IF WE GET TO THEIR LAIR.
BRODERICK & NELSON
TIMBER MERCHANTS

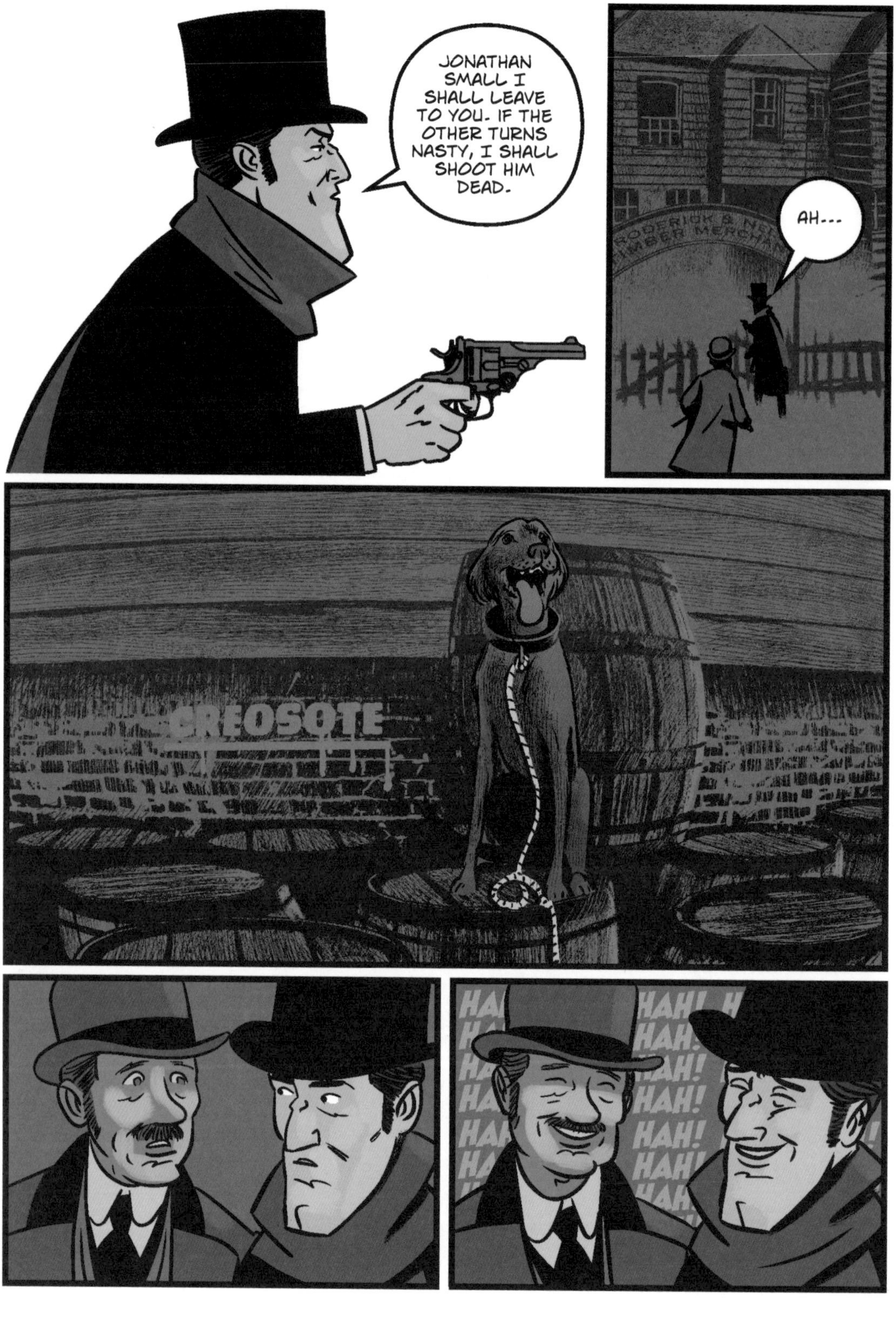
JONATHAN SMALL I SHALL LEAVE TO YOU. IF THE OTHER TURNS NASTY, I SHALL SHOOT HIM DEAD.
AH...
CREOSOTE
HAH! HAH! HAH! HAH! HAH!

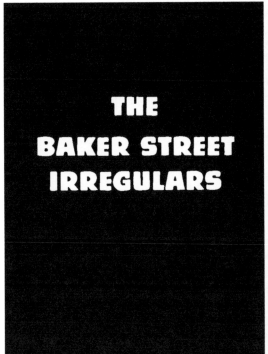

THE
BAKER STREET
IRREGULARS

WHAT NOW? HAS TOBY LOST HIS CHARACTER FOR INFALLIBILITY?

BY NO MEANS. IF YOU CONSIDER HOW MUCH CREOSOTE IS CARTED ABOUT LONDON, IT'S NO WONDER THAT OUR TRAIL WAS CROSSED.

SEE, HE KEEPS TO THE PAVEMENT, WHERE THE BARREL WOULD HAVE PASSED ALONG THE ROADWAY. WE ARE ON THE TRUE SCENT NOW!

BELMONT PLACE

PRINCE'S STREET

BELMONT PLACE AND PRINCE'S STREET. WE ARE MAKING FOR BROAD STREET. AFTER THAT THERE'S BUT ONE DESTINATION...

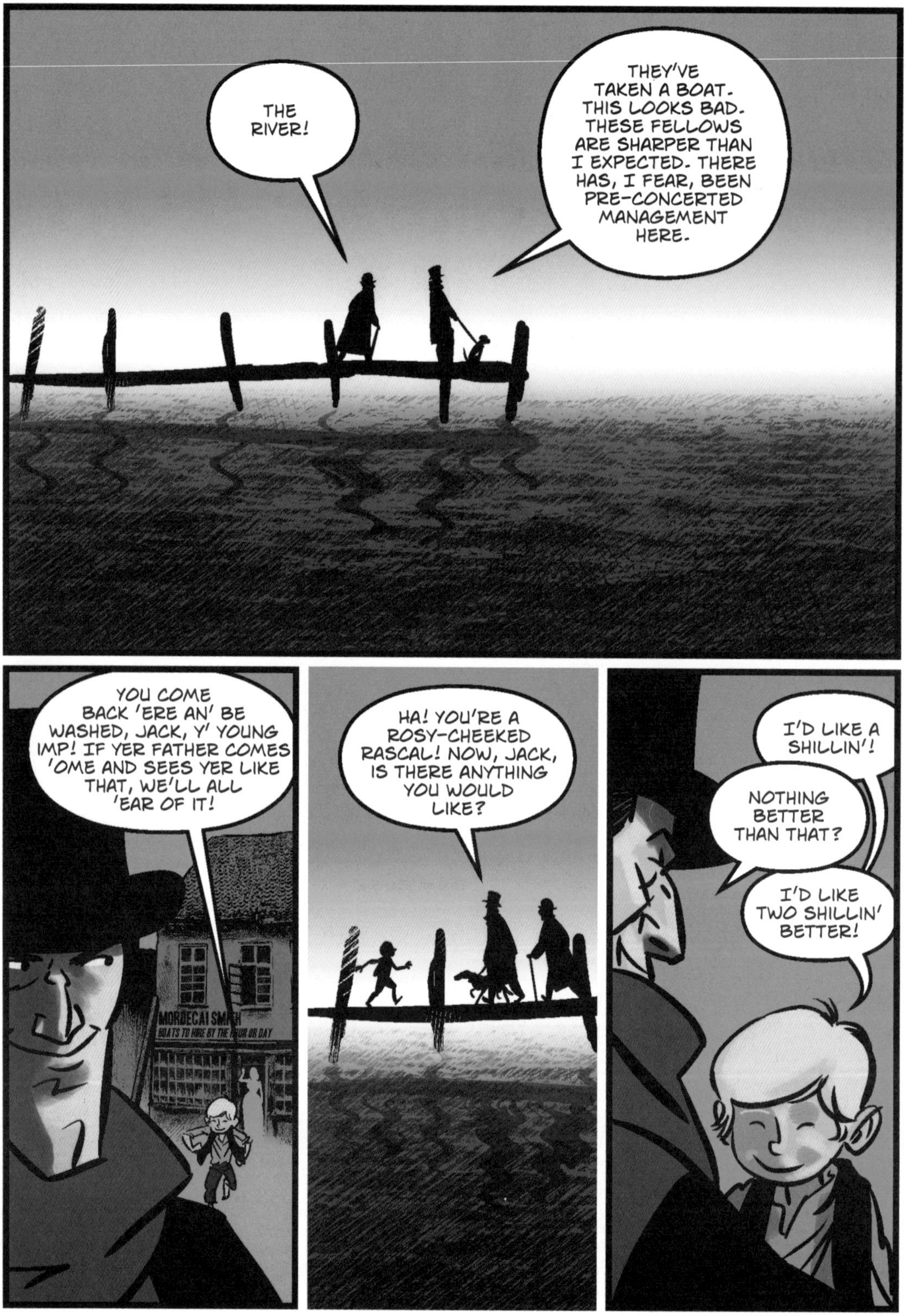
THE RIVER!
THEY'VE TAKEN A BOAT. THIS LOOKS BAD. THESE FELLOWS ARE SHARPER THAN I EXPECTED. THERE HAS, I FEAR, BEEN PRE-CONCERTED MANAGEMENT HERE.
YOU COME BACK 'ERE AN' BE WASHED, JACK, Y' YOUNG IMP! IF YER FATHER COMES 'OME AND SEES YER LIKE THAT, WE'LL ALL 'EAR OF IT!
HA! YOU'RE A ROSY-CHEEKED RASCAL! NOW, JACK, IS THERE ANYTHING YOU WOULD LIKE?
I'D LIKE A SHILLIN'!
NOTHING BETTER THAN THAT?
I'D LIKE TWO SHILLIN' BETTER!

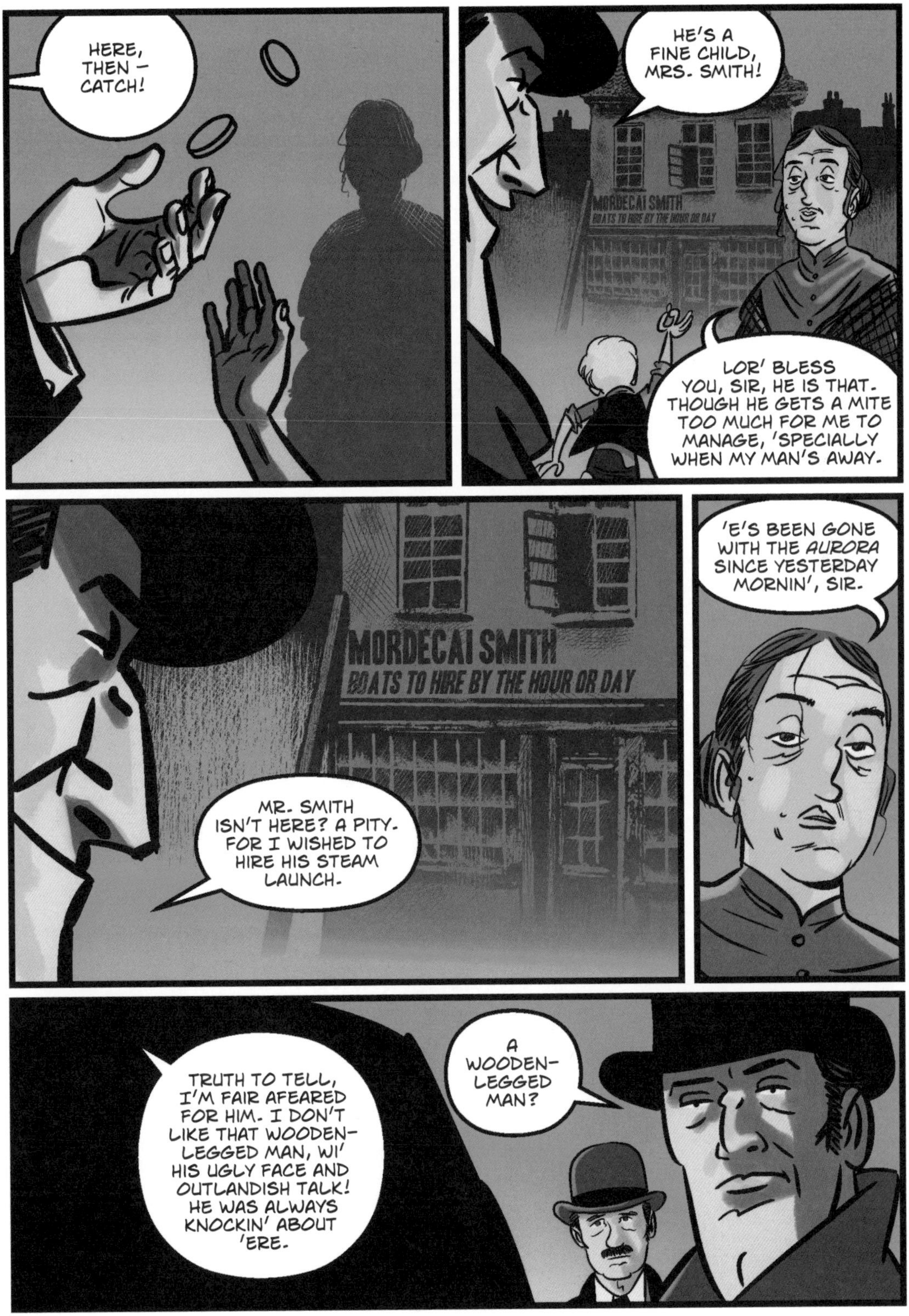
HERE, THEN — CATCH!
HE'S A FINE CHILD, MRS. SMITH!
MORDECAI SMITH
BOATS TO HIRE BY THE HOUR OR DAY
LOR' BLESS YOU, SIR, HE IS THAT. THOUGH HE GETS A MITE TOO MUCH FOR ME TO MANAGE, 'SPECIALLY WHEN MY MAN'S AWAY.
MORDECAI SMITH
BOATS TO HIRE BY THE HOUR OR DAY
MR. SMITH ISN'T HERE? A PITY. FOR I WISHED TO HIRE HIS STEAM LAUNCH.
'E'S BEEN GONE WITH THE *AURORA* SINCE YESTERDAY MORNIN', SIR.
TRUTH TO TELL, I'M FAIR AFEARED FOR HIM. I DON'T LIKE THAT WOODEN-LEGGED MAN, WI' HIS UGLY FACE AND OUTLANDISH TALK! HE WAS ALWAYS KNOCKIN' ABOUT 'ERE.
A WOODEN-LEGGED MAN?

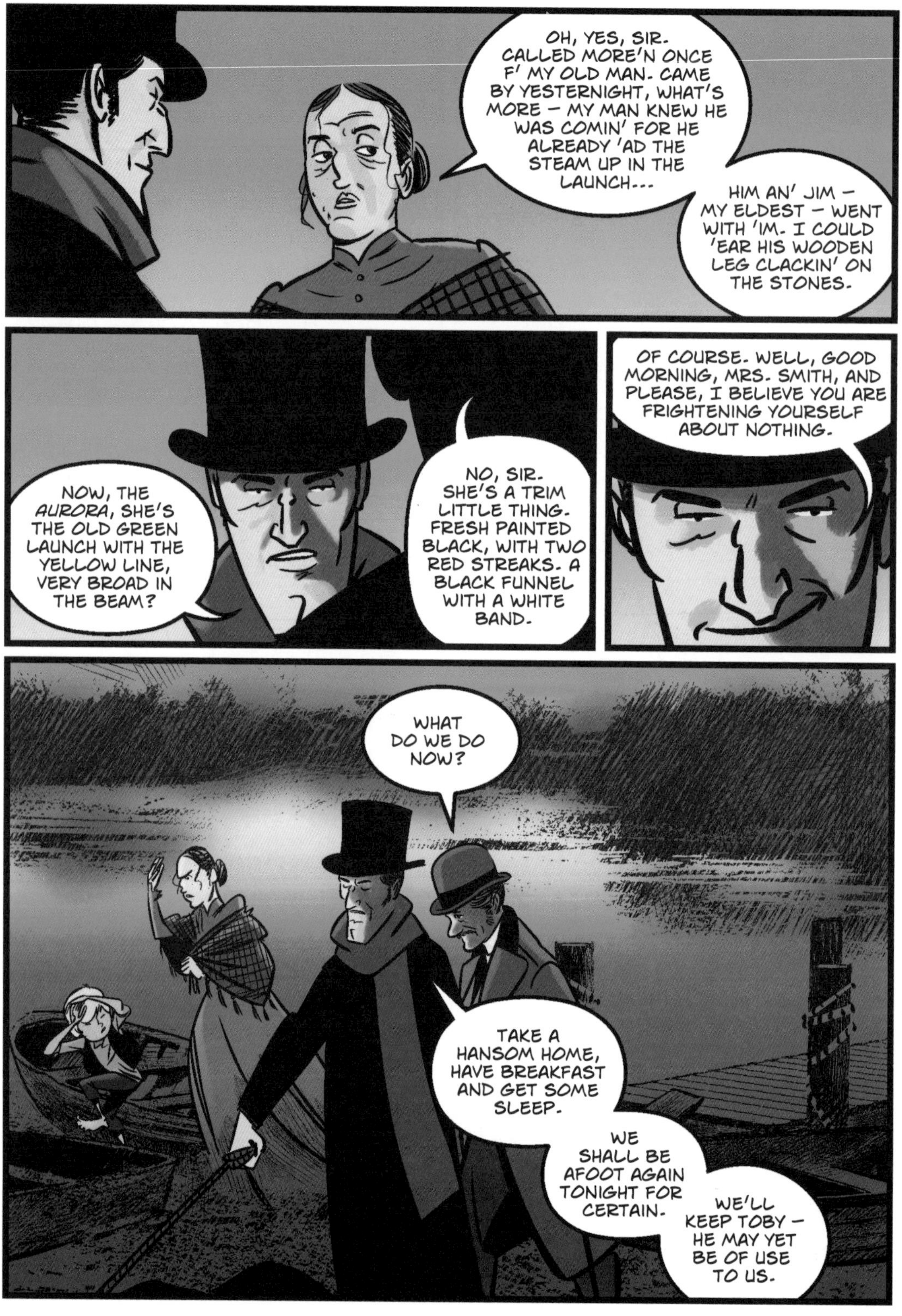
OH, YES, SIR. CALLED MORE'N ONCE F' MY OLD MAN. CAME BY YESTERNIGHT, WHAT'S MORE — MY MAN KNEW HE WAS COMIN' FOR HE ALREADY 'AD THE STEAM UP IN THE LAUNCH...
HIM AN' JIM — MY ELDEST — WENT WITH 'IM. I COULD 'EAR HIS WOODEN LEG CLACKIN' ON THE STONES.
NOW, THE *AURORA*, SHE'S THE OLD GREEN LAUNCH WITH THE YELLOW LINE, VERY BROAD IN THE BEAM?
NO, SIR. SHE'S A TRIM LITTLE THING. FRESH PAINTED BLACK, WITH TWO RED STREAKS. A BLACK FUNNEL WITH A WHITE BAND.
OF COURSE. WELL, GOOD MORNING, MRS. SMITH, AND PLEASE, I BELIEVE YOU ARE FRIGHTENING YOURSELF ABOUT NOTHING.
WHAT DO WE DO NOW?
TAKE A HANSOM HOME, HAVE BREAKFAST AND GET SOME SLEEP.
WE SHALL BE AFOOT AGAIN TONIGHT FOR CERTAIN.
WE'LL KEEP TOBY — HE MAY YET BE OF USE TO US.

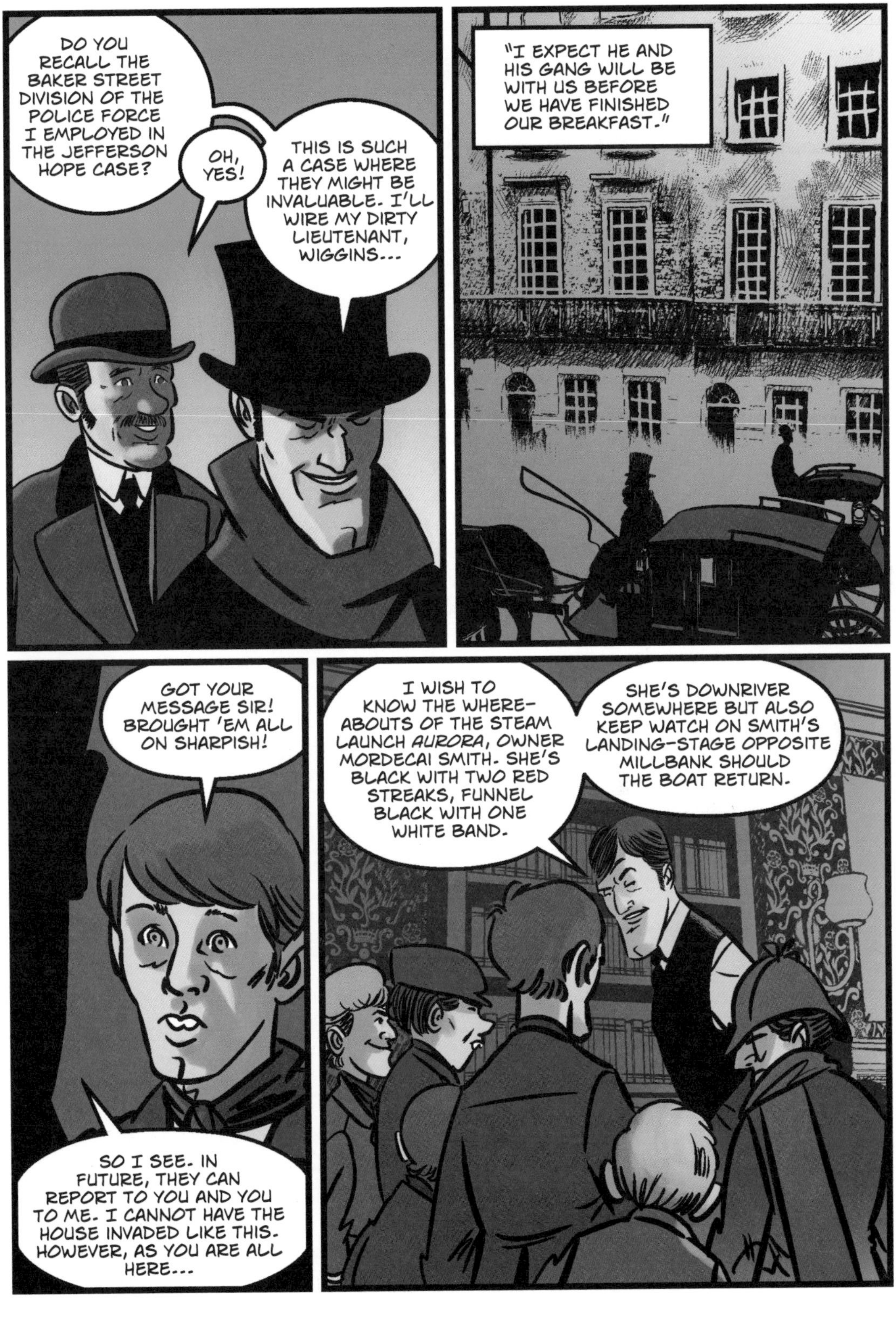
DO YOU RECALL THE BAKER STREET DIVISION OF THE POLICE FORCE I EMPLOYED IN THE JEFFERSON HOPE CASE?
OH, YES!
THIS IS SUCH A CASE WHERE THEY MIGHT BE INVALUABLE. I'LL WIRE MY DIRTY LIEUTENANT, WIGGINS...
"I EXPECT HE AND HIS GANG WILL BE WITH US BEFORE WE HAVE FINISHED OUR BREAKFAST."
GOT YOUR MESSAGE SIR! BROUGHT 'EM ALL ON SHARPISH!
SO I SEE. IN FUTURE, THEY CAN REPORT TO YOU AND YOU TO ME. I CANNOT HAVE THE HOUSE INVADED LIKE THIS. HOWEVER, AS YOU ARE ALL HERE...
I WISH TO KNOW THE WHEREABOUTS OF THE STEAM LAUNCH *AURORA*, OWNER MORDECAI SMITH. SHE'S BLACK WITH TWO RED STREAKS, FUNNEL BLACK WITH ONE WHITE BAND.
SHE'S DOWNRIVER SOMEWHERE BUT ALSO KEEP WATCH ON SMITH'S LANDING-STAGE OPPOSITE MILLBANK SHOULD THE BOAT RETURN.

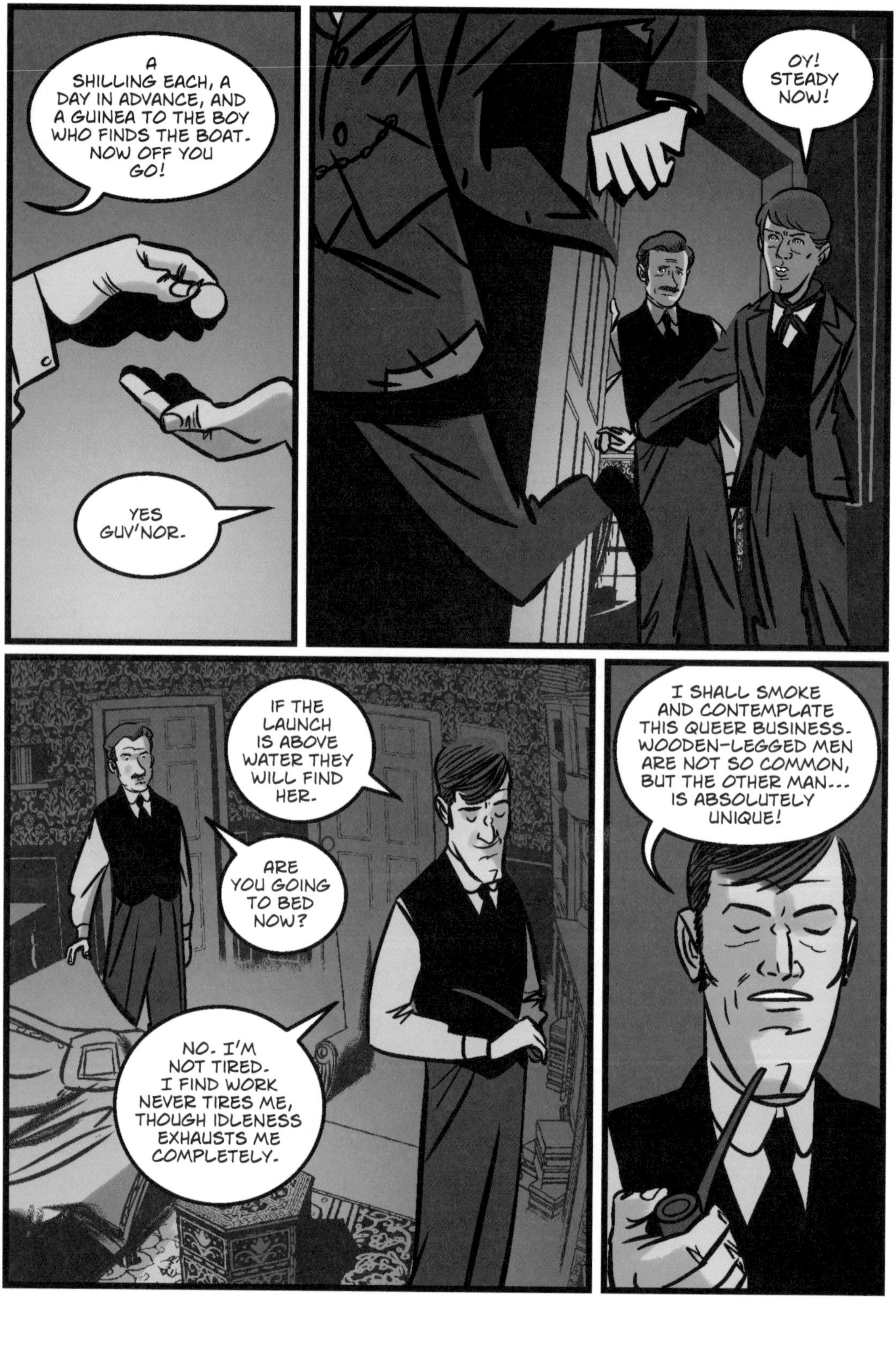
A SHILLING EACH, A DAY IN ADVANCE, AND A GUINEA TO THE BOY WHO FINDS THE BOAT. NOW OFF YOU GO!
YES GUV'NOR.
OY! STEADY NOW!
IF THE LAUNCH IS ABOVE WATER THEY WILL FIND HER.
ARE YOU GOING TO BED NOW?
NO. I'M NOT TIRED. I FIND WORK NEVER TIRES ME, THOUGH IDLENESS EXHAUSTS ME COMPLETELY.
I SHALL SMOKE AND CONTEMPLATE THIS QUEER BUSINESS. WOODEN-LEGGED MEN ARE NOT SO COMMON, BUT THE OTHER MAN... IS ABSOLUTELY UNIQUE!

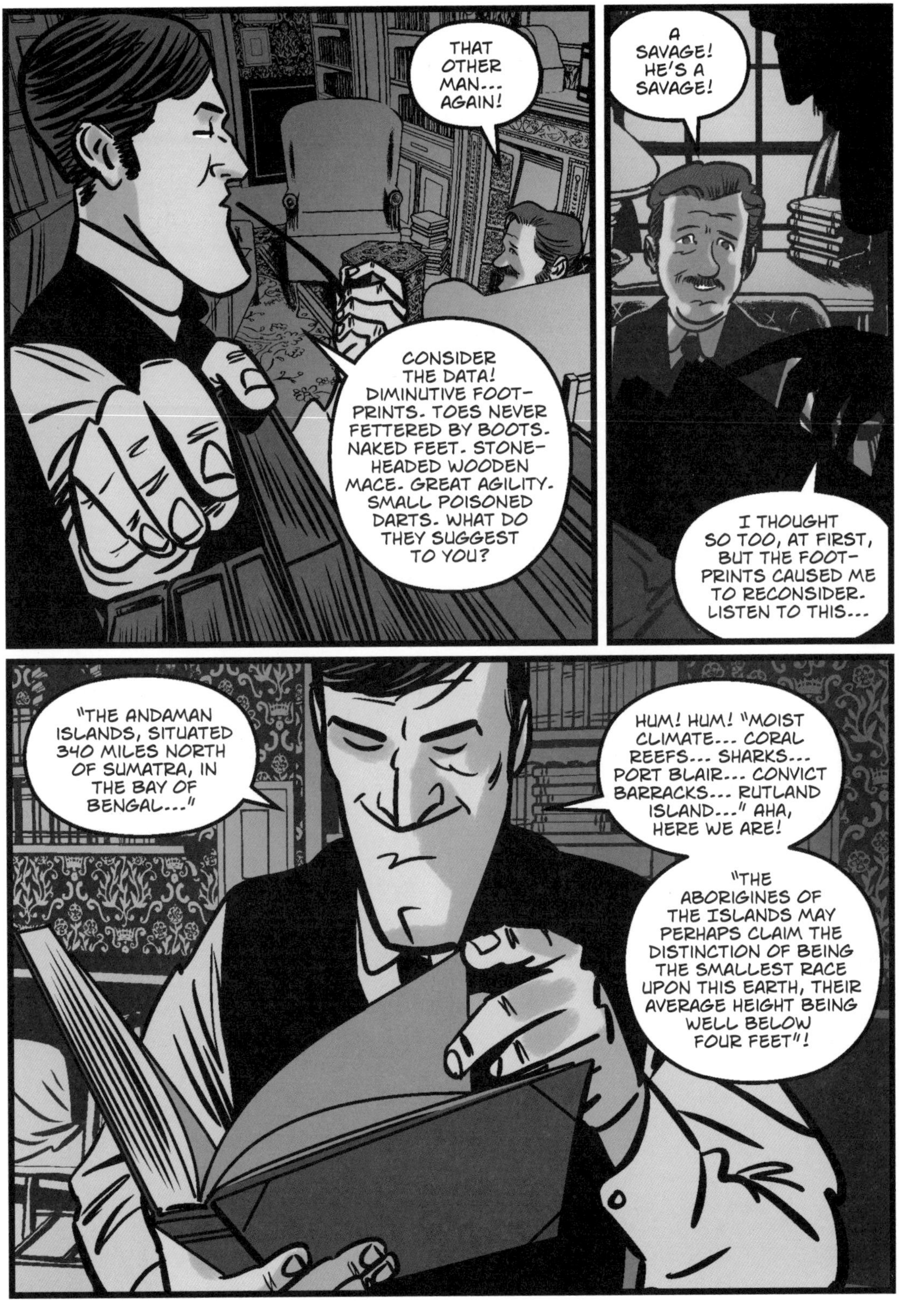
THAT OTHER MAN... AGAIN!
CONSIDER THE DATA! DIMINUTIVE FOOT-PRINTS. TOES NEVER FETTERED BY BOOTS. NAKED FEET. STONE-HEADED WOODEN MACE. GREAT AGILITY. SMALL POISONED DARTS. WHAT DO THEY SUGGEST TO YOU?
A SAVAGE! HE'S A SAVAGE!
I THOUGHT SO TOO, AT FIRST, BUT THE FOOT-PRINTS CAUSED ME TO RECONSIDER. LISTEN TO THIS...
"THE ANDAMAN ISLANDS, SITUATED 340 MILES NORTH OF SUMATRA, IN THE BAY OF BENGAL..."
HUM! HUM! "MOIST CLIMATE... CORAL REEFS... SHARKS... PORT BLAIR... CONVICT BARRACKS... RUTLAND ISLAND..." AHA, HERE WE ARE!
"THE ABORIGINES OF THE ISLANDS MAY PERHAPS CLAIM THE DISTINCTION OF BEING THE SMALLEST RACE UPON THIS EARTH, THEIR AVERAGE HEIGHT BEING WELL BELOW FOUR FEET"!

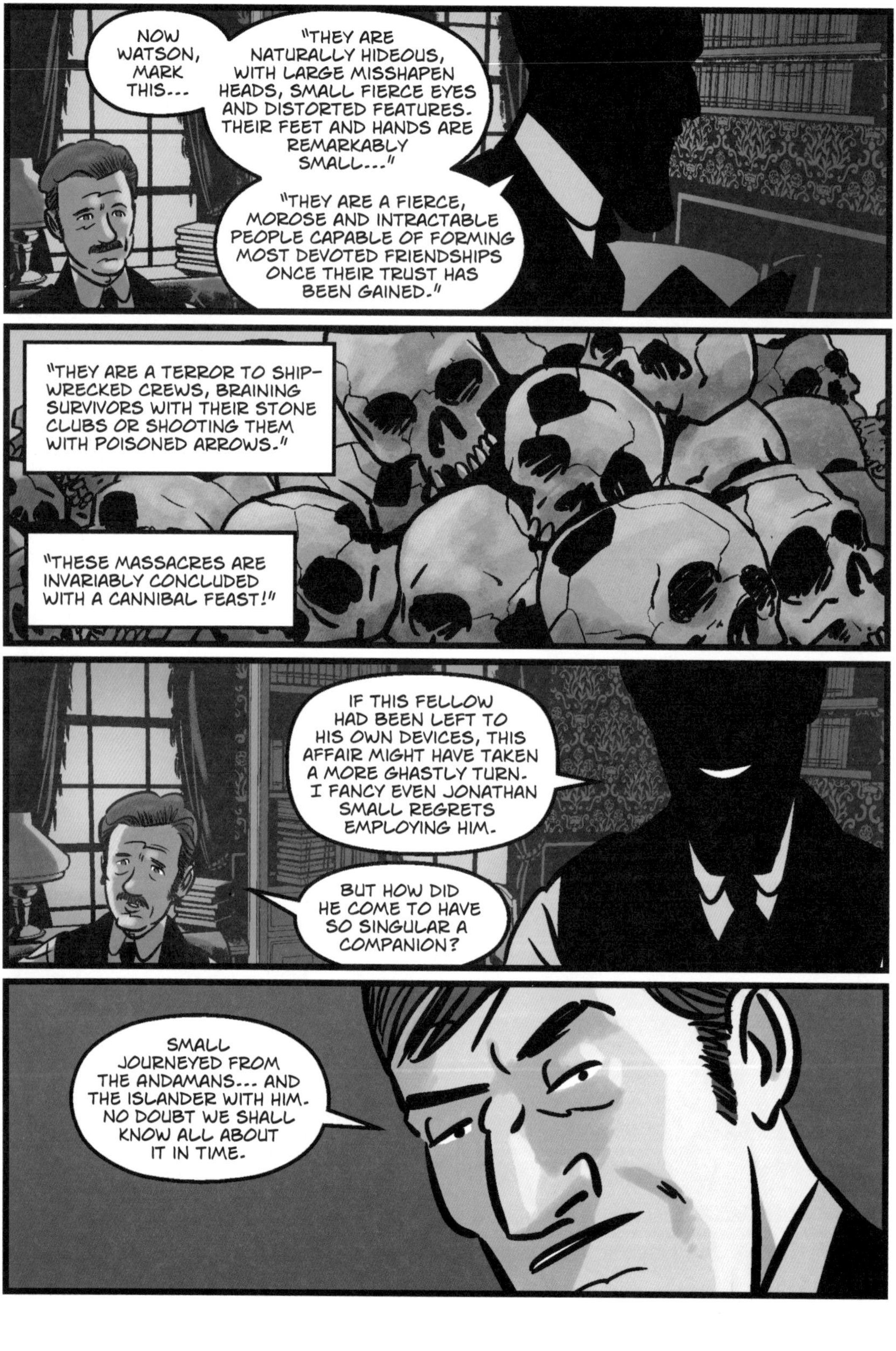
NOW WATSON, MARK THIS...
"THEY ARE NATURALLY HIDEOUS, WITH LARGE MISSHAPEN HEADS, SMALL FIERCE EYES AND DISTORTED FEATURES. THEIR FEET AND HANDS ARE REMARKABLY SMALL..."
"THEY ARE A FIERCE, MOROSE AND INTRACTABLE PEOPLE CAPABLE OF FORMING MOST DEVOTED FRIENDSHIPS ONCE THEIR TRUST HAS BEEN GAINED."
"THEY ARE A TERROR TO SHIP-WRECKED CREWS, BRAINING SURVIVORS WITH THEIR STONE CLUBS OR SHOOTING THEM WITH POISONED ARROWS."
"THESE MASSACRES ARE INVARIABLY CONCLUDED WITH A CANNIBAL FEAST!"
IF THIS FELLOW HAD BEEN LEFT TO HIS OWN DEVICES, THIS AFFAIR MIGHT HAVE TAKEN A MORE GHASTLY TURN. I FANCY EVEN JONATHAN SMALL REGRETS EMPLOYING HIM.
BUT HOW DID HE COME TO HAVE SO SINGULAR A COMPANION?
SMALL JOURNEYED FROM THE ANDAMANS... AND THE ISLANDER WITH HIM. NO DOUBT WE SHALL KNOW ALL ABOUT IT IN TIME.

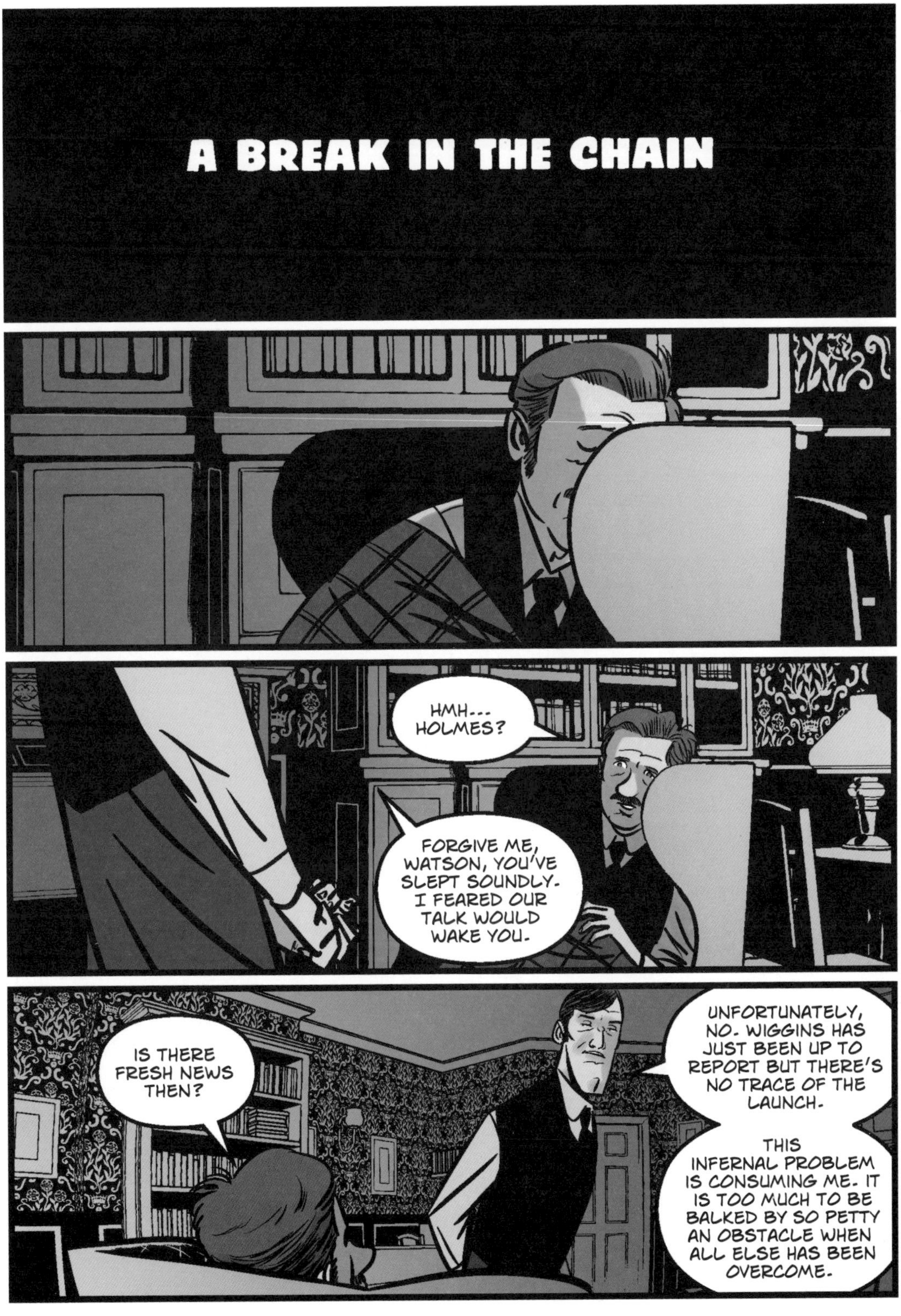
A BREAK IN THE CHAIN
HMH... HOLMES?
FORGIVE ME, WATSON, YOU'VE SLEPT SOUNDLY. I FEARED OUR TALK WOULD WAKE YOU.
IS THERE FRESH NEWS THEN?
UNFORTUNATELY, NO. WIGGINS HAS JUST BEEN UP TO REPORT BUT THERE'S NO TRACE OF THE LAUNCH.
THIS INFERNAL PROBLEM IS CONSUMING ME. IT IS TOO MUCH TO BE BALKED BY SO PETTY AN OBSTACLE WHEN ALL ELSE HAS BEEN OVERCOME.

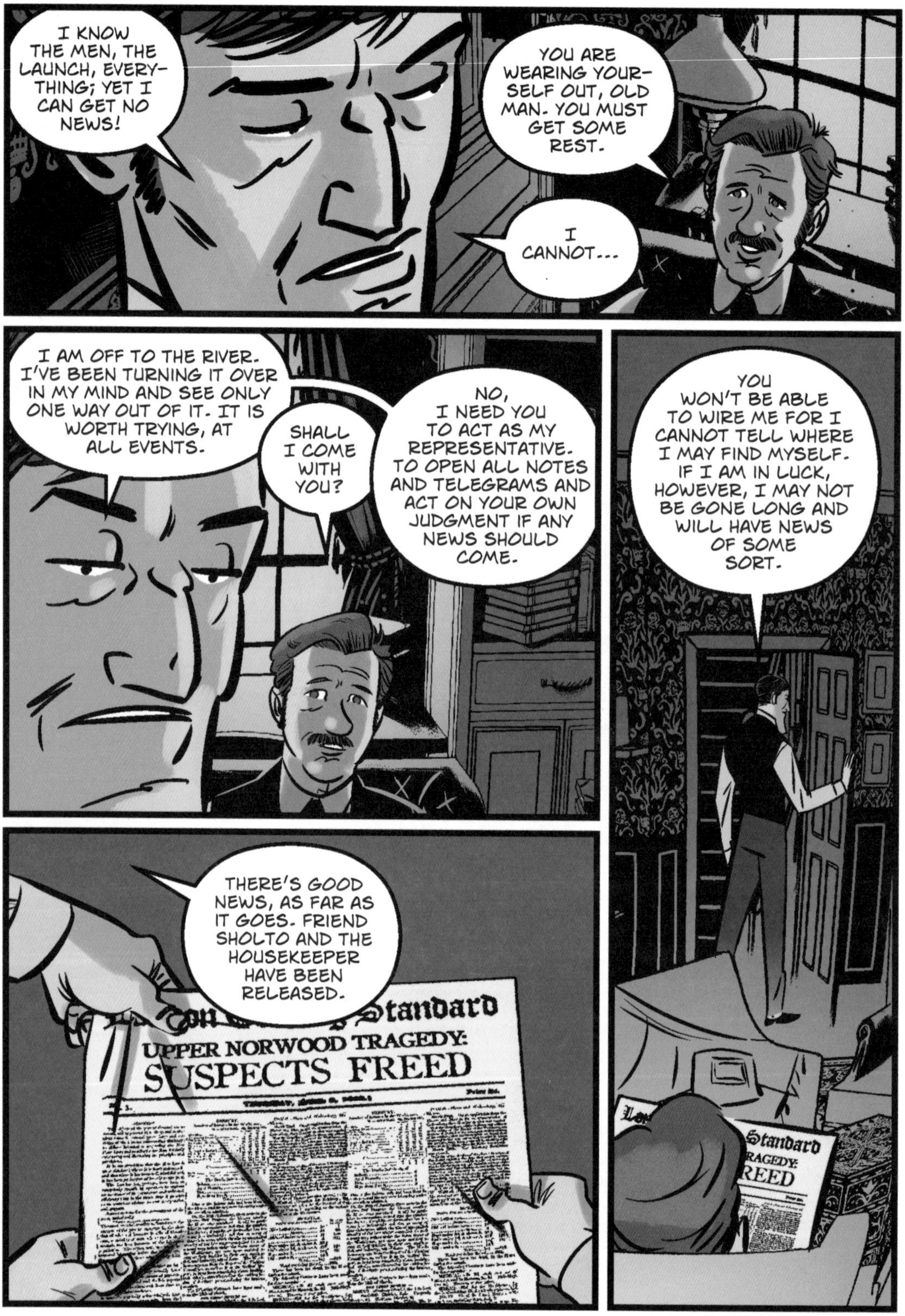
I KNOW THE MEN, THE LAUNCH, EVERY-THING; YET I CAN GET NO NEWS!
YOU ARE WEARING YOUR-SELF OUT, OLD MAN. YOU MUST GET SOME REST.
I CANNOT...
I AM OFF TO THE RIVER. I'VE BEEN TURNING IT OVER IN MY MIND AND SEE ONLY ONE WAY OUT OF IT. IT IS WORTH TRYING, AT ALL EVENTS.
SHALL I COME WITH YOU?
NO, I NEED YOU TO ACT AS MY REPRESENTATIVE. TO OPEN ALL NOTES AND TELEGRAMS AND ACT ON YOUR OWN JUDGMENT IF ANY NEWS SHOULD COME.
YOU WON'T BE ABLE TO WIRE ME FOR I CANNOT TELL WHERE I MAY FIND MYSELF. IF I AM IN LUCK, HOWEVER, I MAY NOT BE GONE LONG AND WILL HAVE NEWS OF SOME SORT.
THERE'S GOOD NEWS, AS FAR AS IT GOES. FRIEND SHOLTO AND THE HOUSEKEEPER HAVE BEEN RELEASED.
Standard
UPPER NORWOOD TRAGEDY:
SUSPECTS FREED

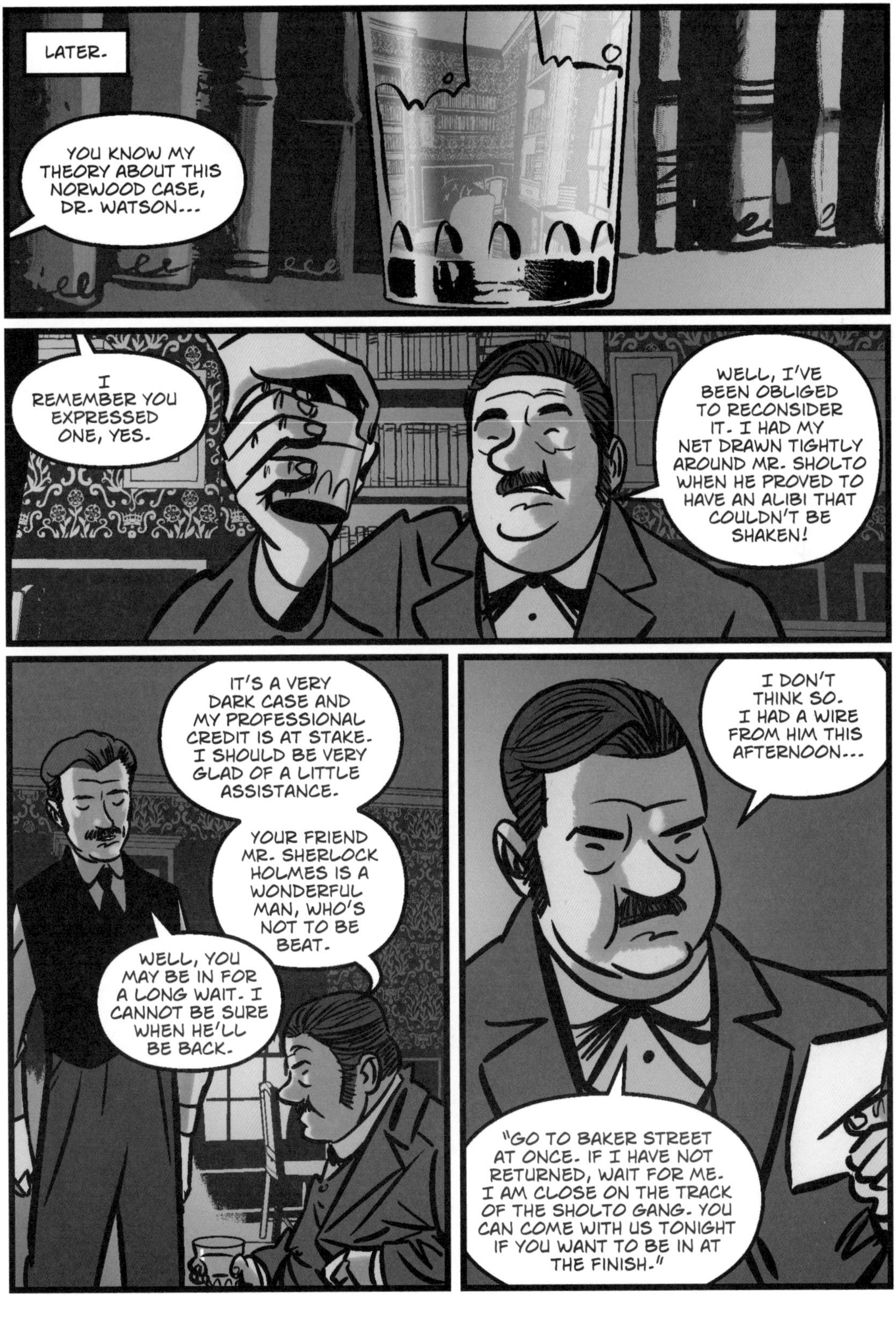
LATER.
YOU KNOW MY THEORY ABOUT THIS NORWOOD CASE, DR. WATSON...
I REMEMBER YOU EXPRESSED ONE, YES.
WELL, I'VE BEEN OBLIGED TO RECONSIDER IT. I HAD MY NET DRAWN TIGHTLY AROUND MR. SHOLTO WHEN HE PROVED TO HAVE AN ALIBI THAT COULDN'T BE SHAKEN!
IT'S A VERY DARK CASE AND MY PROFESSIONAL CREDIT IS AT STAKE. I SHOULD BE VERY GLAD OF A LITTLE ASSISTANCE.
YOUR FRIEND MR. SHERLOCK HOLMES IS A WONDERFUL MAN, WHO'S NOT TO BE BEAT.
WELL, YOU MAY BE IN FOR A LONG WAIT. I CANNOT BE SURE WHEN HE'LL BE BACK.
I DON'T THINK SO. I HAD A WIRE FROM HIM THIS AFTERNOON...
"GO TO BAKER STREET AT ONCE. IF I HAVE NOT RETURNED, WAIT FOR ME. I AM CLOSE ON THE TRACK OF THE SHOLTO GANG. YOU CAN COME WITH US TONIGHT IF YOU WANT TO BE IN AT THE FINISH."

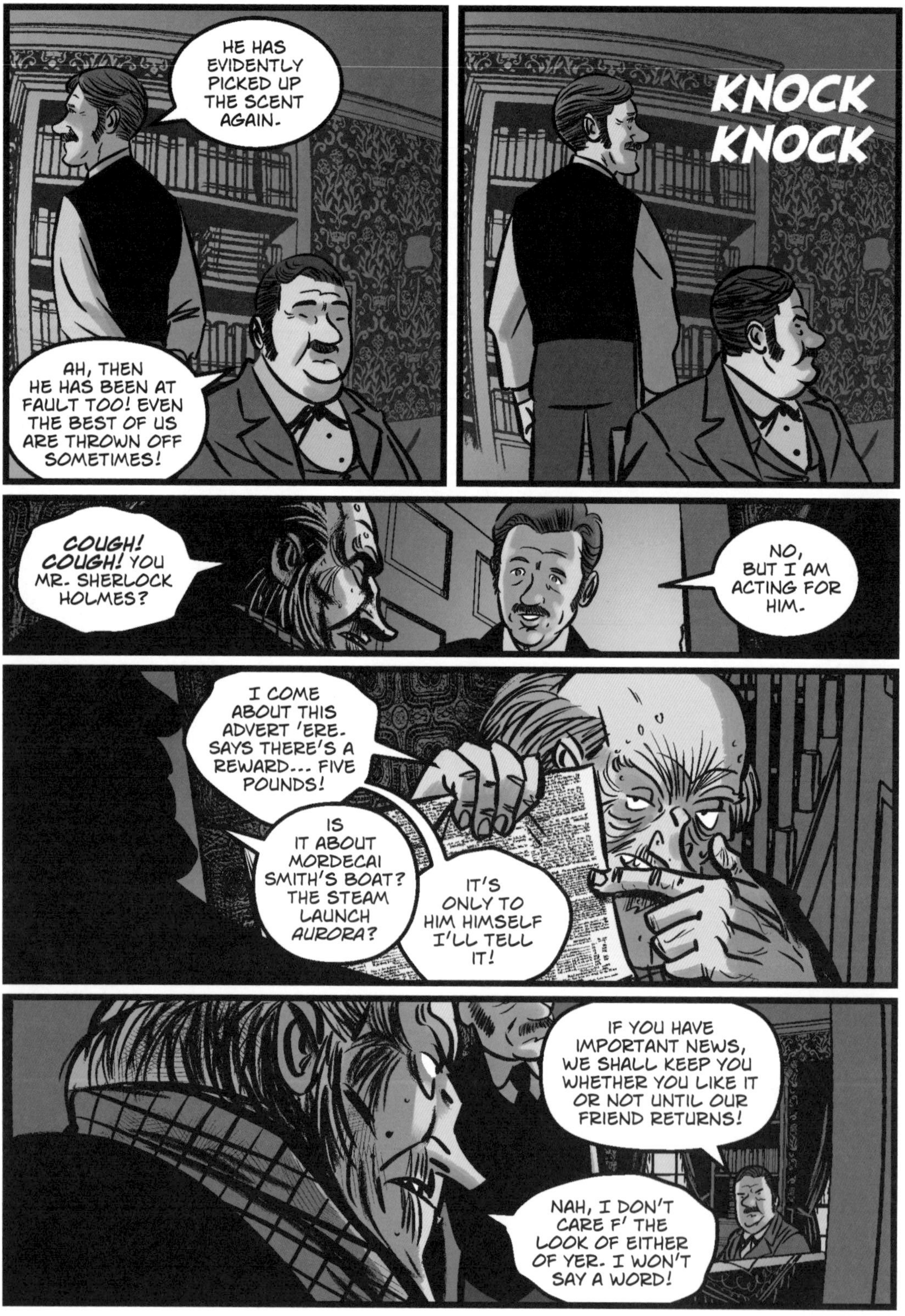
HE HAS EVIDENTLY PICKED UP THE SCENT AGAIN.
AH, THEN HE HAS BEEN AT FAULT TOO! EVEN THE BEST OF US ARE THROWN OFF SOMETIMES!
KNOCK KNOCK
COUGH! COUGH! YOU MR. SHERLOCK HOLMES?
NO, BUT I AM ACTING FOR HIM.
I COME ABOUT THIS ADVERT 'ERE. SAYS THERE'S A REWARD... FIVE POUNDS!
IS IT ABOUT MORDECAI SMITH'S BOAT? THE STEAM LAUNCH AURORA?
IT'S ONLY TO HIM HIMSELF I'LL TELL IT!
IF YOU HAVE IMPORTANT NEWS, WE SHALL KEEP YOU WHETHER YOU LIKE IT OR NOT UNTIL OUR FRIEND RETURNS!
NAH, I DON'T CARE F' THE LOOK OF EITHER OF YER. I WON'T SAY A WORD!

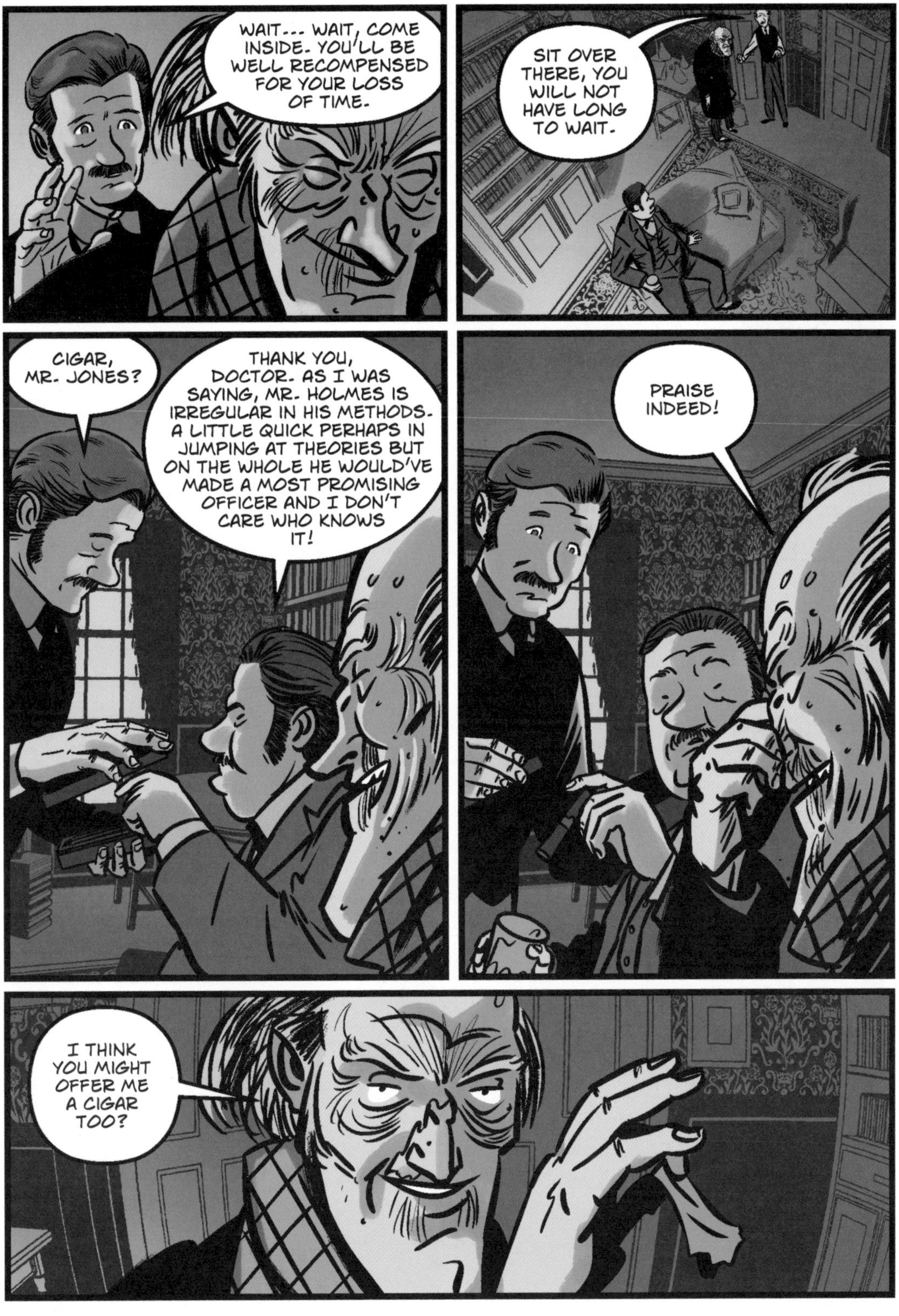
WAIT... WAIT, COME INSIDE. YOU'LL BE WELL RECOMPENSED FOR YOUR LOSS OF TIME.
SIT OVER THERE, YOU WILL NOT HAVE LONG TO WAIT.
CIGAR, MR. JONES?
THANK YOU, DOCTOR. AS I WAS SAYING, MR. HOLMES IS IRREGULAR IN HIS METHODS. A LITTLE QUICK PERHAPS IN JUMPING AT THEORIES BUT ON THE WHOLE HE WOULD'VE MADE A MOST PROMISING OFFICER AND I DON'T CARE WHO KNOWS IT!
PRAISE INDEED!
I THINK YOU MIGHT OFFER ME A CIGAR TOO?

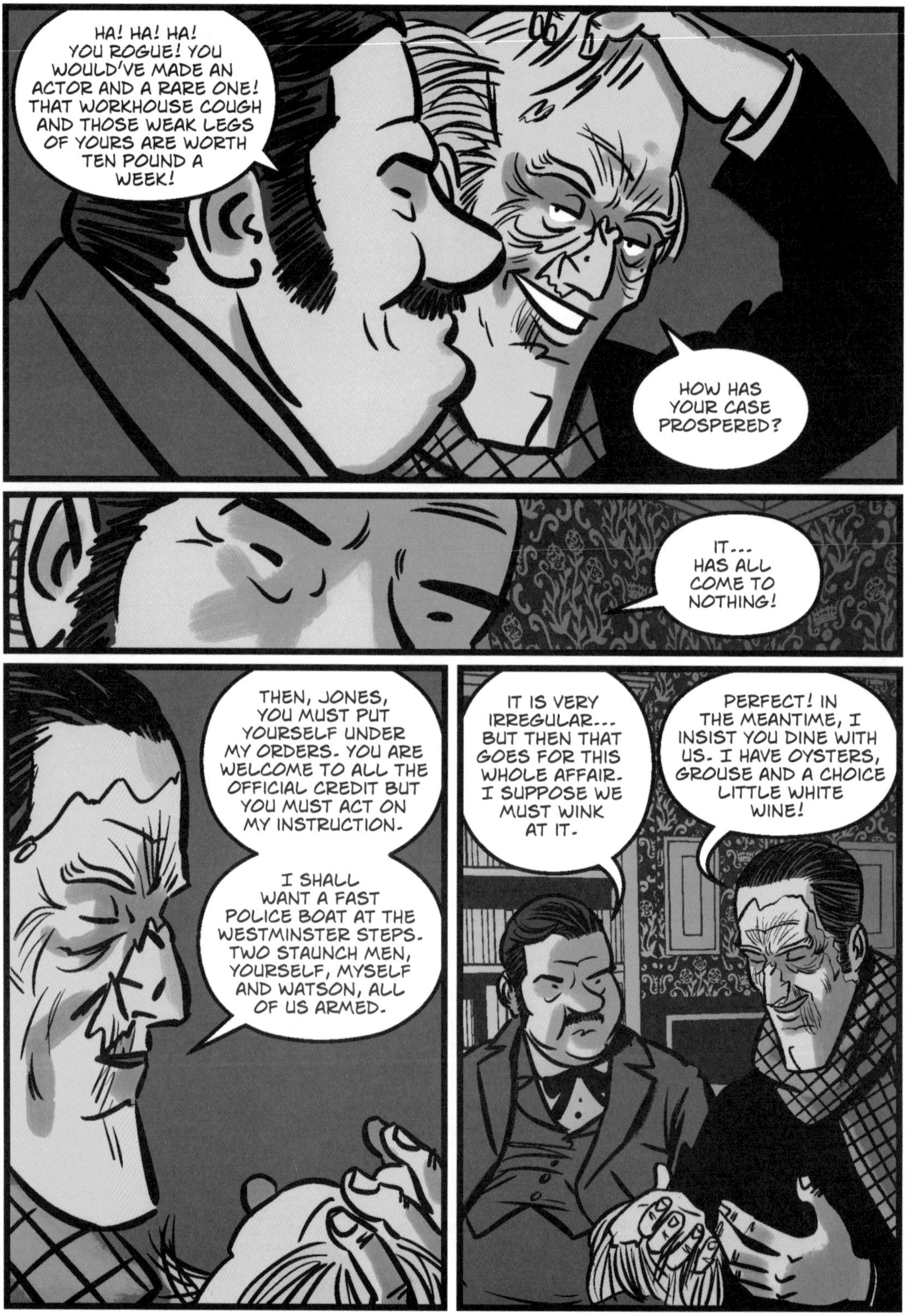
HA! HA! HA! YOU ROGUE! YOU WOULD'VE MADE AN ACTOR AND A RARE ONE! THAT WORKHOUSE COUGH AND THOSE WEAK LEGS OF YOURS ARE WORTH TEN POUND A WEEK!
HOW HAS YOUR CASE PROSPERED?
IT... HAS ALL COME TO NOTHING!
THEN, JONES, YOU MUST PUT YOURSELF UNDER MY ORDERS. YOU ARE WELCOME TO ALL THE OFFICIAL CREDIT BUT YOU MUST ACT ON MY INSTRUCTION.
I SHALL WANT A FAST POLICE BOAT AT THE WESTMINSTER STEPS. TWO STAUNCH MEN, YOURSELF, MYSELF AND WATSON, ALL OF US ARMED.
IT IS VERY IRREGULAR... BUT THEN THAT GOES FOR THIS WHOLE AFFAIR. I SUPPOSE WE MUST WINK AT IT.
PERFECT! IN THE MEANTIME, I INSIST YOU DINE WITH US. I HAVE OYSTERS, GROUSE AND A CHOICE LITTLE WHITE WINE!

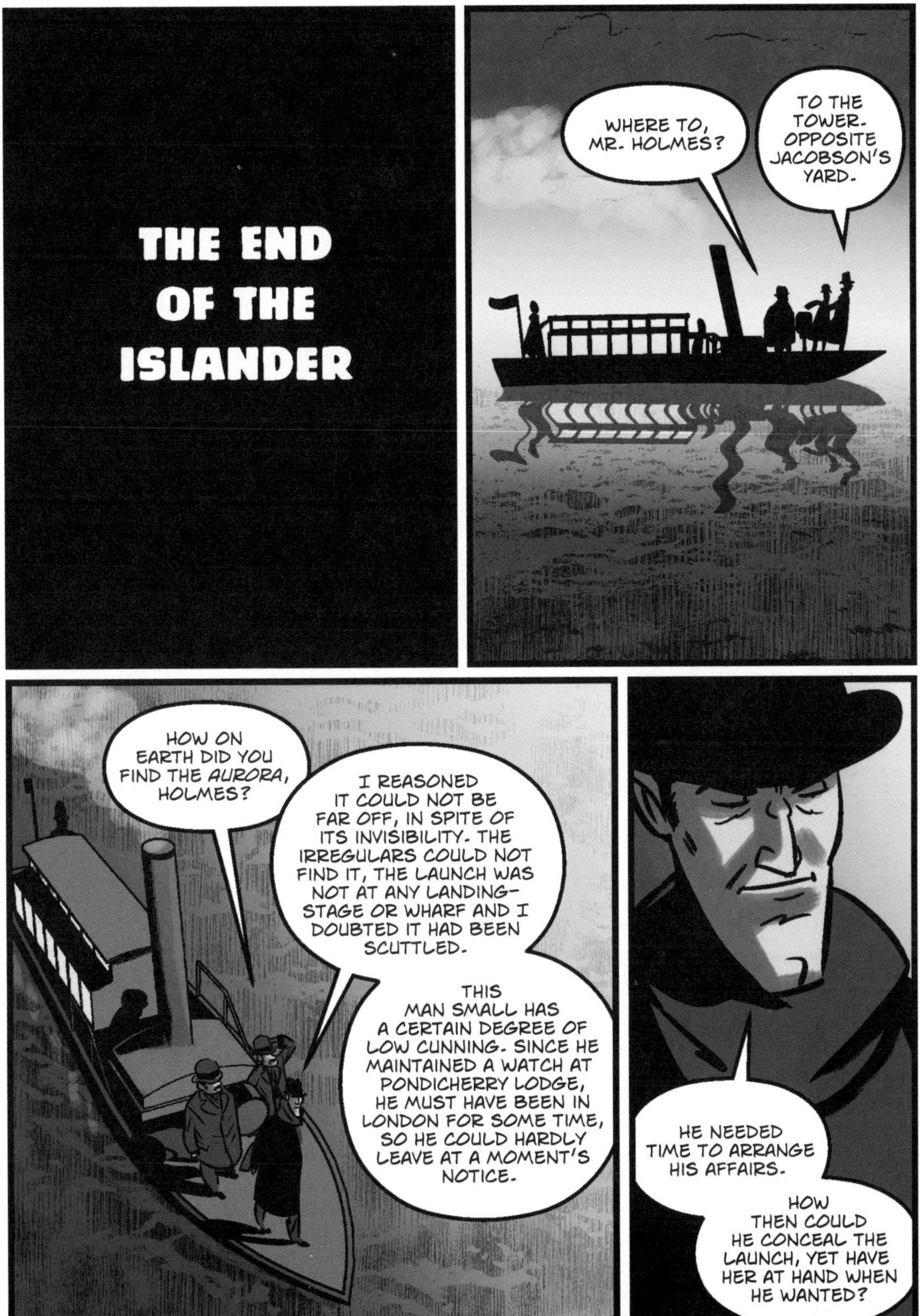
THE END OF THE ISLANDER
WHERE TO, MR. HOLMES?
TO THE TOWER. OPPOSITE JACOBSON'S YARD.
HOW ON EARTH DID YOU FIND THE *AURORA*, HOLMES?
I REASONED IT COULD NOT BE FAR OFF, IN SPITE OF ITS INVISIBILITY. THE IRREGULARS COULD NOT FIND IT, THE LAUNCH WAS NOT AT ANY LANDING-STAGE OR WHARF AND I DOUBTED IT HAD BEEN SCUTTLED.
THIS MAN SMALL HAS A CERTAIN DEGREE OF LOW CUNNING. SINCE HE MAINTAINED A WATCH AT PONDICHERRY LODGE, HE MUST HAVE BEEN IN LONDON FOR SOME TIME, SO HE COULD HARDLY LEAVE AT A MOMENT'S NOTICE.
HE NEEDED TIME TO ARRANGE HIS AFFAIRS.
HOW THEN COULD HE CONCEAL THE LAUNCH, YET HAVE HER AT HAND WHEN HE WANTED?

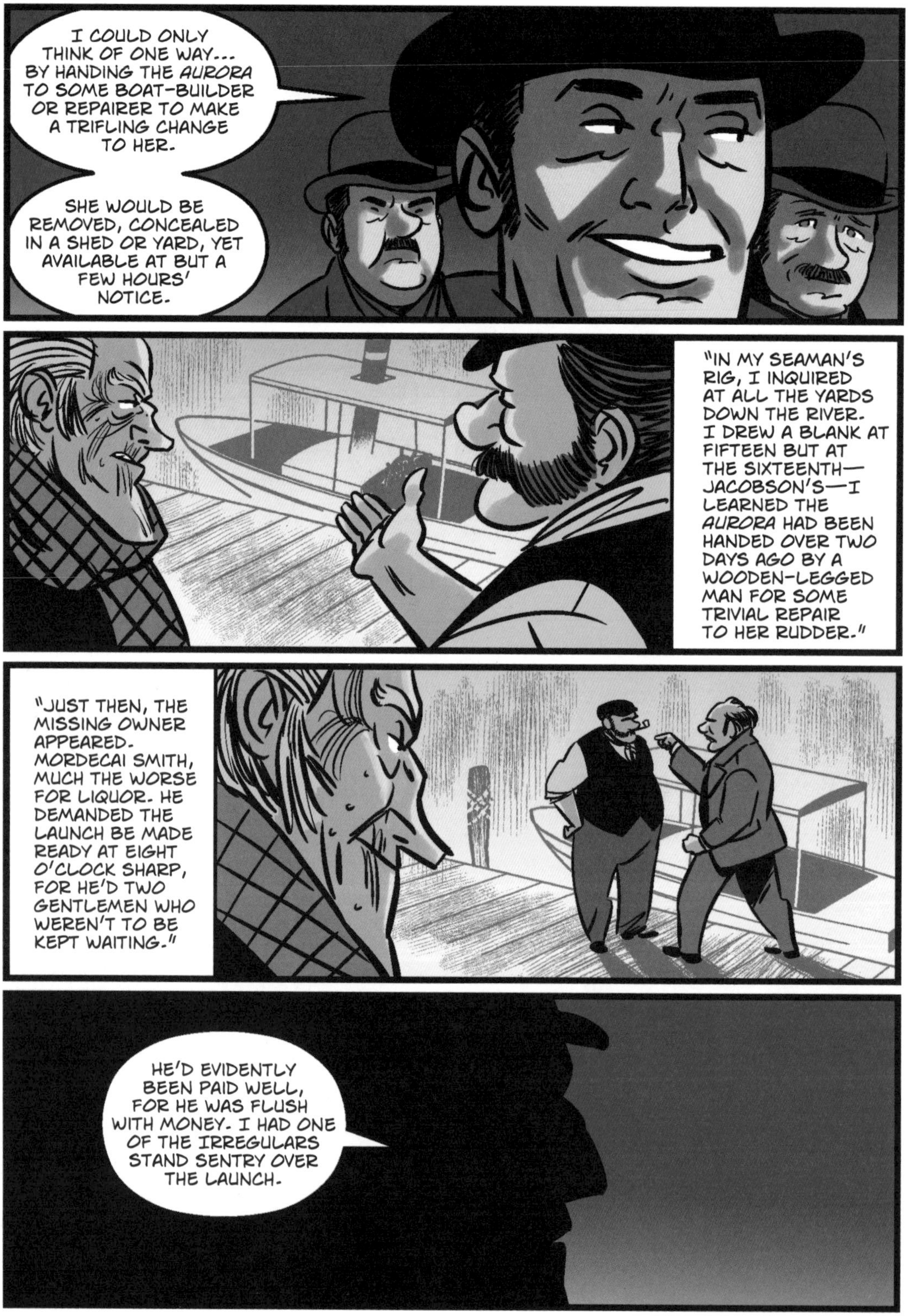
I COULD ONLY THINK OF ONE WAY... BY HANDING THE *AURORA* TO SOME BOAT-BUILDER OR REPAIRER TO MAKE A TRIFLING CHANGE TO HER.
SHE WOULD BE REMOVED, CONCEALED IN A SHED OR YARD, YET AVAILABLE AT BUT A FEW HOURS' NOTICE.
"IN MY SEAMAN'S RIG, I INQUIRED AT ALL THE YARDS DOWN THE RIVER. I DREW A BLANK AT FIFTEEN BUT AT THE SIXTEENTH—JACOBSON'S—I LEARNED THE *AURORA* HAD BEEN HANDED OVER TWO DAYS AGO BY A WOODEN-LEGGED MAN FOR SOME TRIVIAL REPAIR TO HER RUDDER."
"JUST THEN, THE MISSING OWNER APPEARED. MORDECAI SMITH, MUCH THE WORSE FOR LIQUOR. HE DEMANDED THE LAUNCH BE MADE READY AT EIGHT O'CLOCK SHARP, FOR HE'D TWO GENTLEMEN WHO WEREN'T TO BE KEPT WAITING."
HE'D EVIDENTLY BEEN PAID WELL, FOR HE WAS FLUSH WITH MONEY. I HAD ONE OF THE IRREGULARS STAND SENTRY OVER THE LAUNCH.

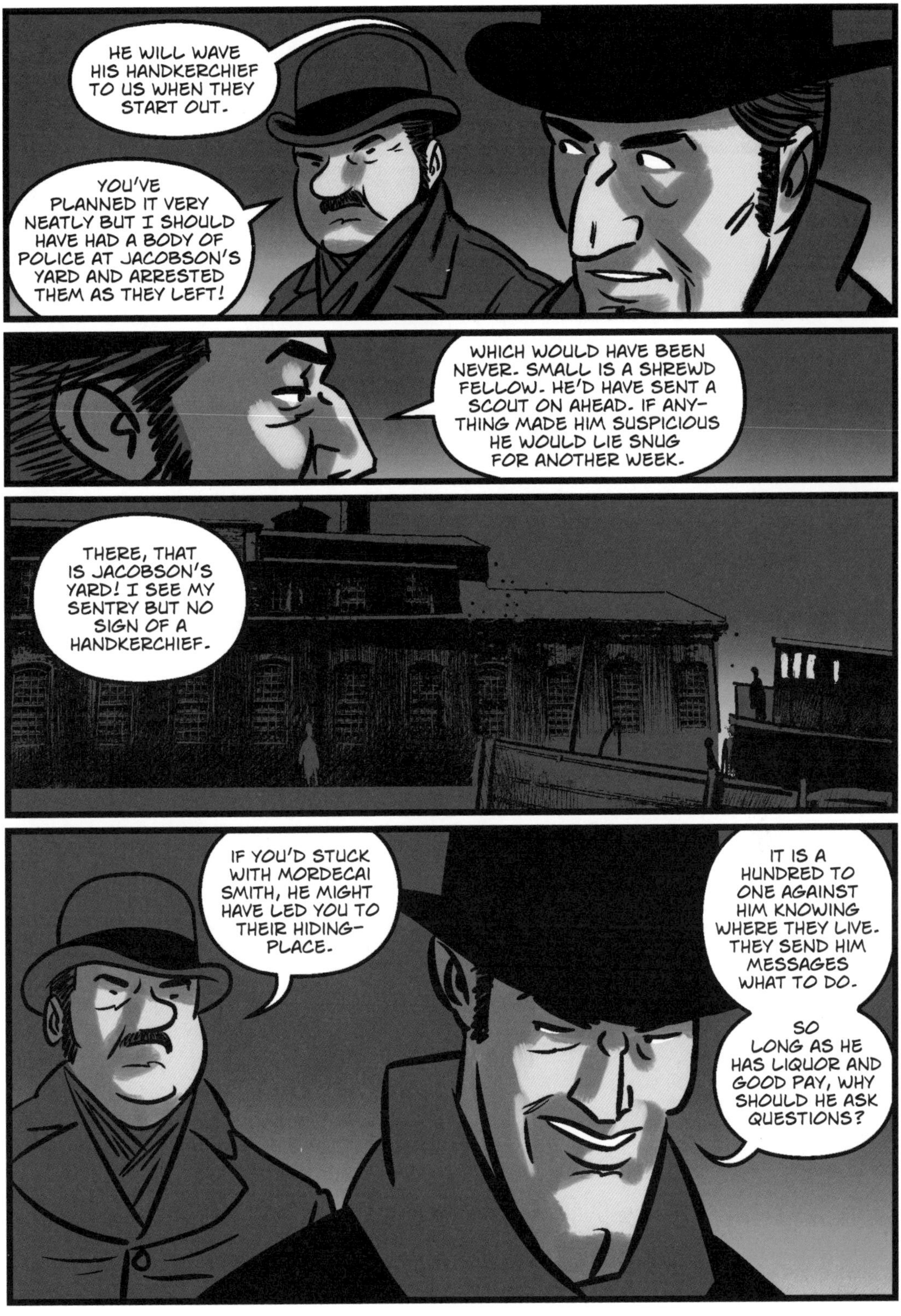
HE WILL WAVE HIS HANDKERCHIEF TO US WHEN THEY START OUT.
YOU'VE PLANNED IT VERY NEATLY BUT I SHOULD HAVE HAD A BODY OF POLICE AT JACOBSON'S YARD AND ARRESTED THEM AS THEY LEFT!
WHICH WOULD HAVE BEEN NEVER. SMALL IS A SHREWD FELLOW. HE'D HAVE SENT A SCOUT ON AHEAD. IF ANY-THING MADE HIM SUSPICIOUS HE WOULD LIE SNUG FOR ANOTHER WEEK.
THERE, THAT IS JACOBSON'S YARD! I SEE MY SENTRY BUT NO SIGN OF A HANDKERCHIEF.
IF YOU'D STUCK WITH MORDECAI SMITH, HE MIGHT HAVE LED YOU TO THEIR HIDING-PLACE.
IT IS A HUNDRED TO ONE AGAINST HIM KNOWING WHERE THEY LIVE. THEY SEND HIM MESSAGES WHAT TO DO.
SO LONG AS HE HAS LIQUOR AND GOOD PAY, WHY SHOULD HE ASK QUESTIONS?

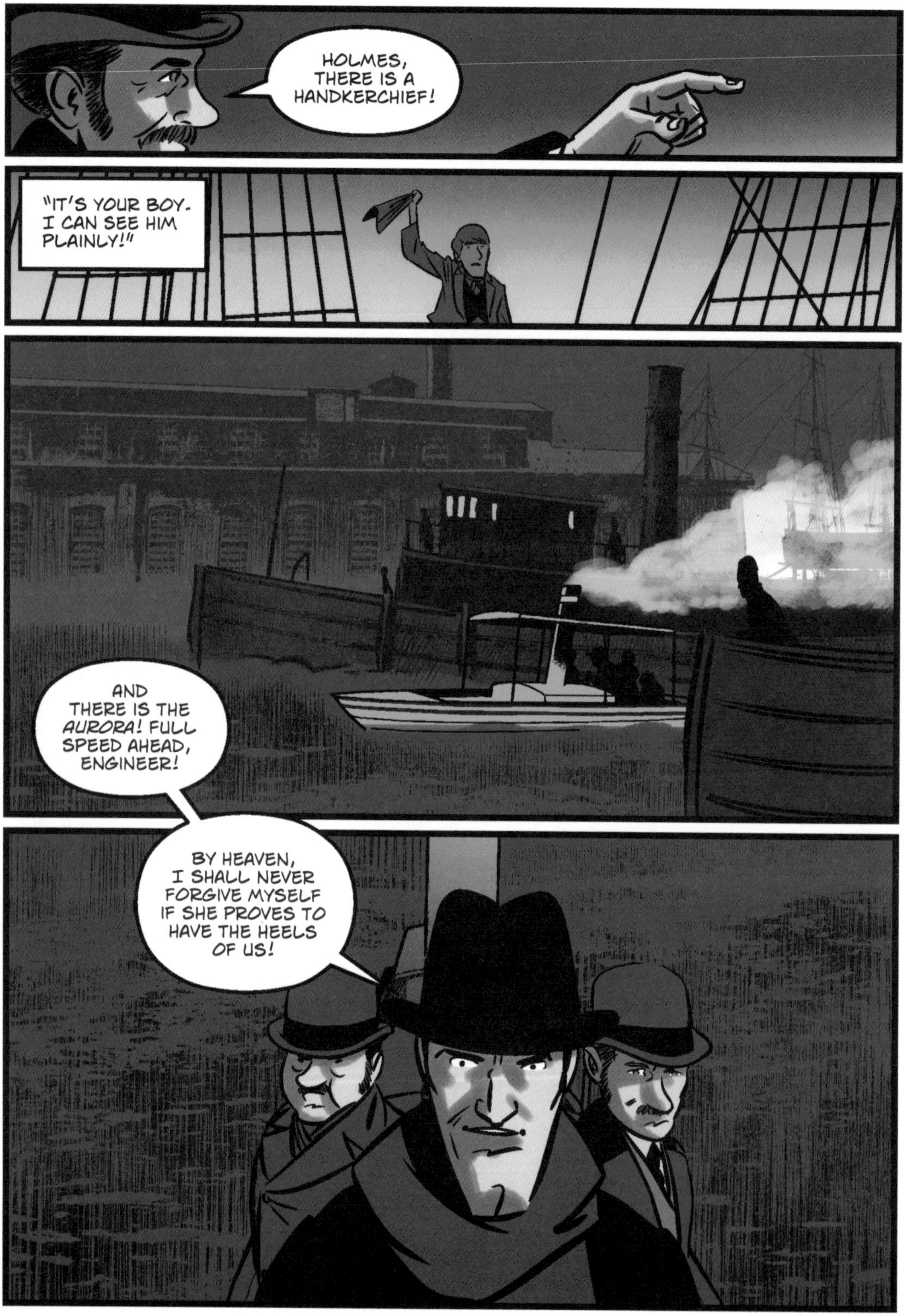
HOLMES, THERE IS A HANDKERCHIEF!
"IT'S YOUR BOY. I CAN SEE HIM PLAINLY!"
AND THERE IS THE *AURORA*! FULL SPEED AHEAD, ENGINEER!
BY HEAVEN, I SHALL NEVER FORGIVE MYSELF IF SHE PROVES TO HAVE THE HEELS OF US!

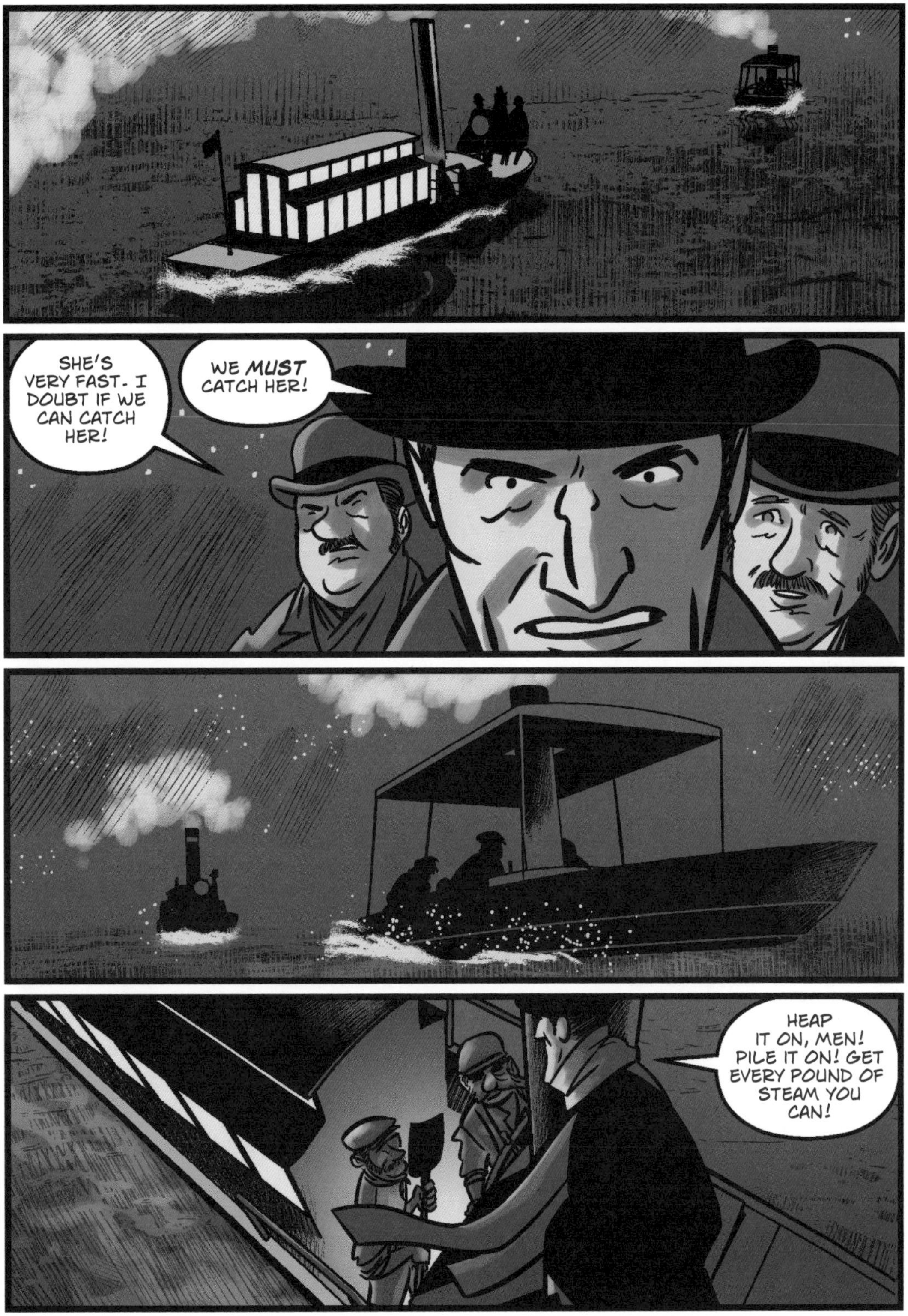
SHE'S VERY FAST. I DOUBT IF WE CAN CATCH HER!
WE MUST CATCH HER!
HEAP IT ON, MEN! PILE IT ON! GET EVERY POUND OF STEAM YOU CAN!

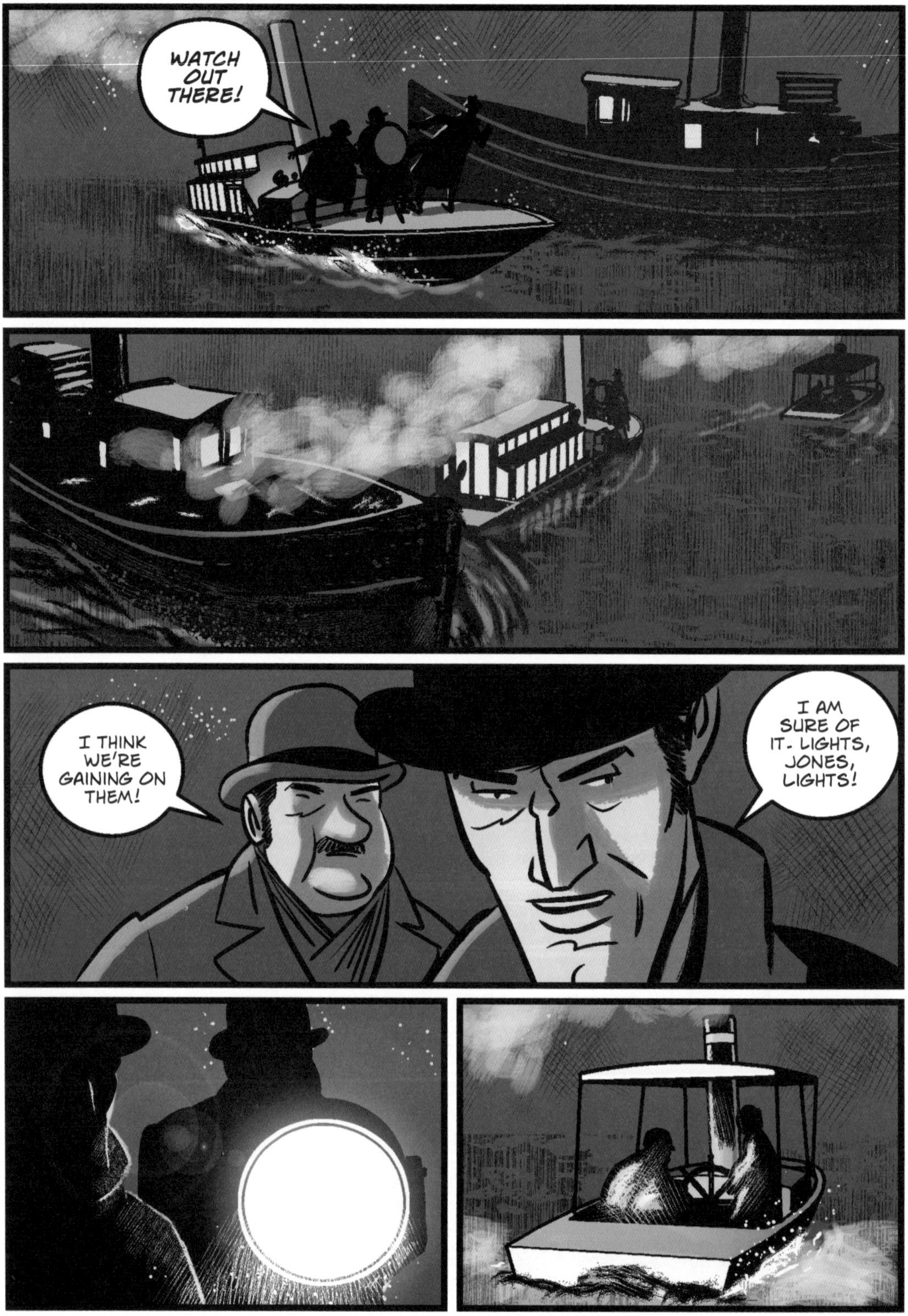
WATCH OUT THERE!
I THINK WE'RE GAINING ON THEM!
I AM SURE OF IT. LIGHTS, JONES, LIGHTS!

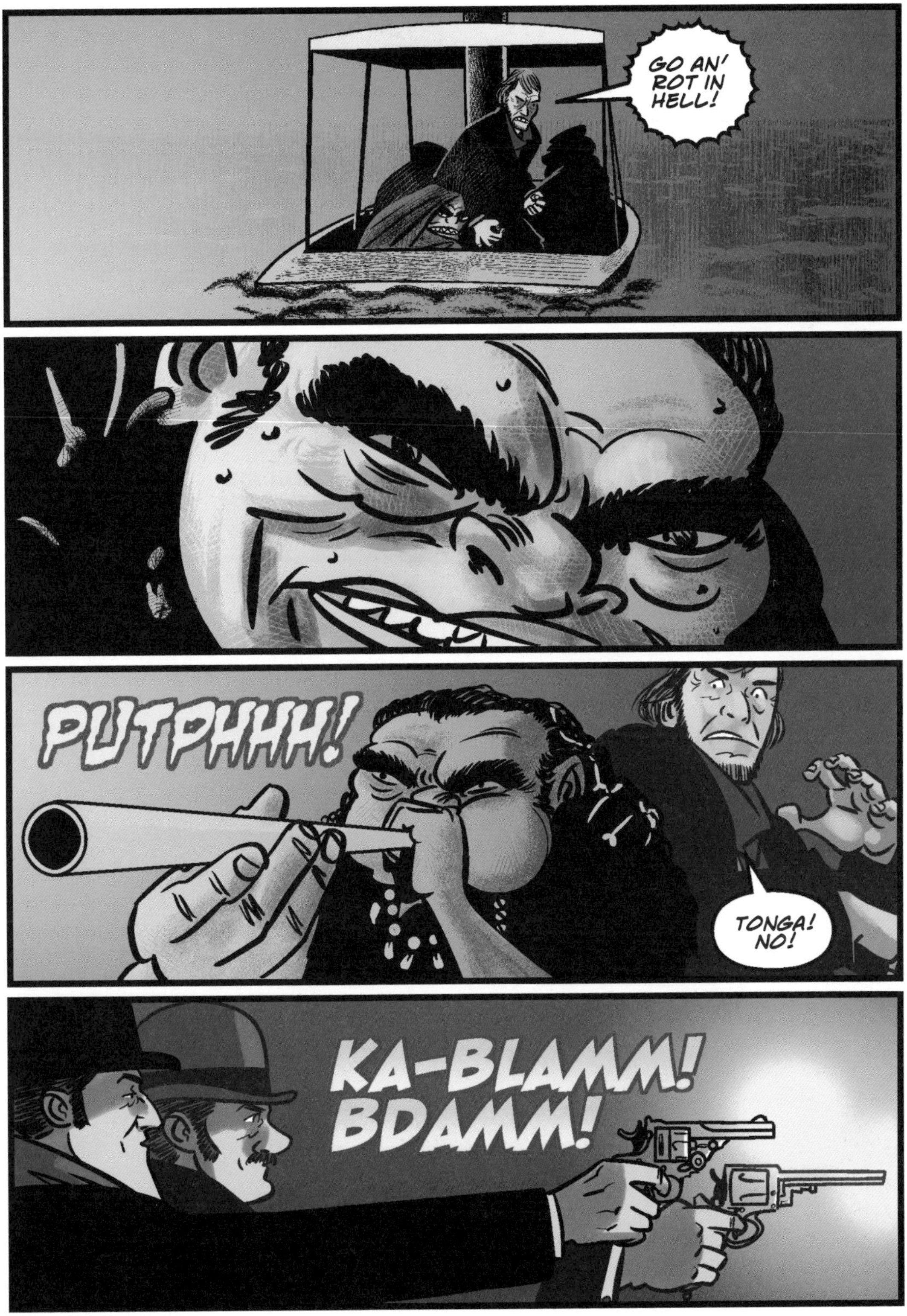
GO AN' ROT IN HELL!
PUTPHHH!
TONGA! NO!
KA-BLAMM! BDAMM!

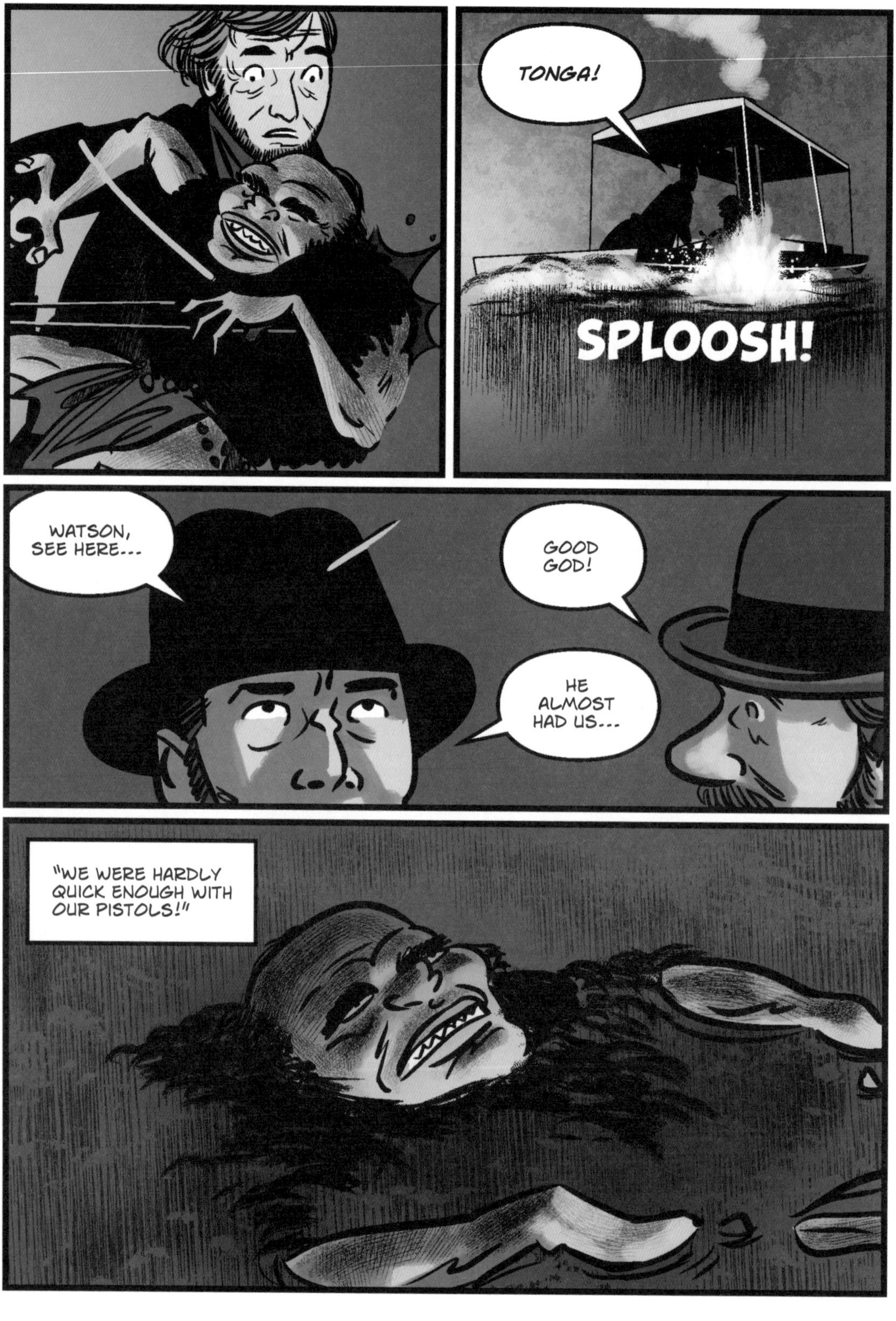
TONGA!
SPLOOSH!
WATSON, SEE HERE...
GOOD GOD!
HE ALMOST HAD US...
"WE WERE HARDLY QUICK ENOUGH WITH OUR PISTOLS!"

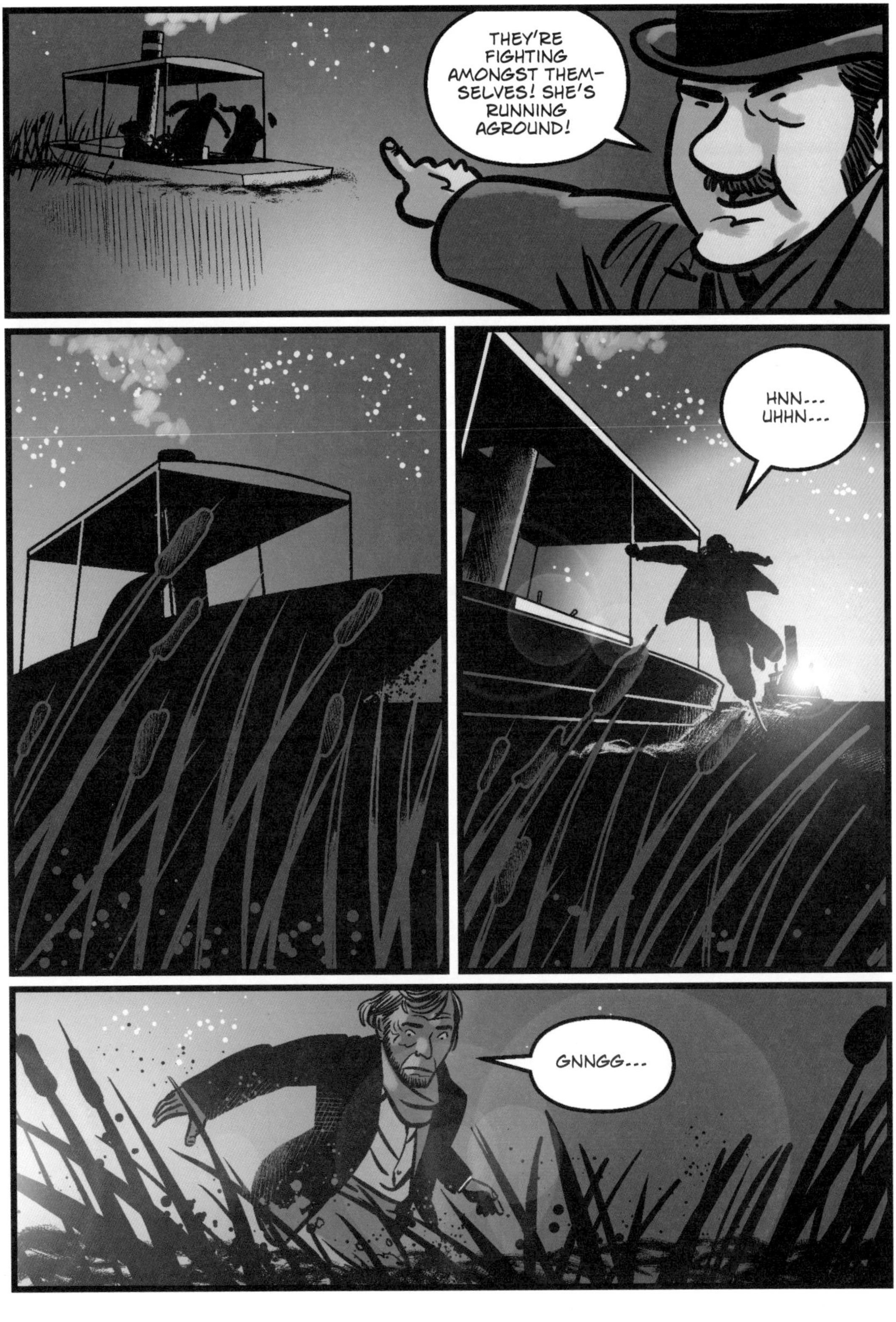
THEY'RE FIGHTING AMONGST THEM-SELVES! SHE'S RUNNING AGROUND!
HNN... UHHN...
GNNGG...

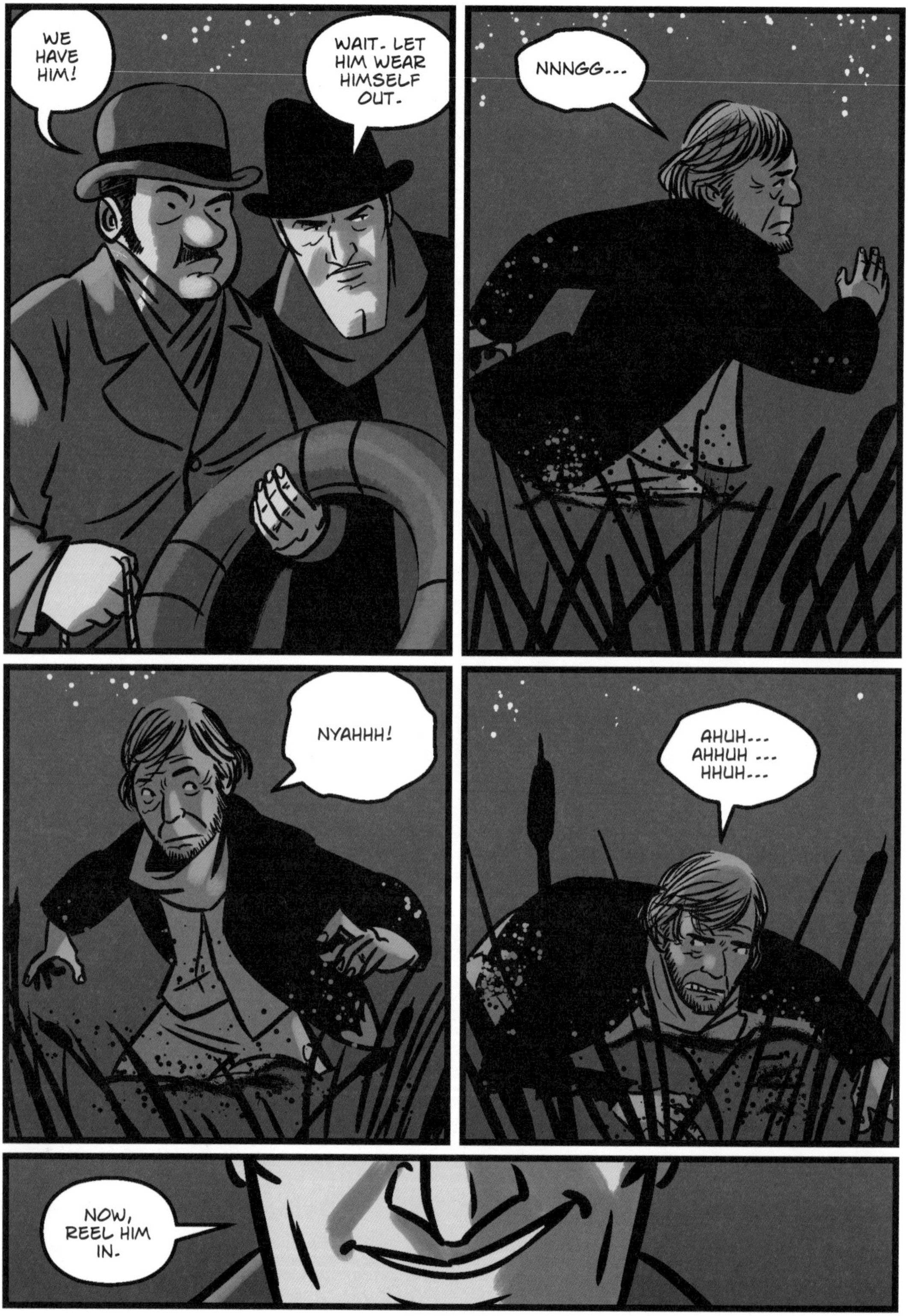
WE HAVE HIM!
WAIT- LET HIM WEAR HIMSELF OUT-
NNNGG...
NYAHHH!
AHUH... AHHUH ... HHUH...
NOW, REEL HIM IN-

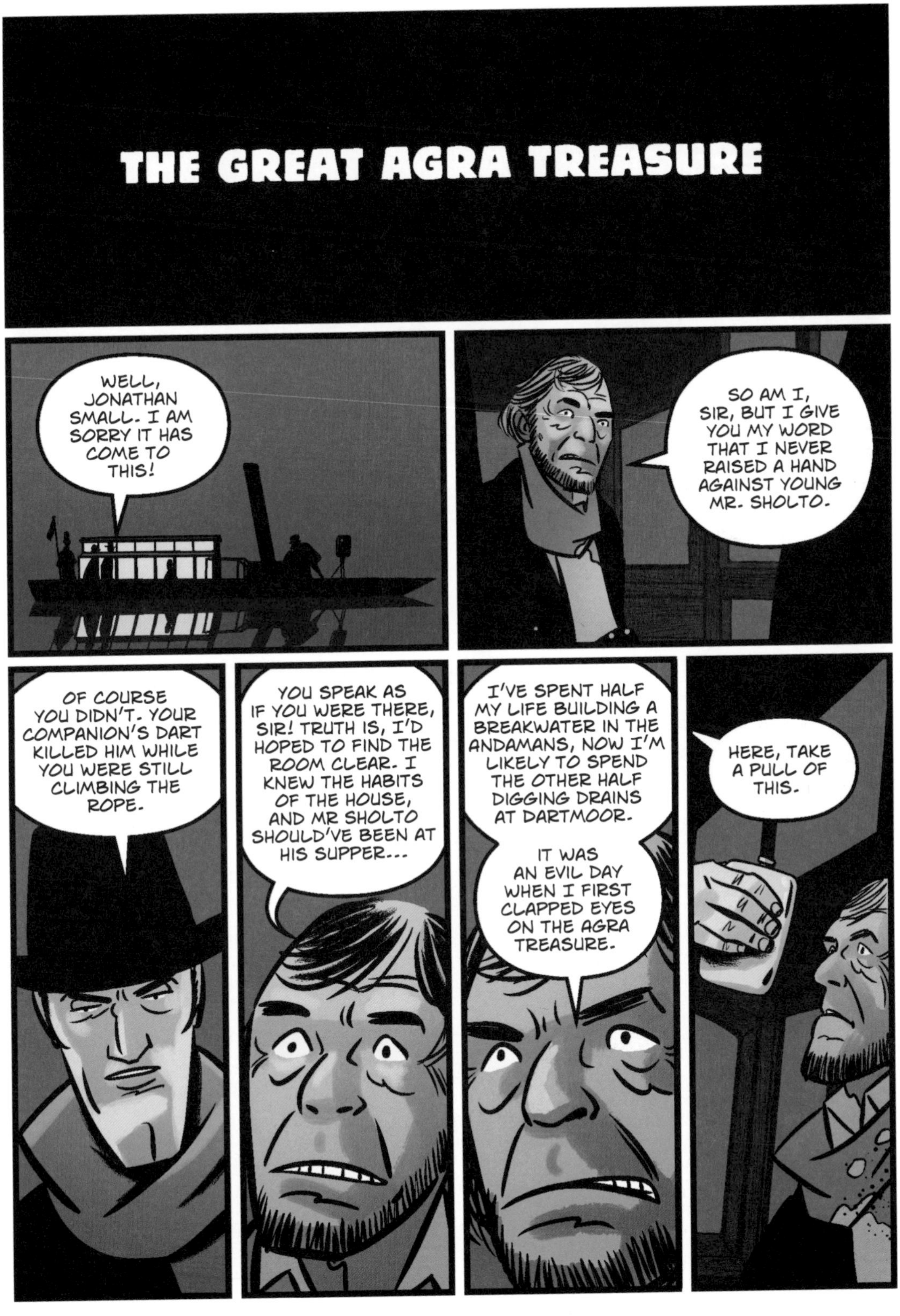
THE GREAT AGRA TREASURE
WELL, JONATHAN SMALL. I AM SORRY IT HAS COME TO THIS!
SO AM I, SIR, BUT I GIVE YOU MY WORD THAT I NEVER RAISED A HAND AGAINST YOUNG MR. SHOLTO.
OF COURSE YOU DIDN'T. YOUR COMPANION'S DART KILLED HIM WHILE YOU WERE STILL CLIMBING THE ROPE.
YOU SPEAK AS IF YOU WERE THERE, SIR! TRUTH IS, I'D HOPED TO FIND THE ROOM CLEAR. I KNEW THE HABITS OF THE HOUSE, AND MR SHOLTO SHOULD'VE BEEN AT HIS SUPPER...
I'VE SPENT HALF MY LIFE BUILDING A BREAKWATER IN THE ANDAMANS, NOW I'M LIKELY TO SPEND THE OTHER HALF DIGGING DRAINS AT DARTMOOR.
IT WAS AN EVIL DAY WHEN I FIRST CLAPPED EYES ON THE AGRA TREASURE.
HERE, TAKE A PULL OF THIS.

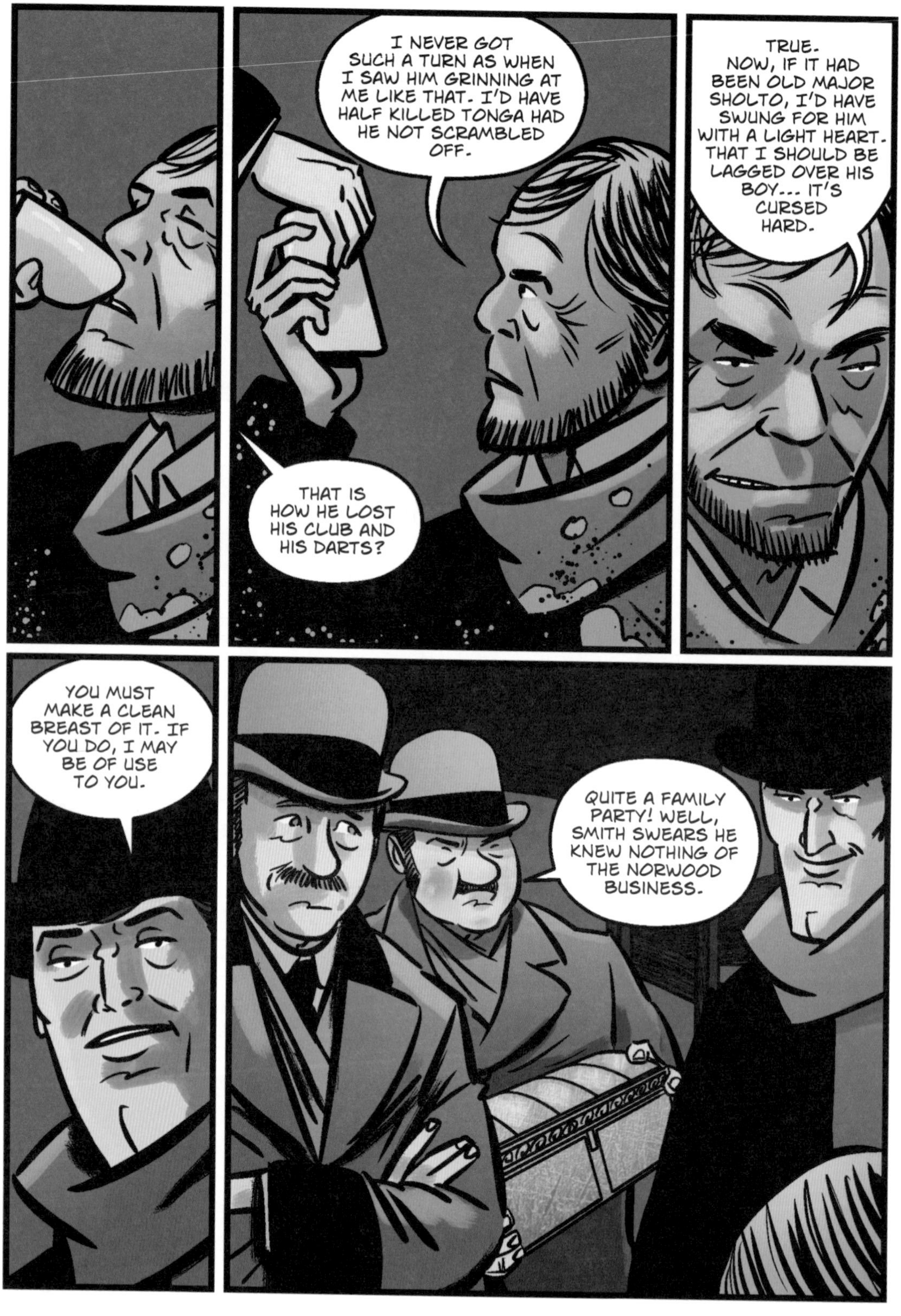
I NEVER GOT SUCH A TURN AS WHEN I SAW HIM GRINNING AT ME LIKE THAT. I'D HAVE HALF KILLED TONGA HAD HE NOT SCRAMBLED OFF.
THAT IS HOW HE LOST HIS CLUB AND HIS DARTS?
TRUE. NOW, IF IT HAD BEEN OLD MAJOR SHOLTO, I'D HAVE SWUNG FOR HIM WITH A LIGHT HEART. THAT I SHOULD BE LAGGED OVER HIS BOY... IT'S CURSED HARD.
YOU MUST MAKE A CLEAN BREAST OF IT. IF YOU DO, I MAY BE OF USE TO YOU.
QUITE A FAMILY PARTY! WELL, SMITH SWEARS HE KNEW NOTHING OF THE NORWOOD BUSINESS.

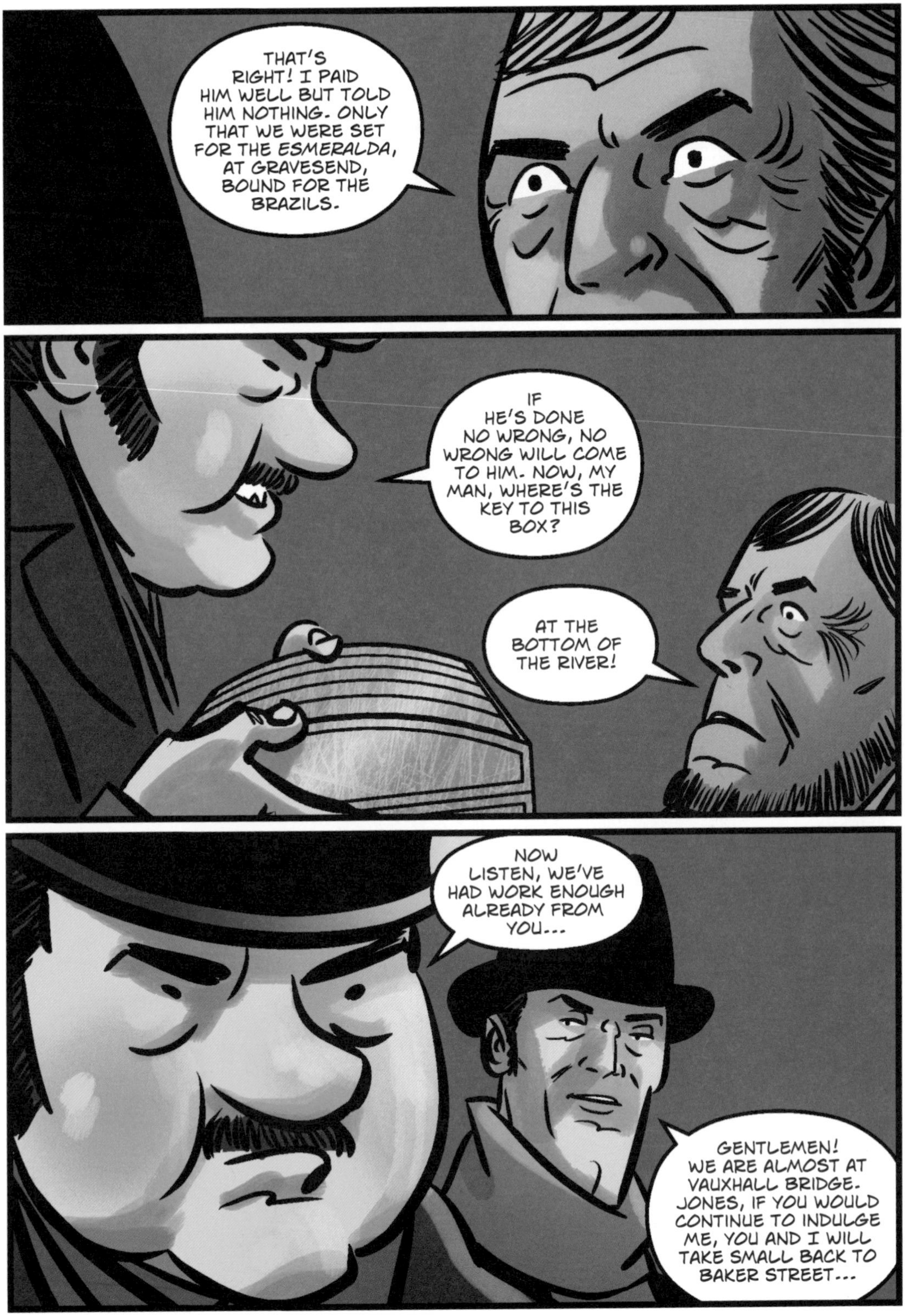
THAT'S RIGHT! I PAID HIM WELL BUT TOLD HIM NOTHING. ONLY THAT WE WERE SET FOR THE ESMERALDA, AT GRAVESEND, BOUND FOR THE BRAZILS.
IF HE'S DONE NO WRONG, NO WRONG WILL COME TO HIM. NOW, MY MAN, WHERE'S THE KEY TO THIS BOX?
AT THE BOTTOM OF THE RIVER!
NOW LISTEN, WE'VE HAD WORK ENOUGH ALREADY FROM YOU...
GENTLEMEN! WE ARE ALMOST AT VAUXHALL BRIDGE. JONES, IF YOU WOULD CONTINUE TO INDULGE ME, YOU AND I WILL TAKE SMALL BACK TO BAKER STREET...

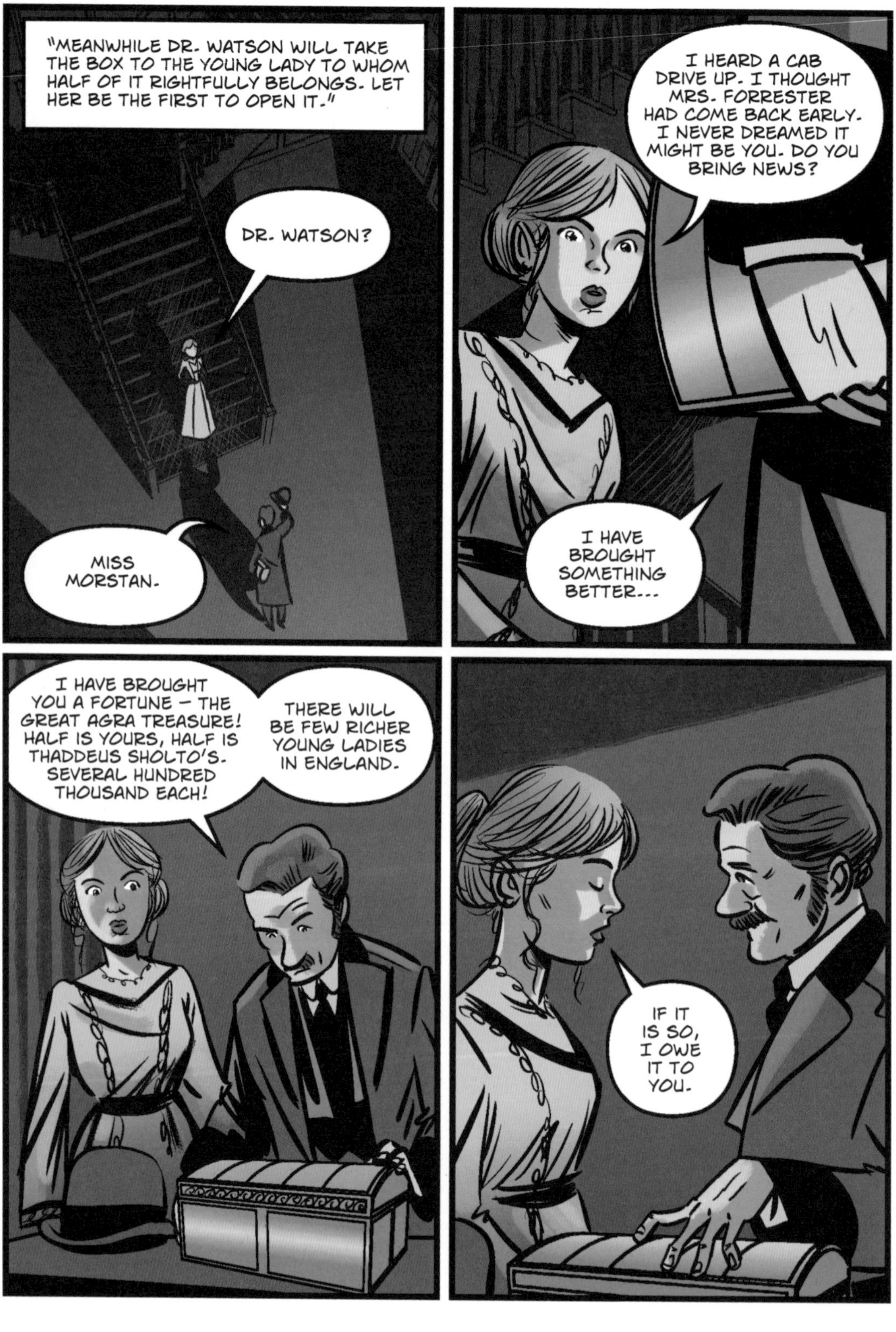
"MEANWHILE DR. WATSON WILL TAKE THE BOX TO THE YOUNG LADY TO WHOM HALF OF IT RIGHTFULLY BELONGS. LET HER BE THE FIRST TO OPEN IT."
DR. WATSON?
MISS MORSTAN.
I HEARD A CAB DRIVE UP. I THOUGHT MRS. FORRESTER HAD COME BACK EARLY. I NEVER DREAMED IT MIGHT BE YOU. DO YOU BRING NEWS?
I HAVE BROUGHT SOMETHING BETTER...
I HAVE BROUGHT YOU A FORTUNE — THE GREAT AGRA TREASURE! HALF IS YOURS, HALF IS THADDEUS SHOLTO'S. SEVERAL HUNDRED THOUSAND EACH!
THERE WILL BE FEW RICHER YOUNG LADIES IN ENGLAND.
IF IT IS SO, I OWE IT TO YOU.

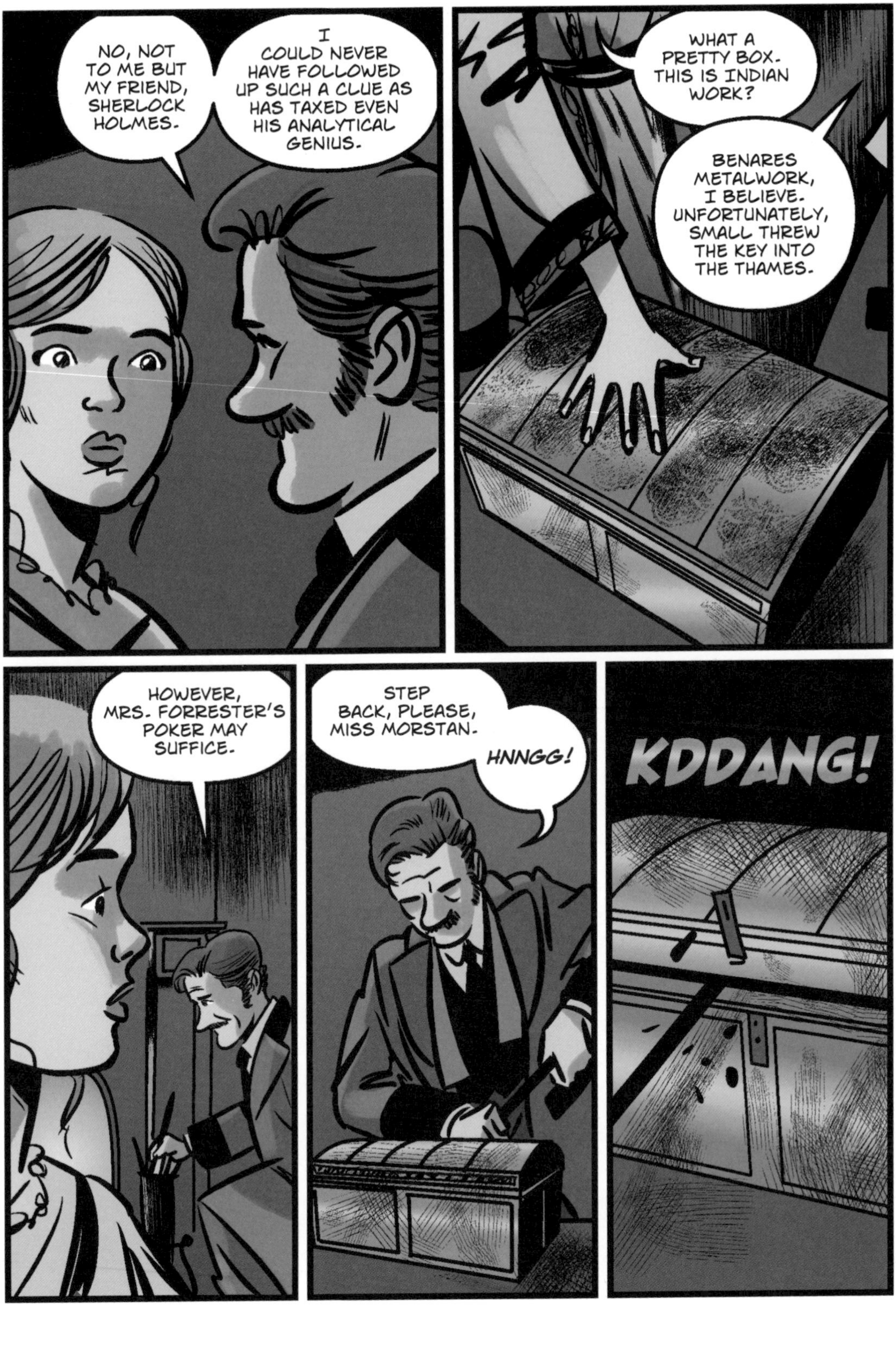
NO, NOT TO ME BUT MY FRIEND, SHERLOCK HOLMES.
I COULD NEVER HAVE FOLLOWED UP SUCH A CLUE AS HAS TAXED EVEN HIS ANALYTICAL GENIUS.
WHAT A PRETTY BOX. THIS IS INDIAN WORK?
BENARES METALWORK, I BELIEVE. UNFORTUNATELY, SMALL THREW THE KEY INTO THE THAMES.
HOWEVER, MRS. FORRESTER'S POKER MAY SUFFICE.
STEP BACK, PLEASE, MISS MORSTAN.
HNNGG!
KDDANG!

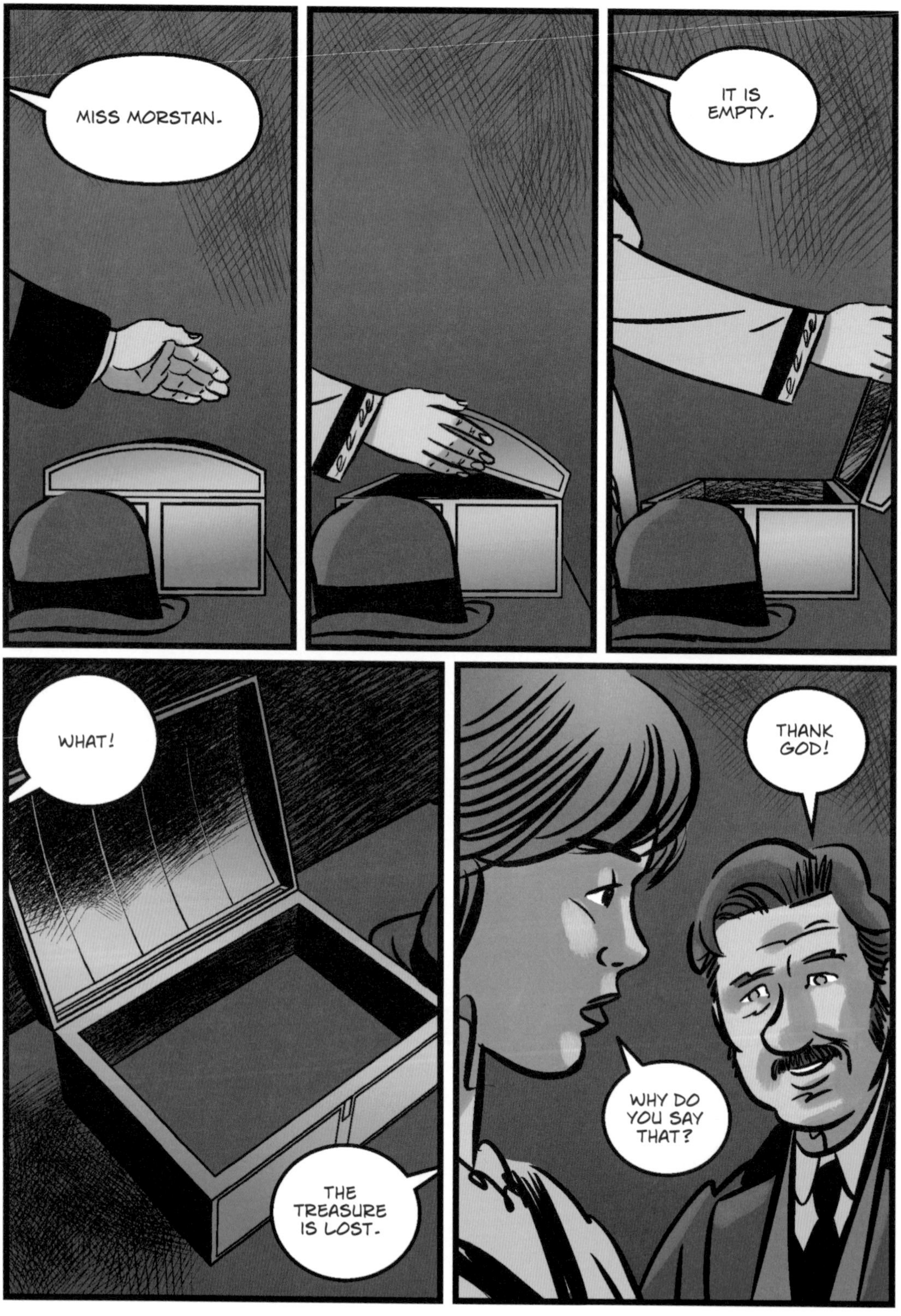
MISS MORSTAN.
IT IS EMPTY.
WHAT!
THE TREASURE IS LOST.
THANK GOD!
WHY DO YOU SAY THAT?

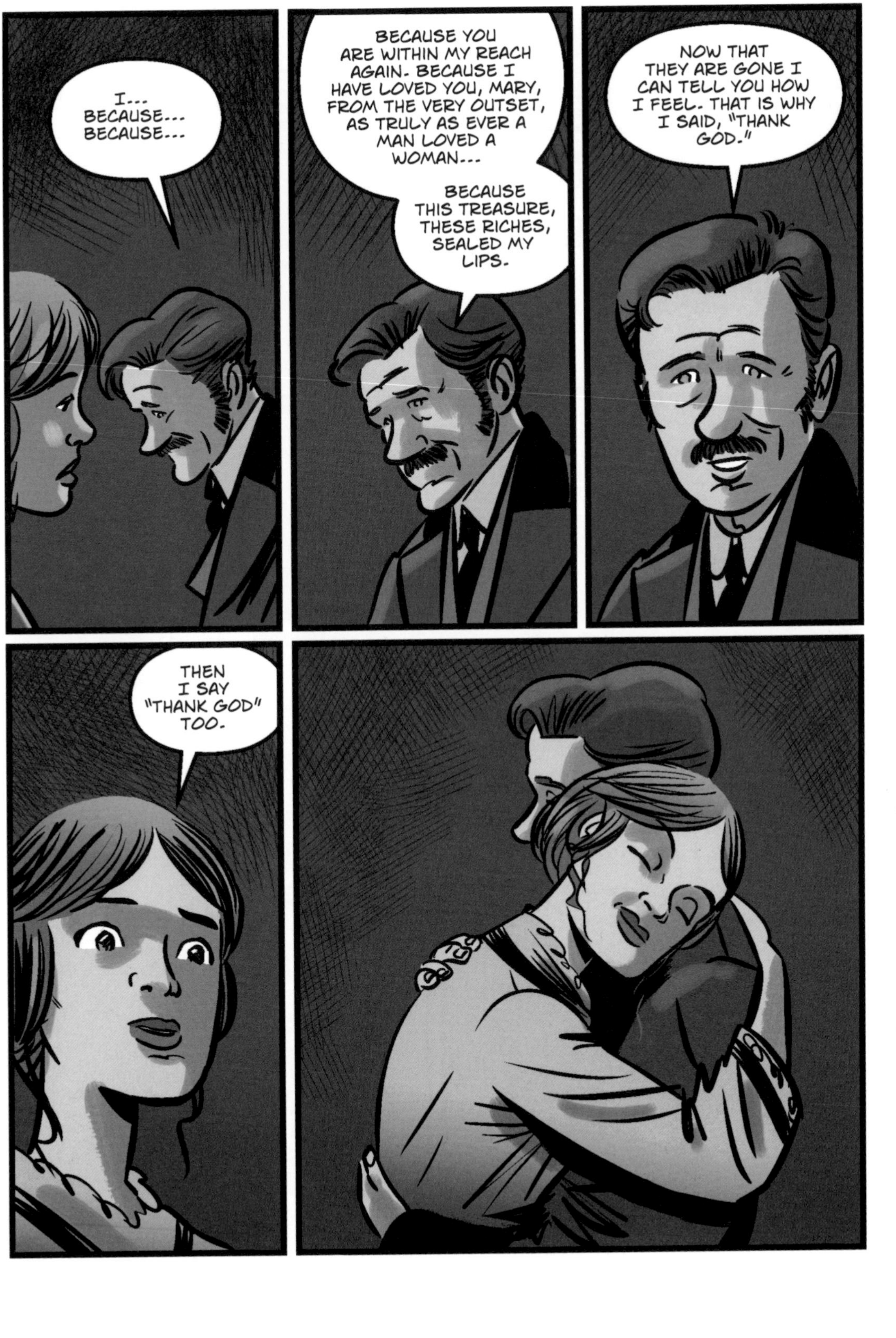
I... BECAUSE... BECAUSE...
BECAUSE YOU ARE WITHIN MY REACH AGAIN. BECAUSE I HAVE LOVED YOU, MARY, FROM THE VERY OUTSET, AS TRULY AS EVER A MAN LOVED A WOMAN...
BECAUSE THIS TREASURE, THESE RICHES, SEALED MY LIPS.
NOW THAT THEY ARE GONE I CAN TELL YOU HOW I FEEL. THAT IS WHY I SAID, "THANK GOD."
THEN I SAY "THANK GOD" TOO.

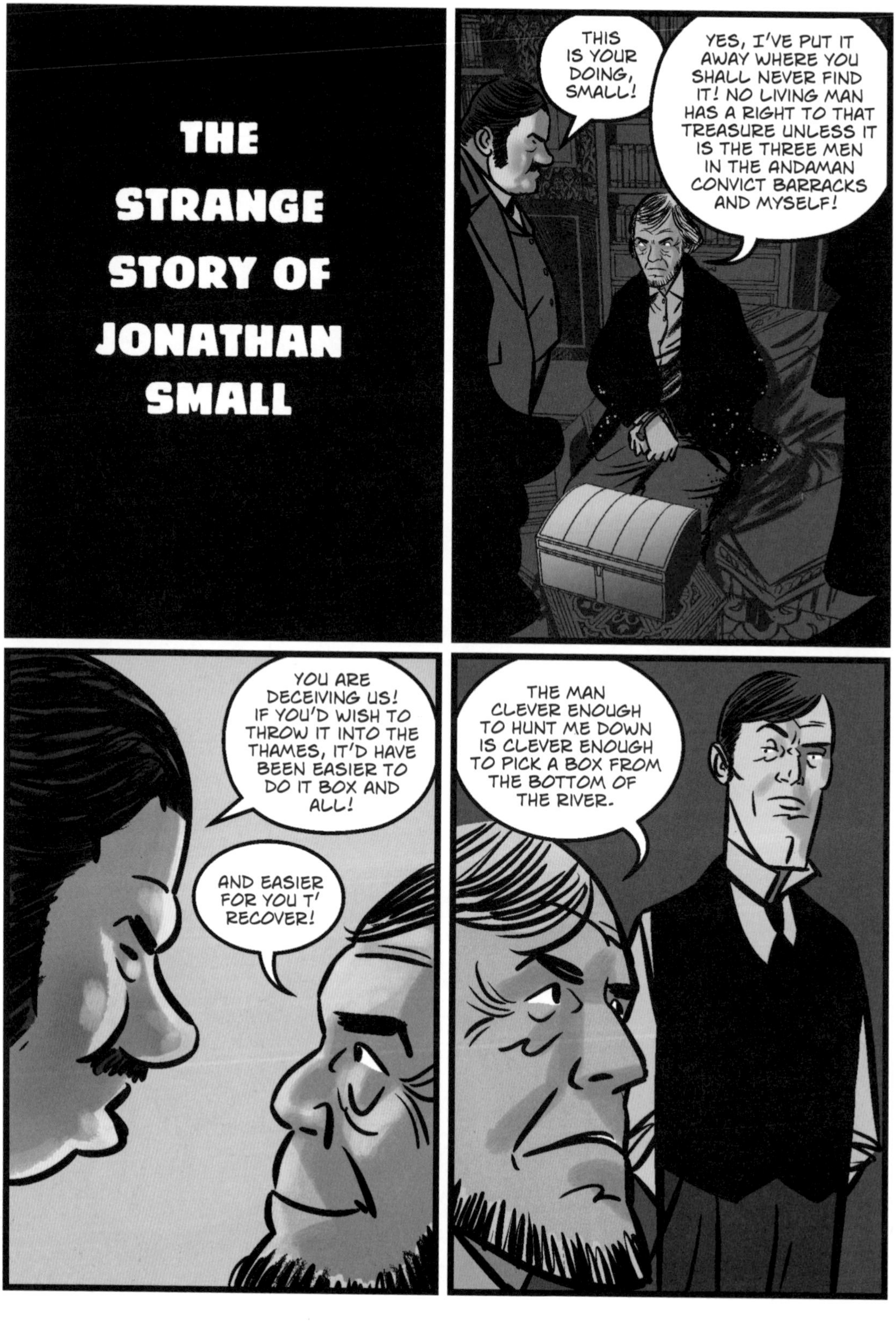
THE STRANGE STORY OF JONATHAN SMALL
THIS IS YOUR DOING, SMALL!
YES, I'VE PUT IT AWAY WHERE YOU SHALL NEVER FIND IT! NO LIVING MAN HAS A RIGHT TO THAT TREASURE UNLESS IT IS THE THREE MEN IN THE ANDAMAN CONVICT BARRACKS AND MYSELF!
YOU ARE DECEIVING US! IF YOU'D WISH TO THROW IT INTO THE THAMES, IT'D HAVE BEEN EASIER TO DO IT BOX AND ALL!
AND EASIER FOR YOU T' RECOVER!
THE MAN CLEVER ENOUGH TO HUNT ME DOWN IS CLEVER ENOUGH TO PICK A BOX FROM THE BOTTOM OF THE RIVER.

THIS IS A SERIOUS MATTER! IF YOU'D HELPED JUSTICE INSTEAD OF THWARTING IT, YOU'D HAVE A BETTER CHANCE AT YOUR TRIAL!

JUSTICE! A PRETTY JUSTICE! WHOSE LOOT IS THIS, IF NOT OURS? SHOULD I GIVE IT UP TO THOSE WHO HAVE NOT EARNED IT?

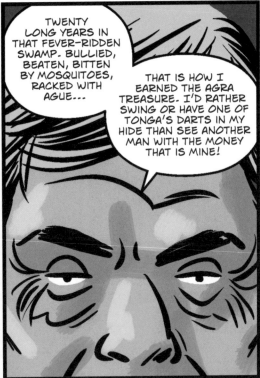

TWENTY LONG YEARS IN THAT FEVER-RIDDEN SWAMP. BULLIED, BEATEN, BITTEN BY MOSQUITOES, RACKED WITH AGUE...

THAT IS HOW I EARNED THE AGRA TREASURE. I'D RATHER SWING OR HAVE ONE OF TONGA'S DARTS IN MY HIDE THAN SEE ANOTHER MAN WITH THE MONEY THAT IS MINE!

YOU FORGET, WE KNOW NOTHING OF THIS MATTER. WE CANNOT TELL HOW FAR JUSTICE MAY HAVE BEEN ORIGINALLY ON YOUR SIDE.

WELL, SIR, YOU'VE BEEN FAIR-SPOKEN TO ME, THOUGH I SEE IT'S YOU I HAVE TO THANK FOR THESE BRACELETS ON MY WRISTS.

STILL, I BEAR NO GRUDGE FOR THAT. IF YOU WANT TO HEAR MY STORY, I'VE NO WISH TO HOLD IT BACK.

WHAT I SAY TO YOU IS GOD'S HONEST TRUTH, EVERY WORD OF IT.

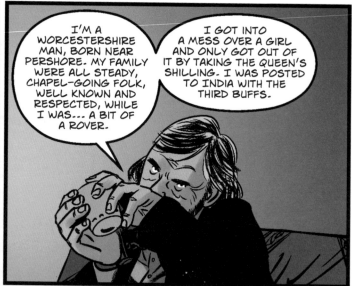

I'M A WORCESTERSHIRE MAN, BORN NEAR PERSHORE. MY FAMILY WERE ALL STEADY, CHAPEL-GOING FOLK, WELL KNOWN AND RESPECTED, WHILE I WAS... A BIT OF A ROVER.

I GOT INTO A MESS OVER A GIRL AND ONLY GOT OUT OF IT BY TAKING THE QUEEN'S SHILLING. I WAS POSTED TO INDIA WITH THE THIRD BUFFS.

A CROCODILE NIPPED THIS OFF WHEN I WAS SWIMMING IN THE GANGES. I WAS FIVE MONTHS IN THE HOSPITAL BEFORE GETTING MY DISCHARGE.

SO, THERE I WAS, A CRIPPLE AT TWENTY, UNFIT FOR ANY ACTIVE OCCUPATION...

"EVEN SO, I FOUND MYSELF A JOB AS AN OVERSEER ON AN INDIGO FARM. I WAS ON HORSEBACK ALL DAY, SO THAT WAS FINE."

"BUT I WAS NEVER IN LUCK FOR LONG. WITHOUT A NOTE OF WARNING, THE GREAT MUTINY WAS ON US. MY MASTER AND HIS FAMILY WERE MURDERED."

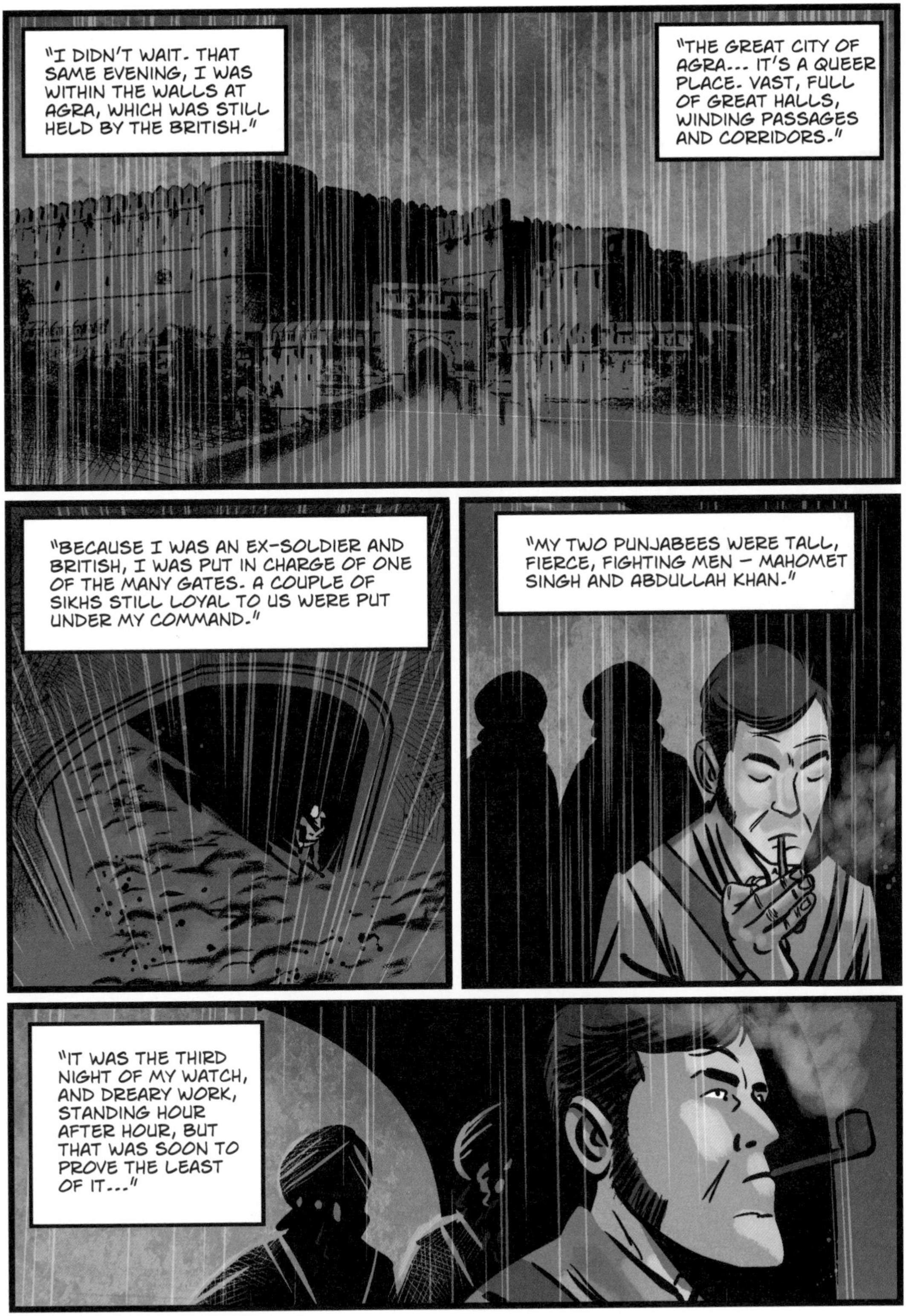
"I DIDN'T WAIT. THAT SAME EVENING, I WAS WITHIN THE WALLS AT AGRA, WHICH WAS STILL HELD BY THE BRITISH."
"THE GREAT CITY OF AGRA... IT'S A QUEER PLACE. VAST, FULL OF GREAT HALLS, WINDING PASSAGES AND CORRIDORS."
"BECAUSE I WAS AN EX-SOLDIER AND BRITISH, I WAS PUT IN CHARGE OF ONE OF THE MANY GATES. A COUPLE OF SIKHS STILL LOYAL TO US WERE PUT UNDER MY COMMAND."
"MY TWO PUNJABEES WERE TALL, FIERCE, FIGHTING MEN — MAHOMET SINGH AND ABDULLAH KHAN."
"IT WAS THE THIRD NIGHT OF MY WATCH, AND DREARY WORK, STANDING HOUR AFTER HOUR, BUT THAT WAS SOON TO PROVE THE LEAST OF IT..."

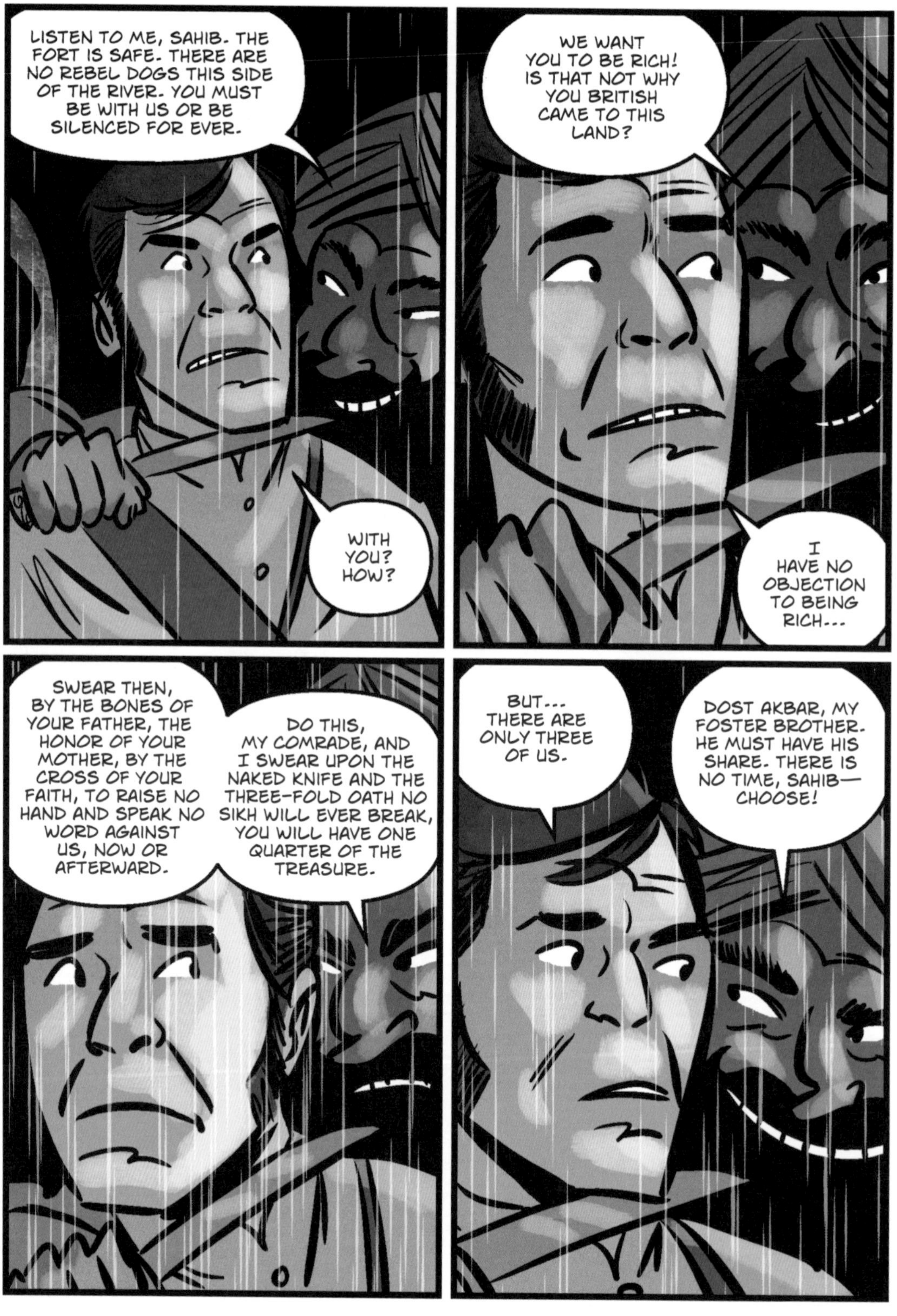
LISTEN TO ME, SAHIB. THE FORT IS SAFE. THERE ARE NO REBEL DOGS THIS SIDE OF THE RIVER. YOU MUST BE WITH US OR BE SILENCED FOR EVER.
WITH YOU? HOW?
WE WANT YOU TO BE RICH! IS THAT NOT WHY YOU BRITISH CAME TO THIS LAND?
I HAVE NO OBJECTION TO BEING RICH...
SWEAR THEN, BY THE BONES OF YOUR FATHER, THE HONOR OF YOUR MOTHER, BY THE CROSS OF YOUR FAITH, TO RAISE NO HAND AND SPEAK NO WORD AGAINST US, NOW OR AFTERWARD.
DO THIS, MY COMRADE, AND I SWEAR UPON THE NAKED KNIFE AND THE THREE-FOLD OATH NO SIKH WILL EVER BREAK, YOU WILL HAVE ONE QUARTER OF THE TREASURE.
BUT... THERE ARE ONLY THREE OF US.
DOST AKBAR, MY FOSTER BROTHER. HE MUST HAVE HIS SHARE. THERE IS NO TIME, SAHIB— CHOOSE!

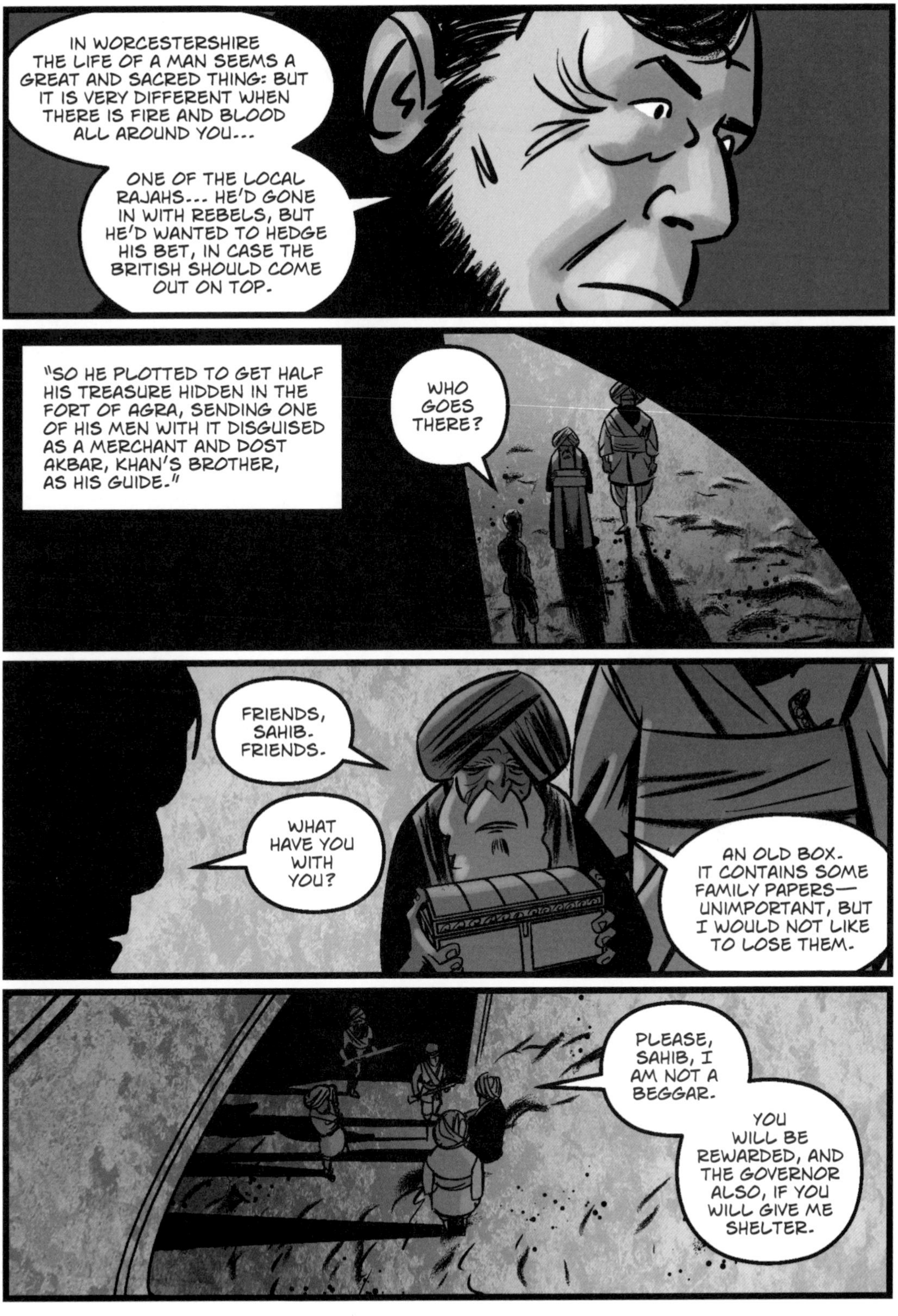
IN WORCESTERSHIRE THE LIFE OF A MAN SEEMS A GREAT AND SACRED THING: BUT IT IS VERY DIFFERENT WHEN THERE IS FIRE AND BLOOD ALL AROUND YOU...
ONE OF THE LOCAL RAJAHS... HE'D GONE IN WITH REBELS, BUT HE'D WANTED TO HEDGE HIS BET, IN CASE THE BRITISH SHOULD COME OUT ON TOP.
"SO HE PLOTTED TO GET HALF HIS TREASURE HIDDEN IN THE FORT OF AGRA, SENDING ONE OF HIS MEN WITH IT DISGUISED AS A MERCHANT AND DOST AKBAR, KHAN'S BROTHER, AS HIS GUIDE."
WHO GOES THERE?
FRIENDS, SAHIB. FRIENDS.
WHAT HAVE YOU WITH YOU?
AN OLD BOX. IT CONTAINS SOME FAMILY PAPERS— UNIMPORTANT, BUT I WOULD NOT LIKE TO LOSE THEM.
PLEASE, SAHIB, I AM NOT A BEGGAR.
YOU WILL BE REWARDED, AND THE GOVERNOR ALSO, IF YOU WILL GIVE ME SHELTER.

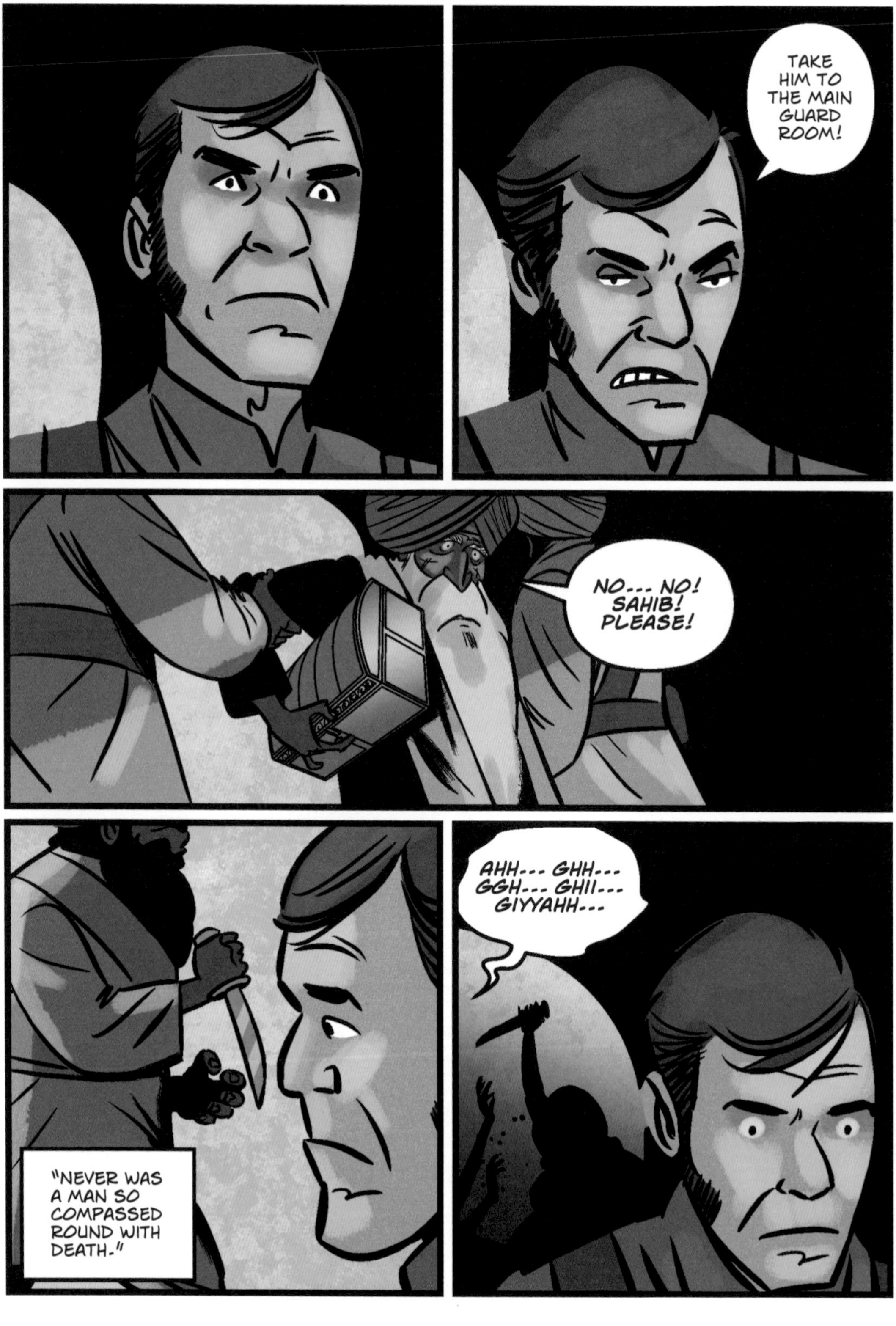
TAKE HIM TO THE MAIN GUARD ROOM!
NO... NO! SAHIB! PLEASE!
"NEVER WAS A MAN SO COMPASSED ROUND WITH DEATH."
AHH... GHH... GGH... GHII... GIYYAHH...

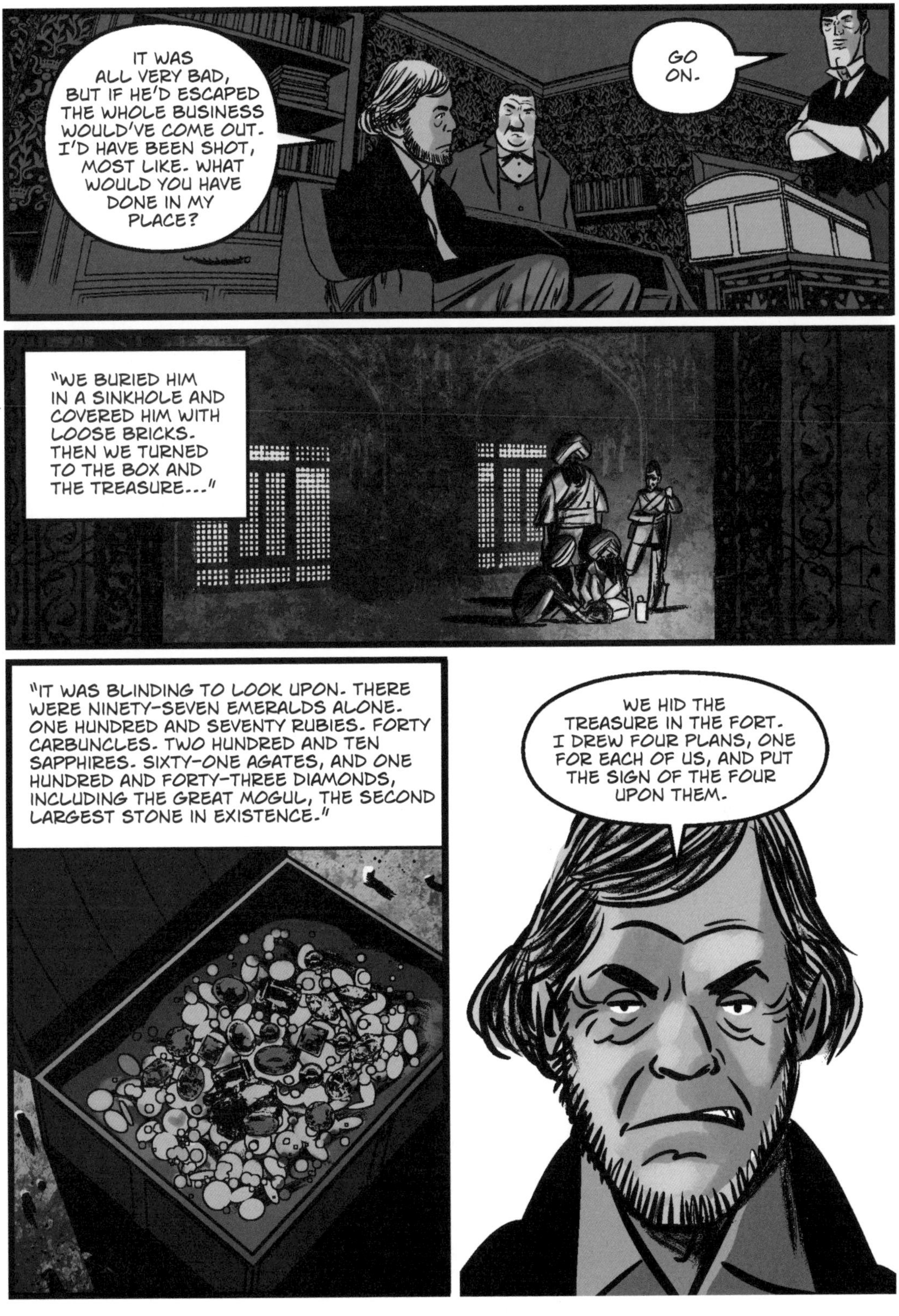
IT WAS ALL VERY BAD, BUT IF HE'D ESCAPED THE WHOLE BUSINESS WOULD'VE COME OUT. I'D HAVE BEEN SHOT, MOST LIKE. WHAT WOULD YOU HAVE DONE IN MY PLACE?
GO ON.
"WE BURIED HIM IN A SINKHOLE AND COVERED HIM WITH LOOSE BRICKS. THEN WE TURNED TO THE BOX AND THE TREASURE..."
"IT WAS BLINDING TO LOOK UPON. THERE WERE NINETY-SEVEN EMERALDS ALONE. ONE HUNDRED AND SEVENTY RUBIES. FORTY CARBUNCLES. TWO HUNDRED AND TEN SAPPHIRES. SIXTY-ONE AGATES, AND ONE HUNDRED AND FORTY-THREE DIAMONDS, INCLUDING THE GREAT MOGUL, THE SECOND LARGEST STONE IN EXISTENCE."
WE HID THE TREASURE IN THE FORT. I DREW FOUR PLANS, ONE FOR EACH OF US, AND PUT THE SIGN OF THE FOUR UPON THEM.

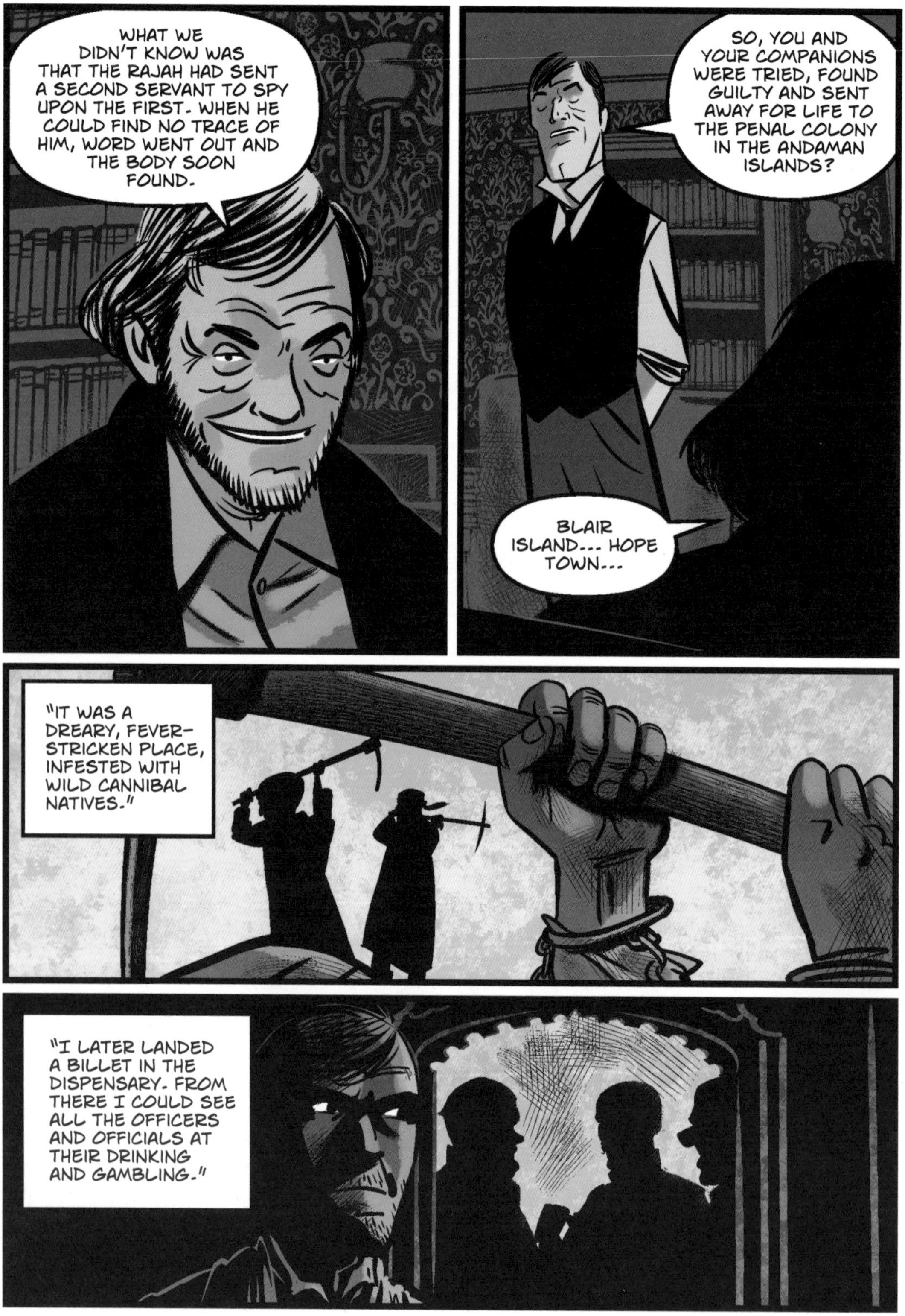
WHAT WE DIDN'T KNOW WAS THAT THE RAJAH HAD SENT A SECOND SERVANT TO SPY UPON THE FIRST. WHEN HE COULD FIND NO TRACE OF HIM, WORD WENT OUT AND THE BODY SOON FOUND.
SO, YOU AND YOUR COMPANIONS WERE TRIED, FOUND GUILTY AND SENT AWAY FOR LIFE TO THE PENAL COLONY IN THE ANDAMAN ISLANDS?
BLAIR ISLAND... HOPE TOWN...
"IT WAS A DREARY, FEVER-STRICKEN PLACE, INFESTED WITH WILD CANNIBAL NATIVES."
"I LATER LANDED A BILLET IN THE DISPENSARY. FROM THERE I COULD SEE ALL THE OFFICERS AND OFFICIALS AT THEIR DRINKING AND GAMBLING."

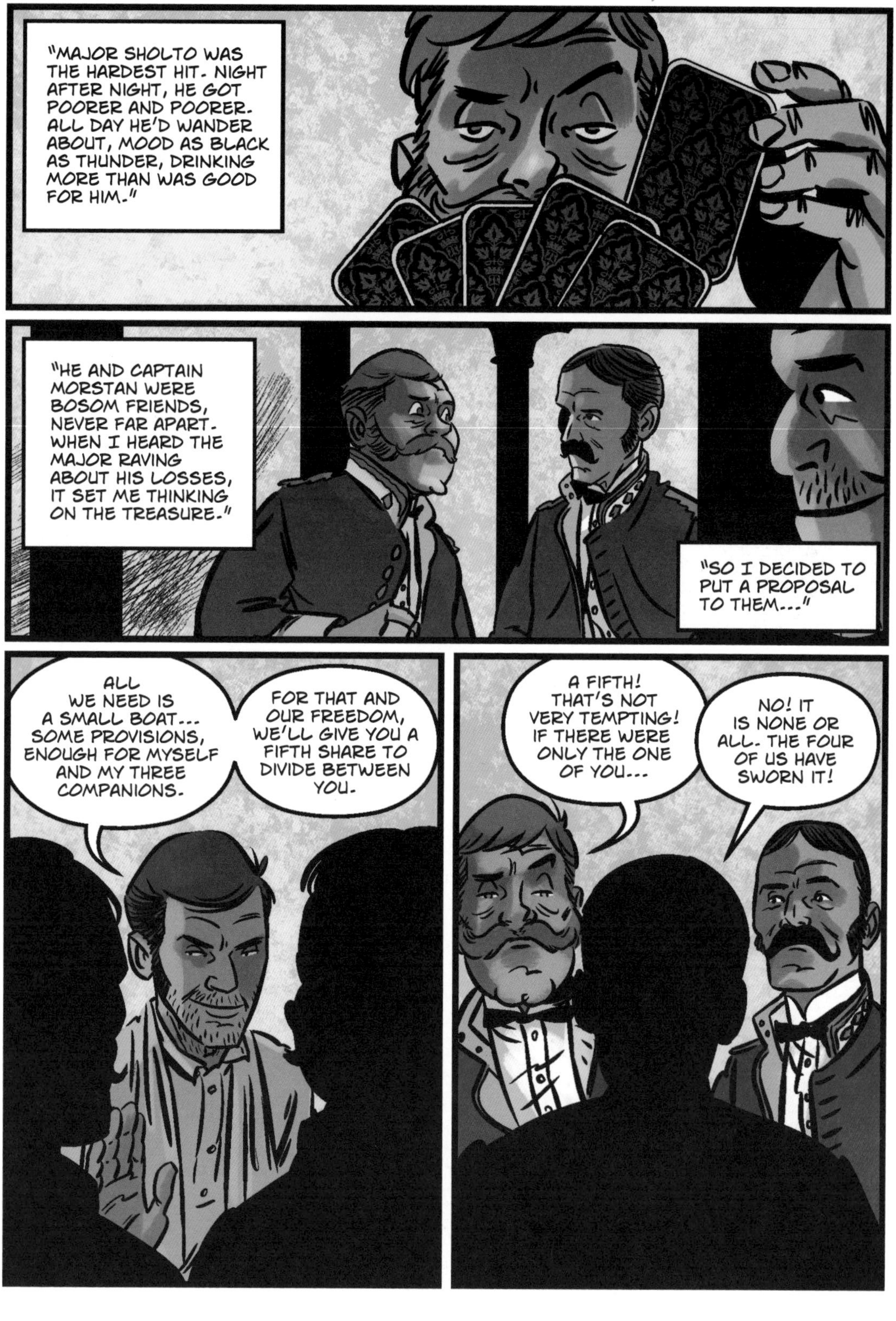
"MAJOR SHOLTO WAS THE HARDEST HIT. NIGHT AFTER NIGHT, HE GOT POORER AND POORER. ALL DAY HE'D WANDER ABOUT, MOOD AS BLACK AS THUNDER, DRINKING MORE THAN WAS GOOD FOR HIM."
"HE AND CAPTAIN MORSTAN WERE BOSOM FRIENDS, NEVER FAR APART. WHEN I HEARD THE MAJOR RAVING ABOUT HIS LOSSES, IT SET ME THINKING ON THE TREASURE."
"SO I DECIDED TO PUT A PROPOSAL TO THEM..."
ALL WE NEED IS A SMALL BOAT... SOME PROVISIONS, ENOUGH FOR MYSELF AND MY THREE COMPANIONS.
FOR THAT AND OUR FREEDOM, WE'LL GIVE YOU A FIFTH SHARE TO DIVIDE BETWEEN YOU.
A FIFTH! THAT'S NOT VERY TEMPTING! IF THERE WERE ONLY THE ONE OF YOU...
NO! IT IS NONE OR ALL. THE FOUR OF US HAVE SWORN IT!

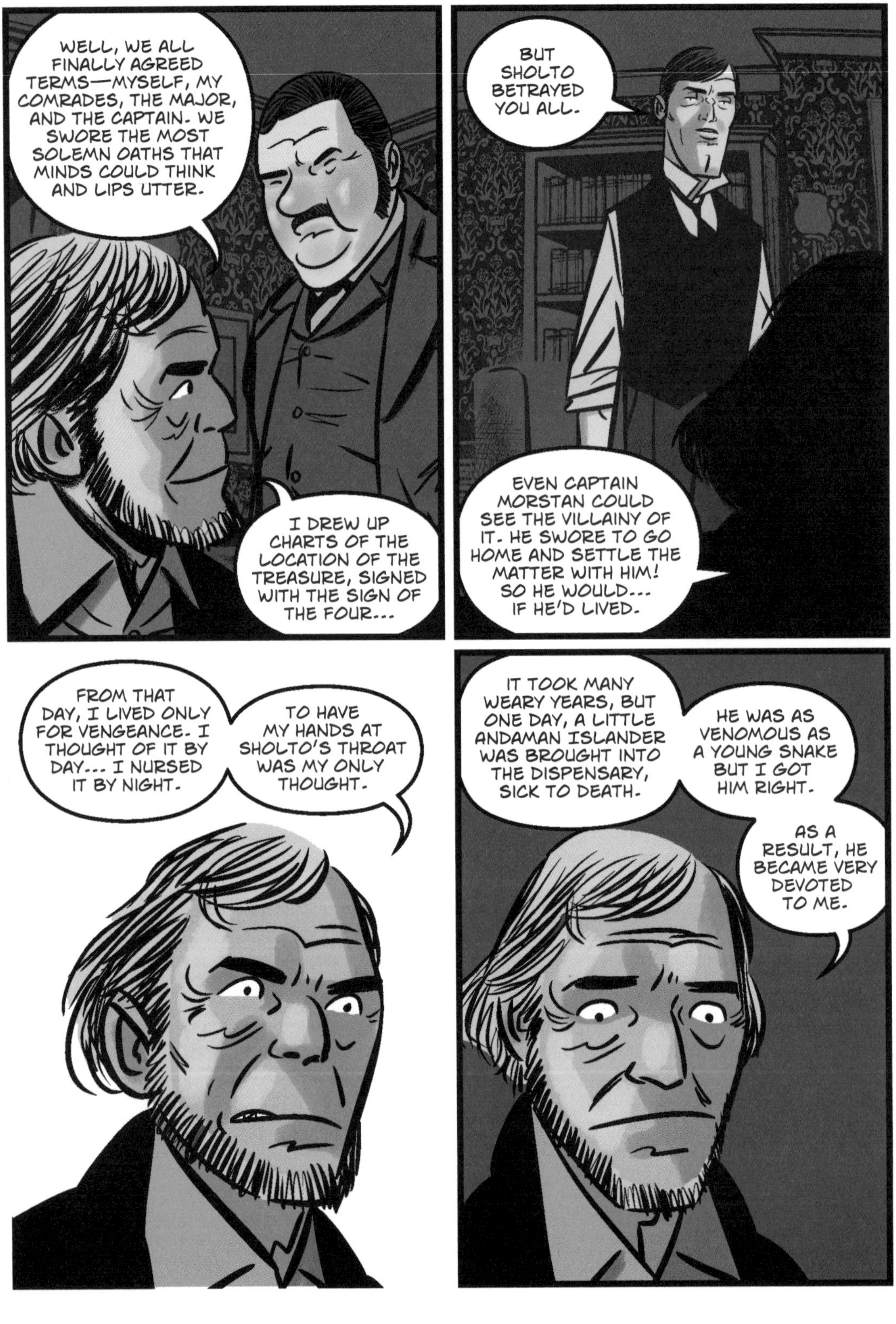
WELL, WE ALL FINALLY AGREED TERMS—MYSELF, MY COMRADES, THE MAJOR, AND THE CAPTAIN. WE SWORE THE MOST SOLEMN OATHS THAT MINDS COULD THINK AND LIPS UTTER.
I DREW UP CHARTS OF THE LOCATION OF THE TREASURE, SIGNED WITH THE SIGN OF THE FOUR...
BUT SHOLTO BETRAYED YOU ALL.
EVEN CAPTAIN MORSTAN COULD SEE THE VILLAINY OF IT. HE SWORE TO GO HOME AND SETTLE THE MATTER WITH HIM! SO HE WOULD... IF HE'D LIVED.
FROM THAT DAY, I LIVED ONLY FOR VENGEANCE. I THOUGHT OF IT BY DAY... I NURSED IT BY NIGHT.
TO HAVE MY HANDS AT SHOLTO'S THROAT WAS MY ONLY THOUGHT.
IT TOOK MANY WEARY YEARS, BUT ONE DAY, A LITTLE ANDAMAN ISLANDER WAS BROUGHT INTO THE DISPENSARY, SICK TO DEATH.
HE WAS AS VENOMOUS AS A YOUNG SNAKE BUT I GOT HIM RIGHT.
AS A RESULT, HE BECAME VERY DEVOTED TO ME.

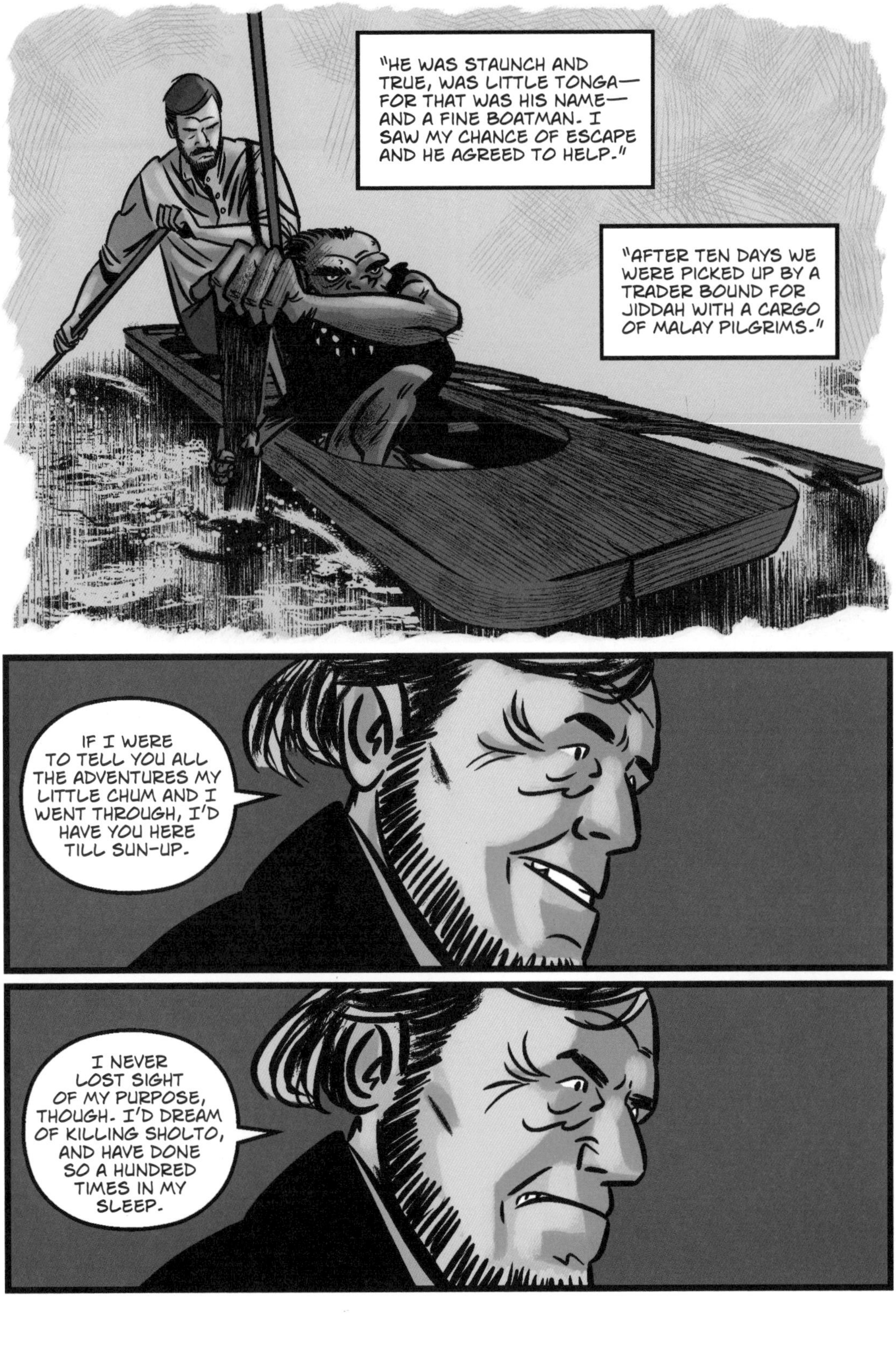
"HE WAS STAUNCH AND TRUE, WAS LITTLE TONGA— FOR THAT WAS HIS NAME— AND A FINE BOATMAN. I SAW MY CHANCE OF ESCAPE AND HE AGREED TO HELP."
"AFTER TEN DAYS WE WERE PICKED UP BY A TRADER BOUND FOR JIDDAH WITH A CARGO OF MALAY PILGRIMS."
IF I WERE TO TELL YOU ALL THE ADVENTURES MY LITTLE CHUM AND I WENT THROUGH, I'D HAVE YOU HERE TILL SUN-UP.
I NEVER LOST SIGHT OF MY PURPOSE, THOUGH. I'D DREAM OF KILLING SHOLTO, AND HAVE DONE SO A HUNDRED TIMES IN MY SLEEP.

"THREE OR FOUR YEARS AGO, WE FOUND OURSELVES IN LONDON. I'D NO TROUBLE IN FINDING SHOLTO, BUT I NEEDED TO KNOW IF HE HAD REALIZED THE TREASURE, OR IF HE STILL HAD IT."

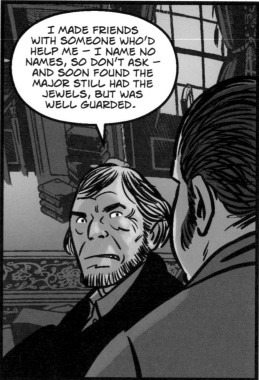

I MADE FRIENDS WITH SOMEONE WHO'D HELP ME — I NAME NO NAMES, SO DON'T ASK — AND SOON FOUND THE MAJOR STILL HAD THE JEWELS, BUT WAS WELL GUARDED.

"WHEN I HEARD HE WAS DYING, I HURRIED TO THE HOUSE BUT ARRIVED TOO LATE. I PINNED THE SIGN OF THE FOUR TO HIS BOSOM, THAT HE SHOULD TAKE TO THE GRAVE A TOKEN FROM THE MEN HE'D ROBBED."

WHEN WORD CAME THE TREASURE HAD BEEN FOUND AT THE TOP OF THE HOUSE, I REASONED HOW TO REACH IT... WITH TONGA'S HELP.

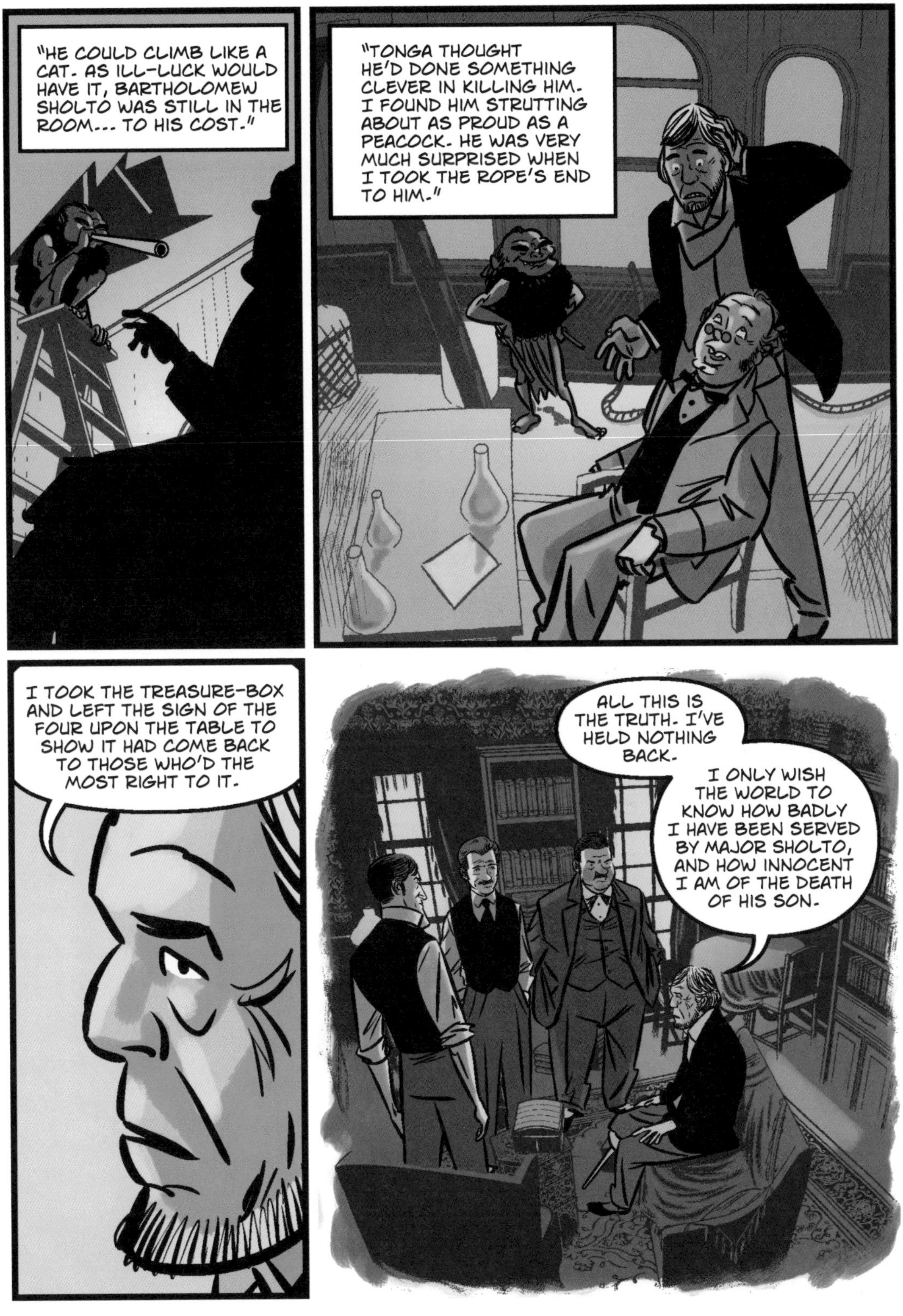
"HE COULD CLIMB LIKE A CAT. AS ILL-LUCK WOULD HAVE IT, BARTHOLOMEW SHOLTO WAS STILL IN THE ROOM... TO HIS COST."
"TONGA THOUGHT HE'D DONE SOMETHING CLEVER IN KILLING HIM. I FOUND HIM STRUTTING ABOUT AS PROUD AS A PEACOCK. HE WAS VERY MUCH SURPRISED WHEN I TOOK THE ROPE'S END TO HIM."
I TOOK THE TREASURE-BOX AND LEFT THE SIGN OF THE FOUR UPON THE TABLE TO SHOW IT HAD COME BACK TO THOSE WHO'D THE MOST RIGHT TO IT.
ALL THIS IS THE TRUTH. I'VE HELD NOTHING BACK.
I ONLY WISH THE WORLD TO KNOW HOW BADLY I HAVE BEEN SERVED BY MAJOR SHOLTO, AND HOW INNOCENT I AM OF THE DEATH OF HIS SON.

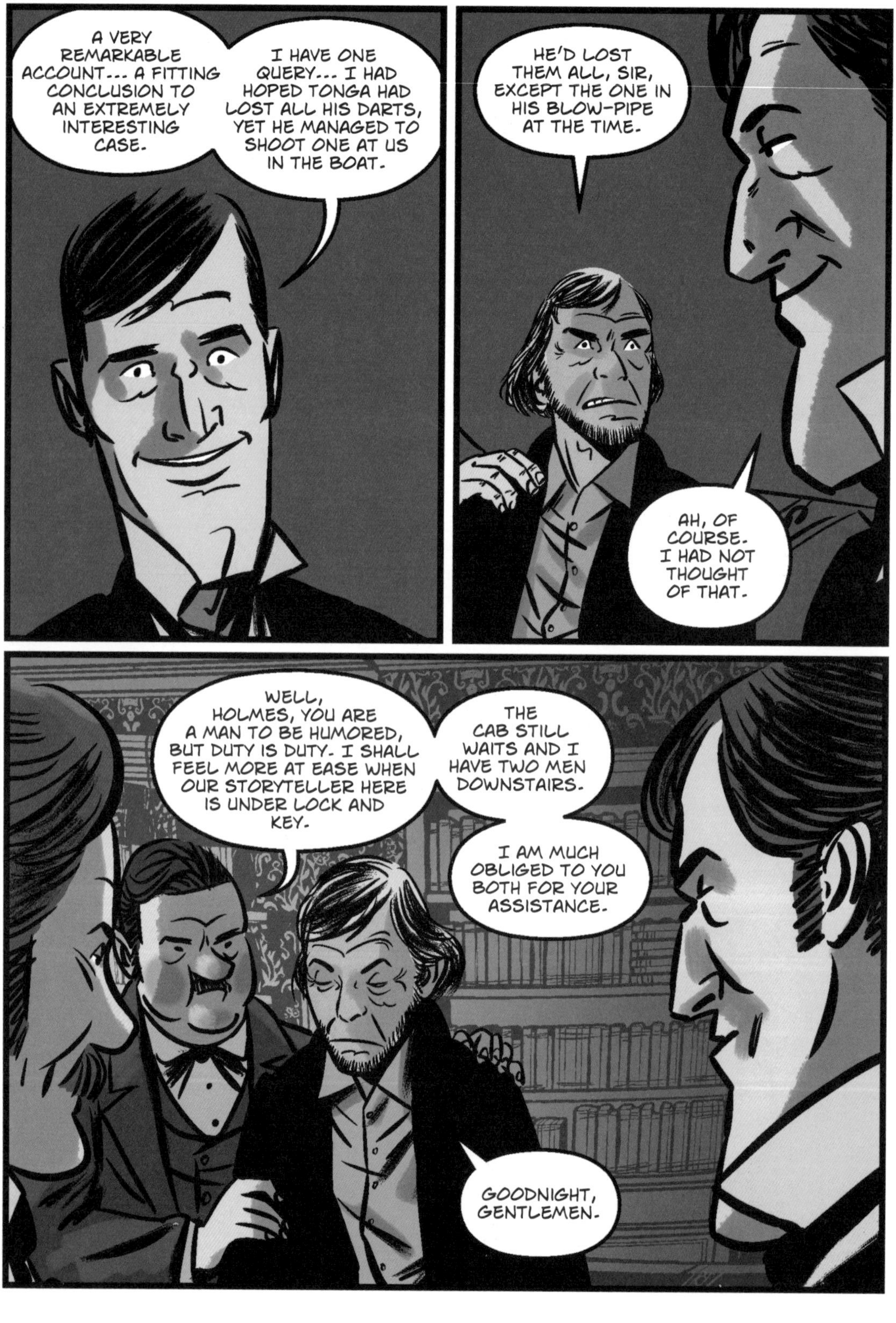
A VERY REMARKABLE ACCOUNT... A FITTING CONCLUSION TO AN EXTREMELY INTERESTING CASE.
I HAVE ONE QUERY... I HAD HOPED TONGA HAD LOST ALL HIS DARTS, YET HE MANAGED TO SHOOT ONE AT US IN THE BOAT.
HE'D LOST THEM ALL, SIR, EXCEPT THE ONE IN HIS BLOW-PIPE AT THE TIME.
AH, OF COURSE. I HAD NOT THOUGHT OF THAT.
WELL, HOLMES, YOU ARE A MAN TO BE HUMORED, BUT DUTY IS DUTY. I SHALL FEEL MORE AT EASE WHEN OUR STORYTELLER HERE IS UNDER LOCK AND KEY.
THE CAB STILL WAITS AND I HAVE TWO MEN DOWNSTAIRS.
I AM MUCH OBLIGED TO YOU BOTH FOR YOUR ASSISTANCE.
GOODNIGHT, GENTLEMEN.

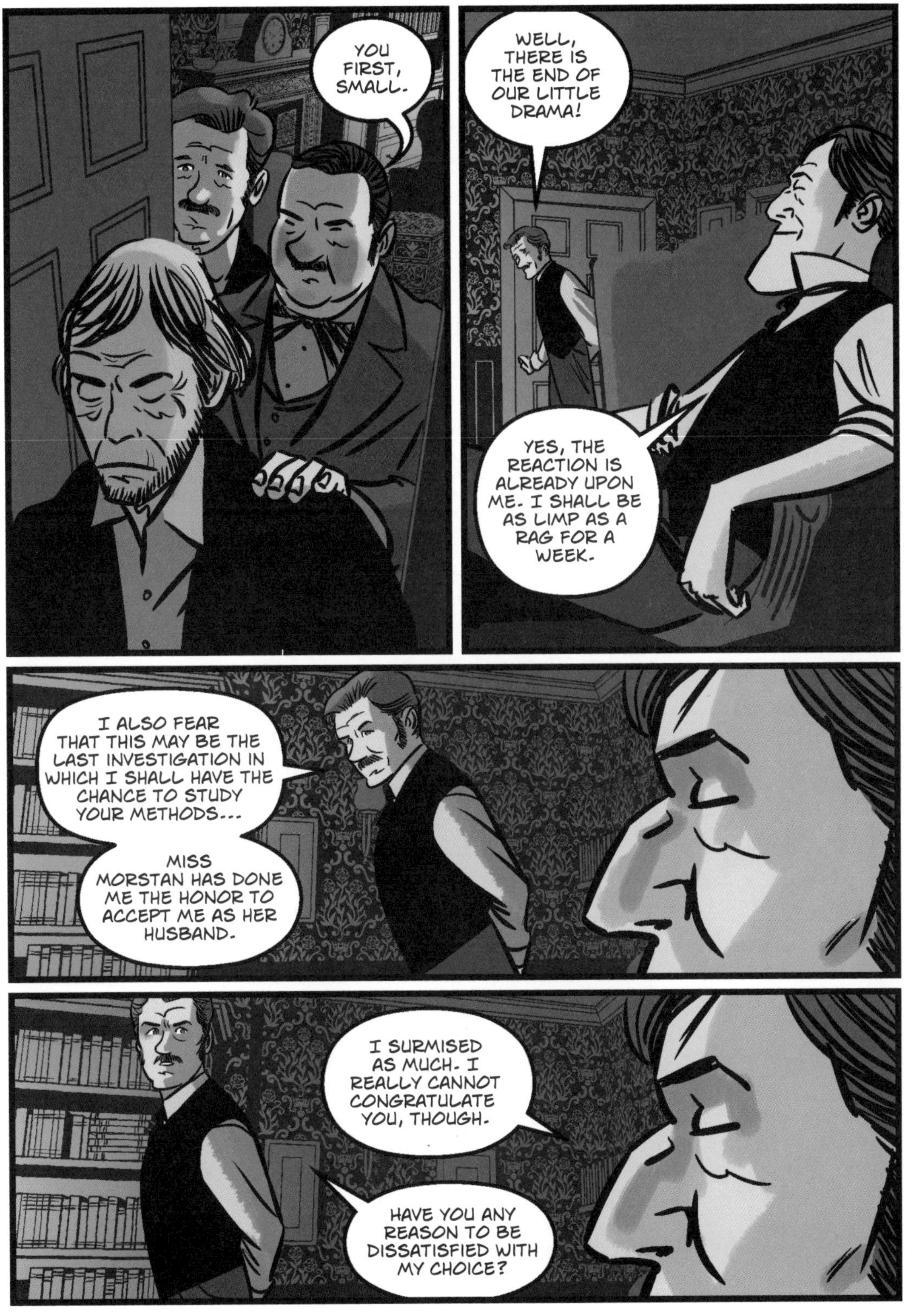
YOU FIRST, SMALL.
WELL, THERE IS THE END OF OUR LITTLE DRAMA!
YES, THE REACTION IS ALREADY UPON ME. I SHALL BE AS LIMP AS A RAG FOR A WEEK.
I ALSO FEAR THAT THIS MAY BE THE LAST INVESTIGATION IN WHICH I SHALL HAVE THE CHANCE TO STUDY YOUR METHODS...
MISS MORSTAN HAS DONE ME THE HONOR TO ACCEPT ME AS HER HUSBAND.
I SURMISED AS MUCH. I REALLY CANNOT CONGRATULATE YOU, THOUGH.
HAVE YOU ANY REASON TO BE DISSATISFIED WITH MY CHOICE?

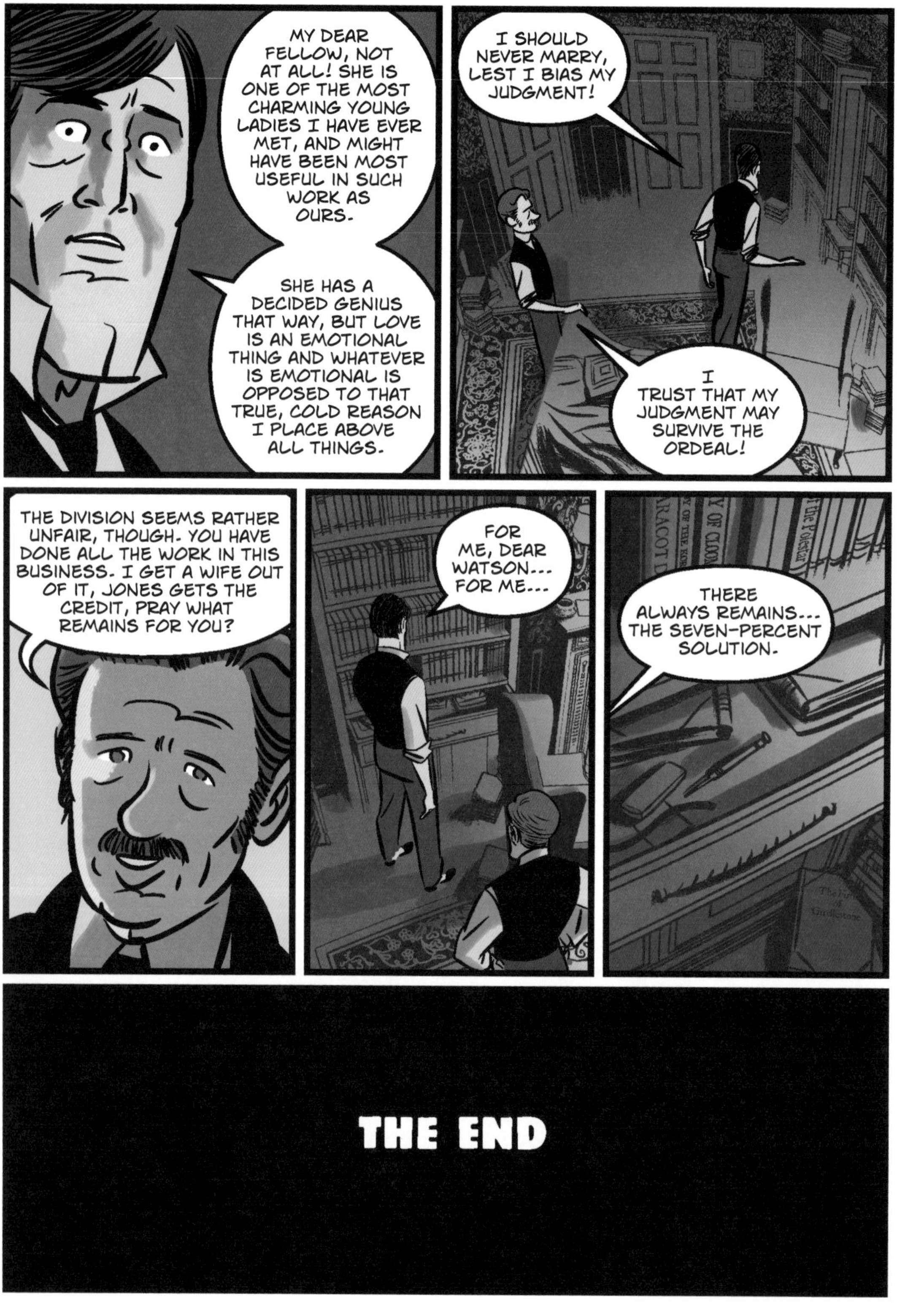
MY DEAR FELLOW, NOT AT ALL! SHE IS ONE OF THE MOST CHARMING YOUNG LADIES I HAVE EVER MET, AND MIGHT HAVE BEEN MOST USEFUL IN SUCH WORK AS OURS.
SHE HAS A DECIDED GENIUS THAT WAY, BUT LOVE IS AN EMOTIONAL THING AND WHATEVER IS EMOTIONAL IS OPPOSED TO THAT TRUE, COLD REASON I PLACE ABOVE ALL THINGS.
I SHOULD NEVER MARRY, LEST I BIAS MY JUDGMENT!
I TRUST THAT MY JUDGMENT MAY SURVIVE THE ORDEAL!
THE DIVISION SEEMS RATHER UNFAIR, THOUGH. YOU HAVE DONE ALL THE WORK IN THIS BUSINESS. I GET A WIFE OUT OF IT, JONES GETS THE CREDIT, PRAY WHAT REMAINS FOR YOU?
FOR ME, DEAR WATSON... FOR ME...
THERE ALWAYS REMAINS... THE SEVEN-PERCENT SOLUTION.
THE END

THE VALLEY OF FEAR

OF FEAR

PREVIEW . . .

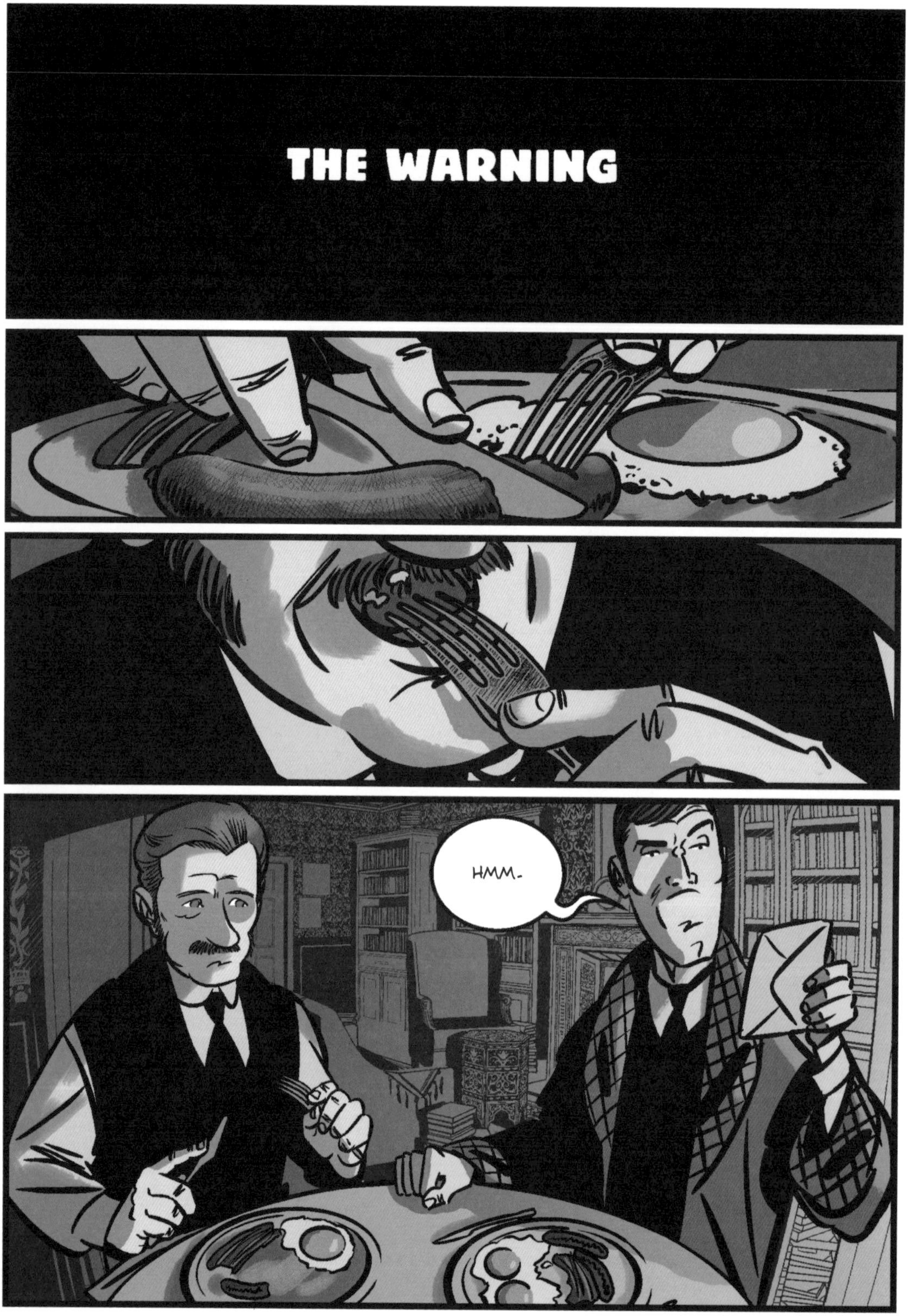
THE WARNING
HMM.

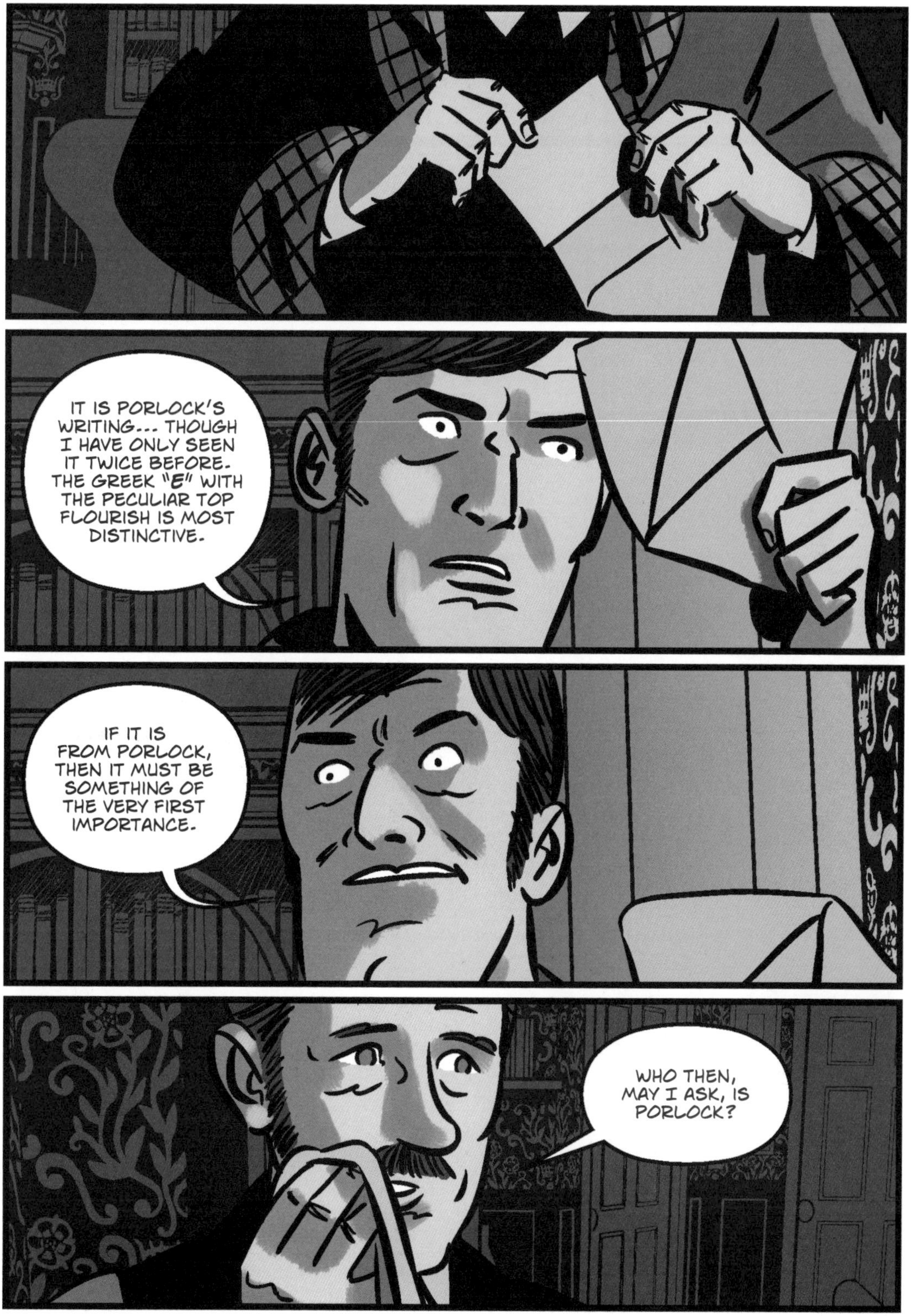
IT IS PORLOCK'S WRITING... THOUGH I HAVE ONLY SEEN IT TWICE BEFORE. THE GREEK "E" WITH THE PECULIAR TOP FLOURISH IS MOST DISTINCTIVE.
IF IT IS FROM PORLOCK, THEN IT MUST BE SOMETHING OF THE VERY FIRST IMPORTANCE.
WHO THEN, MAY I ASK, IS PORLOCK?

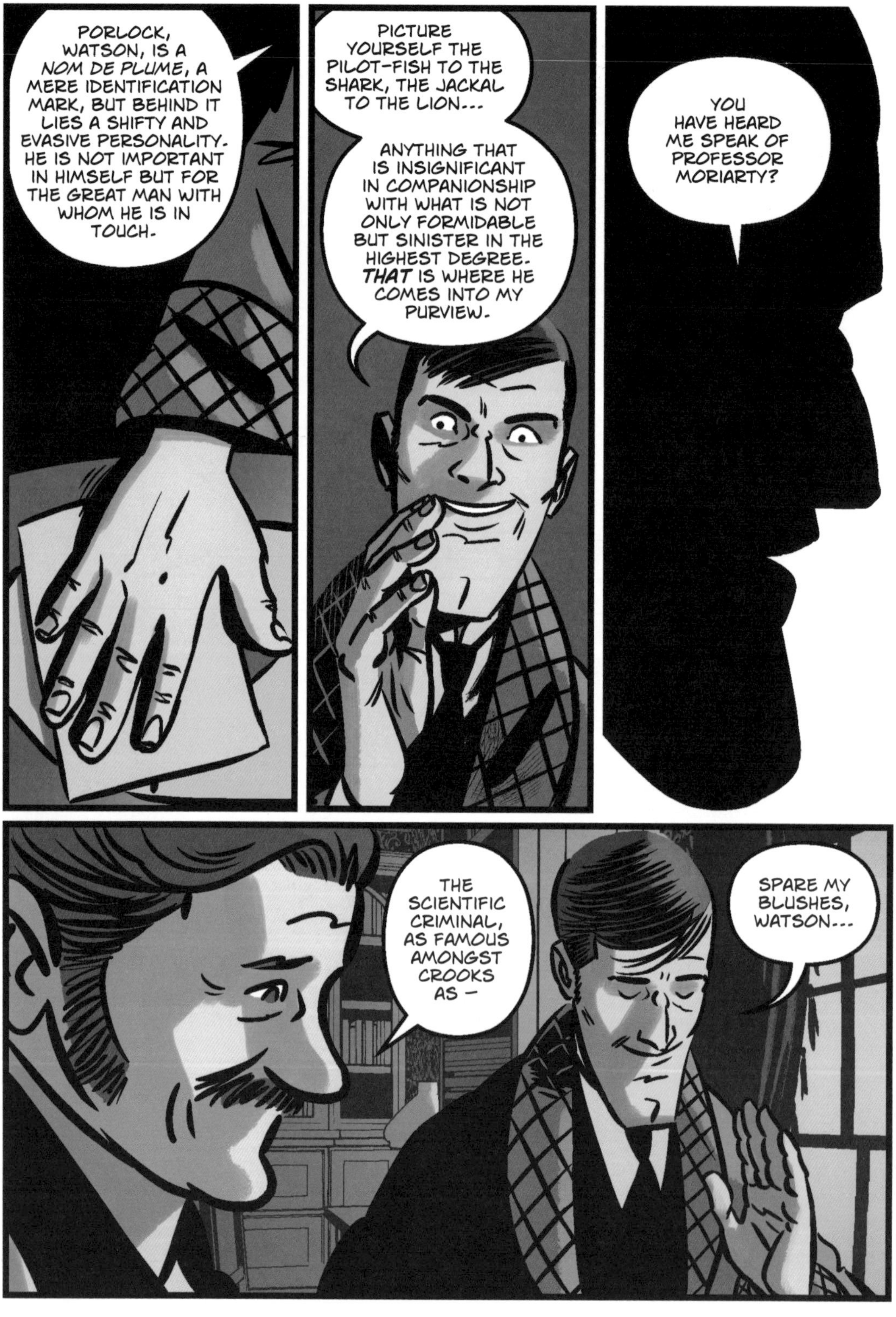
PORLOCK, WATSON, IS A *NOM DE PLUME*, A MERE IDENTIFICATION MARK, BUT BEHIND IT LIES A SHIFTY AND EVASIVE PERSONALITY. HE IS NOT IMPORTANT IN HIMSELF BUT FOR THE GREAT MAN WITH WHOM HE IS IN TOUCH.
PICTURE YOURSELF THE PILOT-FISH TO THE SHARK, THE JACKAL TO THE LION...
ANYTHING THAT IS INSIGNIFICANT IN COMPANIONSHIP WITH WHAT IS NOT ONLY FORMIDABLE BUT SINISTER IN THE HIGHEST DEGREE. *THAT* IS WHERE HE COMES INTO MY PURVIEW.
YOU HAVE HEARD ME SPEAK OF PROFESSOR MORIARTY?
THE SCIENTIFIC CRIMINAL, AS FAMOUS AMONGST CROOKS AS –
SPARE MY BLUSHES, WATSON...

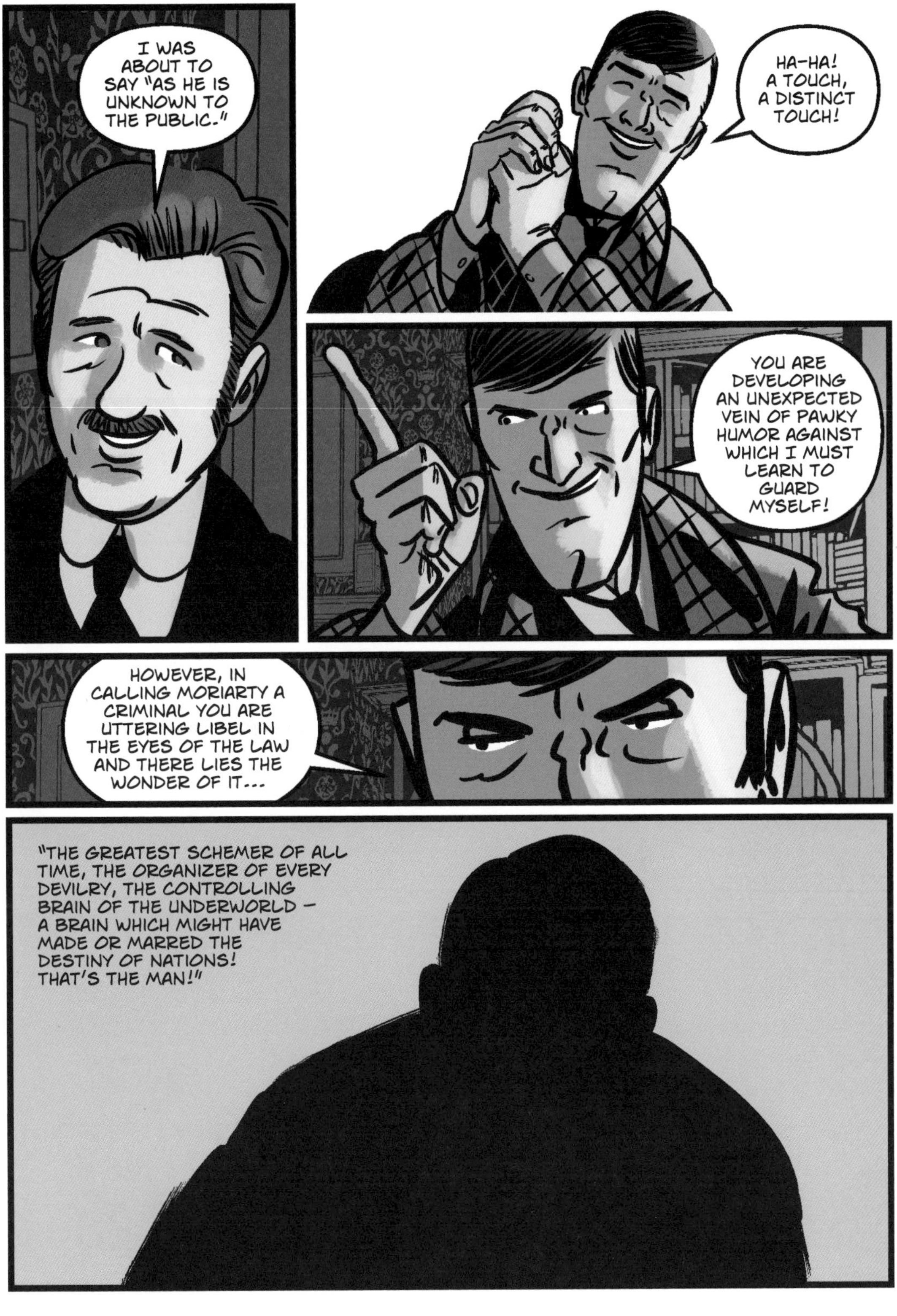
I WAS ABOUT TO SAY "AS HE IS UNKNOWN TO THE PUBLIC."
HA-HA! A TOUCH, A DISTINCT TOUCH!
YOU ARE DEVELOPING AN UNEXPECTED VEIN OF PAWKY HUMOR AGAINST WHICH I MUST LEARN TO GUARD MYSELF!
HOWEVER, IN CALLING MORIARTY A CRIMINAL YOU ARE UTTERING LIBEL IN THE EYES OF THE LAW AND THERE LIES THE WONDER OF IT...
"THE GREATEST SCHEMER OF ALL TIME, THE ORGANIZER OF EVERY DEVILRY, THE CONTROLLING BRAIN OF THE UNDERWORLD – A BRAIN WHICH MIGHT HAVE MADE OR MARRED THE DESTINY OF NATIONS! THAT'S THE MAN!"